Encountering Women of Faith

ENCOUNTERING
Women of Faith

THE ST. CATHERINE'S VISION COLLECTION
VOLUME 2

Kyriaki Karidoyanes FitzGerald
Editor

HC
ORTHODOX
PRESS
HOLY CROSS ORTHODOX PRESS
Brookline, Massachusetts

© 2011 Kyriaki FitzGerald
Published by Holy Cross Orthodox Press
50 Goddard Avenue
Brookline, Massachusetts 02445

ISBN-13 978-1-935317-21-0
ISBN-10 1-935317-21-0

On the cover (clockwise from the top left): the Prophetess Anna, St. Mary of Egypt,
St. Thekla, St. Catherine the Great Martyr, and St. Barbara. Courtesy of The Greek
Orthodox Archdiocese of America.

Library of Congress Cataloging-in-Publication Data

The St. Catherine's vision collection /
Kyriaki Karidoyanes FitzGerald, editor.
v. cm.
Includes bibliographical references and index.
Contents: v. 1. Encountering women of faith.
ISBN 1-932401-07-5 (pbk. : v. 1 : alk. paper)
1. Christian women saints--Biography. 2. Women in the Orthodox
Eastern Church. I. FitzGerald, Kyriaki Karidoyanes, 1956- . II. Title: Saint
Catherine's vision collection.
BX393.S73 2005
281.909212--dc22
2005029016

*To the faithful men and women
who have been supporting the many ways
women and men are called to serve
within the life of the Church, today.*

and

*Clara Nickolson
We are forever grateful
to the loving Lord, thrice-holy,
for your faith, vision,
courage, and perseverance
on behalf of St. Catherine's Vision.
Memory eternal!*

Contents

Foreword
Metropolitan Maximos of Pittsburgh

Encountering Women of Faith, volume 2, is a remarkable and inspiring book that introduces to us the lives of a number of women saints and points to the contemporary significance of their witness. This collection of thoughtful essays is the fruit of the collaboration of ten authors who are members of St. Catherine's Vision, an association founded by Orthodox women, most of whom are graduates of Orthodox theological schools.

The authors introduce us to the distinctive witness of St. Christina of Tyre, St. Thekla, St. Juliana the Merciful, SS. Perpetua and Felicitas, St. Anna the Prophetess, St. Paula, St. Barbara, and St. Mary of Egypt. With a scholarly appreciation of their social and cultural contexts, these saints are presented to us as authentic persons. Each saint is unique in her own historical and cultural context, yet these saints are bound together in Christ across space and time. In Him, they become our contemporaries in faith and in witness. As His faithful followers, the saints present Christ and His gospel to us. Each saint sought to serve her Lord with faith and love in the midst of the responsibilities and obligations of life. As we proclaim through our hymns, God is "wondrous in His saints." In this book, we truly have the opportunity to "encounter women of faith."

This collection is distinctive also because the authors present these saints as faithful witnesses who help us to appreciate challenges of our day. With thoughtful and rich insight, each author writes in her own voice and offers a deeply personal reflection on the significance of her saint. These moving and powerful reflections connect the historic witness of the saint with contemporary issues facing believers today. Each essay in *Encountering Women of Faith* conscientiously and faithfully engages subjects such as dedicating one's life to Christ, becoming an Orthodox Christian, solitude, motherhood and loss, widowhood, serving the poor, radical forgiveness, confronting worldly expectations and corrupt authority, personal sacrifice and the gospel, trusting God through the noise of the fallen world, and seeking the music of His silence. Through these pages, the authors courageously address issues such as poverty, racism, classism, sexism, abuse of power, war, genocide and the cultivation of forgiveness, overcoming child sexual abuse, and the nature of authentic spiritual authority.

This book is the second in the series produced by St. Catherine's Vision. Like the first book, published in 2005 and reprinted in 2010, this book is the result of a deeply consultative process of theological reflection. Each author is solely responsible for her research and the subsequent essay. Yet, the reflections of each author have been discussed by all the authors through a series of writing retreats. This distinctive process strengthens the contribution of each author with the insight of all the authors.

These two volumes are a profound fruit of the ministry of St. Catherine's Vision. The name of this association refers to the vision of Christ that was experienced by St. Catherine the Great Martyr. A well-educated believer, she is remembered because of her defense of the Christian faith in opposition to pagan philosophers. She is frequently honored as a patron of Christian theologians and teachers.

St. Catherine's Vision (SCV) is a unique association established in 2004 and formally endorsed in 2007 by the Standing Conference of Canonical Orthodox Bishops of America (SCOBA) [now the Assembly of Canonical Orthodox Bishops of North and Central America – ed.]. Since its inception, the members of St. Catherine's Vision have been committed to projects that serve three important objectives: Orthodox unity, spiritual renewal, and education. *Encountering Women of Faith* is a collaborative act of love that addresses in a powerful and graceful way each of these objectives. To the best of my knowledge, there is no comparable book by theologically educated Orthodox writers that addresses the vital and challenging issues related to holiness and faithful life today.

For serious students of theology, thoughtful believers, religious educators, adult study groups, and concerned inquirers who wonder how the saints "of old" may have any relevance for the issues we face today, *Encountering Women of Faith* is a two-volume jewel! As a body of work that richly introduces the reader to the "cloud of witnesses" (Heb 12:1)— that is, the saints, the holy women and men of God—the stories related through this series speak to our own context with clarity, immediacy, and vibrancy, all the while urging each one of us to "hear the word of God and keep it" (Luke 11:28).

+ Maximos, Metropolitan of Pittsburgh
Greek Orthodox Archdiocese of America
Pittsburgh, Pennsylvania
September 1, 2010

Surprised by Joy

This volume has been slow in the making. It is produced with deep love and concern for those who may be reading and benefiting from it. This is a gift offered to you, the reader. It was written following the same principled discipline of writing in community described in the introduction of volume 1 of *Encountering Women of Faith*.

Each author is solely responsible for articulating her own perspectives. Even so, we listened to one another, deeply considering one another's study and reflection, while offering support, constructive criticism, and advice. Furthermore, we challenged one another to state what we each really desired to say as best we were able. In a number of cases, the results of these exchanges have been extraordinary.

THE FIRST SURPRISE: A DESIRE FOR CREDIBLE CONTEMPORARY CHRISTIAN WITNESS

As a consequence of this deliberate, collaborative process, there are at least three surprises that have struck us while writing this two-volume series. The first surprise comes from the feedback we collected regarding our first volume. We received many comments from readers of various faith backgrounds indicating that they appreciated the inclusion of the authors' personal experiences alongside the examinations of the saints' lives. We soon understood that this phenomenon points to many readers' desire to better appreciate the mystery of "the cloud of witnesses" (Heb 12:1), that is, the saints of God, in contemporary life. More than we anticipated, these readers sought to be edified by and to learn through the authors' candid reflections and questions.

THE SECOND SURPRISE: MORE RISKS, DIVERSE VOICES AND WRITING STYLES

A second surprise was a direct consequence of the first. As a response to the desire for credible contemporary Christian witness, the authors took greater personal risks of self-revelation in the sharing and writing process. The ways authors risked themselves also varied. Because of this, the writing styles and voices in this text are even more diverse than in our previous volume, and the stories are different—sometimes *very* different—from one another. The various perspectives, styles of writing, personal sharing, and voices that appear in this second volume provide a small, yet solid, demonstration of the many ways God works in the lives of people and the many ways human beings respond to His love. Even through this rich demonstration of human diversity, the book provides a testimony to "the one thing necessary" (Luke 10:42).

Some of the chapters in this book affectionately embrace the reader, offering encouragement, consolation, and hope. Others gently inspire and challenge. Still others powerfully provoke the reader to reconsider certain ways we think and act today. Every chapter, in its own way, bears a unique witness to the depth and breadth of Christian life and history. In totality, these accounts bear a powerful witness to the way in which "God is wondrous in His saints."

THE THIRD SURPRISE: "ANGELIC" SUPPORT

This second book began through generous encouragement and seed money grants awarded to us through the Valparaiso Project of Valparaiso University, the Falls Family Foundation, the Farah Foundation, and other gracious benefactors who wish to remain anonymous. Our third surprise concerns this small, yet growing, group of faithful benefactors, who through their personal and financial efforts have helped sustain our initiative. We would never have been able to complete this book without them! Attracted to our mission and to our work, they have quietly befriended us over the years and have encouraged us with sincere expressions of their trust and love. They have shared a vast array of personal resources, including their prayer, presence, time, expertise, and material assistance.

They told us that they joined this initiative because they profoundly care about the future of the Church, especially for their daughters and sons. They hope that their children's spiritual needs and gifts will be discerned and responded to authentically, in ways that bear witness to the life-giving Tradition of the Church, and they see the chapters in both these volumes as bearing a small witness to this living Tradition. They have quietly urged us to trust the loving God who called us to engage in this unique work. They have modeled for us the humility, perseverance, and love to carry on even when impasses presented themselves.

HOW TO READ THIS BOOK

Feel free to "pick and choose" chapters to read. The great variety of writing styles and perspectives may make one particular chapter a better "fit" at any given time. We hope that you will eventually benefit from engaging every chapter in the time and manner that is good for you.

Although each of the chapters stands solely on its own integrity, they have been placed in the existing sequence intentionally. It was our experience while working together that the sum of our efforts was greater than the total of the individual parts. We hope that this book, read in the order provided, may offer the reader a kind of restorative spiritual journey on which he or she is accompanied by all of us together in the presence of God and His saints.

THE JOURNEY'S OVERVIEW: WHO WILL MEET
AND GREET YOU

The book begins with a lyrical, almost whimsical welcome in the form of questions posed to us by author Eleni Simmons. She initiates our journey by pondering if and how God may be speaking to us today. We are led down a path on which she depicts her own spiritual "personal labyrinth" while sharing examples of how God's saints, including St. Christina of Tyre, are converted by God. Our path then takes a turn to the contemporary Middle East, with Hilary Chala guiding us through an exploration of past and present desert Christian spirituality. Here she shares the life of St. Thekla, "Equal to the Apostles," and the community of holy monastic

women and others who continue to bear faithful witness today to the
God who loves and heals us.

Our route veers once again as Susan Arida leads us to a small section
of racially divided, poverty-stricken urban America. Through the life of
St. Juliana the Merciful, in this chapter we come face to face with pow-
erlessness, personified by women past and present who weep, but who
dare to trust in the loving God "anyway." Our journey now turns, and we
are led by Valerie Karras, who confronts us with the lives of SS. Perpetua
and Felicitas, mothers who surrendered their children and endured a
savage martyrdom rather than forsake Christ. She explores in a challenging and personal manner what can happen when people defy, for the
sake of the gospel, those who abuse their authority. The stakes, in the
past as well as in our own day, have been very high.

At this point, we are greeted by Nikki Stournaras, who shares her
study of the Prophetess Anna. In this chapter, while identifying distracting "noises" of this world, the author powerfully presents us with
the need for silence before God. This is a silence that is powerfully depicted through the story of St. Anna. From here, Stefanie Yazge leads us
through the engaging life of St. Paula, friend of St. Jerome, who helped
him translate the Bible into Latin (a translation that came to be known
as the "Vulgate"). St. Paula's life led this author to examine the ancient
Christian "Order of Widows." Her study invites us to reflect more deeply
on the challenges and sacrifices of widows today, and to wonder how the
Church may better address the pastoral needs that widows represent.

Next, Valerie Zahirsky directs our attention to "Four Who Said
'No.'" This part of our travel becomes almost "a book within the book."
We are introduced to four women saints from various points in history
who said "no" to corrupt authority out of obedience to the will of God.
The author leaves us with the last, but not least, of the four: Mother
Maria Skobtsova. Now our book journey becomes even more delicate
and immediate as Barbara K. Harris shares the story of the martyrdom
of her patron saint and examines the early twentieth-century genocide
of Armenians by the Ottoman Turks. This historical investigation is set
within the larger context of exploring the Christian virtue of forgiveness, through which we and the entire world are invited by the loving
God, for whom nothing is impossible, to do the impossible: forgive.

The passage continues. At this point we are met by Iulia Corduneanu Curtright, who explores in a profound manner Christian "bold-

ness" (*parrhesia*), which is exhibited especially through the life of St. Mary of Egypt, who spent her early adult years as a hardened prostitute and, after being confronted by God, became an example of repentance. In this chapter the author engages us in the doxology of silence. Looking to the witness of the saints and especially this St. Mary, we are exhorted to boldly approach God today "with a pure heart" and "with uncovered face." The volume ends with my chapter, which strives to tell St. Mary of Egypt's life in her own words. The manner by which the Church preserves her life story powerfully indicates that she survived horrific, ongoing abuse; and so this version of her life is recorded in the first person. She shares her experience in some detail, thus identifying how persons may be affected by abuse and how God heals and changes their lives for the sake of His love "anyway."

FINAL THANKS

We pray you will enjoy this and other volumes we anticipate writing. We hope your reading will offer you a taste of the gifts we enjoyed while we were together writing, and we sincerely desire that these written "encounters" will benefit your life.

A few more thanks are in order, first to our dear friend and publisher, Dr. Anton Vrame, for publishing this second volume. We appreciate very much the time he has taken over the years to visit with us, to offer advice and friendship, and to attend to the production of this volume, among other things. We also wish to thank His Eminence Archbishop Demetrios, Chairman of the Assembly of Canonical Orthodox Bishops of North and Central America; Rev. Fr. Mark Arey; His Grace Bishop Dimitrios of Xanthos; Rev. Fr. Nicholas Triantafilou, President of Hellenic College-Holy Cross Greek Orthodox School of Theology; Rev. Fr. Thomas FitzGerald, Dean of Holy Cross Greek Orthodox School of Theology; Rev. Fr. Nicholas Manikas; Rev. Fr. Ephraim Peters; Herald Gjura; Marilyn Rouvelas; Joan Caradonna; Estelle MacDonald; Mary Danckaert; Joan Pohas; Joseph Carlson; Tony Gleason; Martha Shadan; Kara Matty; Gabriela Fulton, who has been wonderfully professional and competent through this whole project; and Steven Klund, the Holy Cross seminarian and graphic artist who did such a fabulous job with the new cover for volume 1 and with the volume 2 cover.

Sincere thanks are expressed here to each member of the SCV Board for the extra time that was given to review and support the editing of this volume, especially to Valerie Zahirsky, Eleni Simmons, and Clara Nickolson, and to the staff members of Sacred Hearts' Retreat Center in Wareham, Massachusetts, our "home away from home," whose cherished friendship, support, and encouragement have helped sustain us. It is apropos here to make a special mention of gratitude to Rev. Fr. Stan Kolasa, Sister Claire Bouchard, and Rev. Deacon Frank Tremblay.

If St. Catherine's Vision is to grow, we need more people to join us in our initiative. If you wish to learn more about and assist in the work of St. Catherine's Vision, please consult the epilogue of this book for information and suggestions.

Kyriaki Karidoyanes FitzGerald, editor
Feast day of St. Catherine the Great Martyr,
November 25, 2010
Sagamore, Massachusetts

St. Catherine's Vision Board
2008–2011

Susan Arida

Hilary Chala

Iulia Corduneanu Curtright

Kyriaki Karidoyanes FitzGerald

Barbara K. Harris

Clara Nickolson

Alexandra Safchuk

Eleni Simmons

Victoria Trbuhovich

Valerie G. Zahirsky

St. Christina of Tyre
and Miraculous Conversions
Eleni Simmons

*H*ave you ever wondered why God no longer speaks out loud to people, as He did to Moses on the mountain? Or why angels don't appear, seemingly in the flesh, to convey messages to those on earth? You sometimes hear or read about people receiving messages in dreams, but has it ever happened to you? In this day and age, if you heard a voice coming from inside a burning bush, you'd probably put out the fire and start looking for the hidden microphone. Instead of thinking of God, you'd be asking, "Am I on *Candid Camera*?"

When you hear someone say that God has called him or her to serve Him, do you wonder how God "spoke"? What makes that person so sure it was God? It might be one of those voices that are a symptom of mental illness. Indeed, many who suffer from that form of mental illness do interpret the voices as coming from God. Someone like Jim Jones—who led hundreds to kill themselves because God told him the only *real* heaven was aboard a space ship that they would meet after their deaths—certainly puts the whole idea of God "speaking" to mankind in question. It's tempting to "tar everyone with the same brush" and consider anyone

Eleni Simmons received a bachelor of business administration in accounting and worked as an accountant for thirty-two years, including sixteen years with a non-profit agency in Boston. While working in Boston she attended Holy Cross Greek Orthodox School of Theology, where she specialized in the writings of the Fathers, receiving the master of divinity (MDiv) and master of theology (ThM) degrees. She lives in Atlanta, where she works as a customer service assistant/billing coordinator for an international corporation, and sings in the choir at Annunciation Greek Orthodox Cathedral. Eleni also serves on the Board of St. Catherine's Vision.

who claims to have heard directly from God or an angel as not just a kook, but perhaps even a danger to society.

A PERSONAL CALLING

In the 1950s I saw the movie *A Man Called Peter*, about Peter Marshall, minister of New York Avenue Presbyterian Church in Washington, DC, who was twice chosen as chaplain of the US Senate. Early in the movie he announced to his mother that he had been called to be a minister. It was the first time I had heard anyone say that, and I wondered how he got this call. Did he hear directly from God, like Moses? Was he called in a dream, as Joseph was warned to take Mary and Jesus to Egypt?

Over the years I kept coming back to this question. Looking back now, after receiving my own "call," it seems a little strange that a movie I saw when I was less than ten years old would make such an impression on me. Was this the beginning of God's attempts to get my attention? Perhaps it was.

My attendance at various Protestant churches and Sunday schools was sporadic until I was seventeen, when I vehemently rejected all "organized" religion. I continued to believe in God but felt no need for churches to tell me how to live, and no need to go through someone else (specifically Jesus) when I prayed. I did not doubt the existence of Jesus as a historical figure, but I thought of him as a good man, sort of like Moses. Things went along fine for the next seven years, until about the time I turned twenty-four, when something happened in my life that left me questioning whether I really believed in God. I began to wonder if I said I did because it was the socially accepted thing to say in the South at that time. I can't really find the words to explain what I was feeling, except to say that my world felt very dark.

In the midst of that darkness, my best friend became engaged to a Roman Catholic man. The first time she was to attend Mass with him, she begged me to go with them so that she would not be the only non-Catholic there. After Mass my friend's fiancé took us on a tour of the Sunday school wing, and I was impressed with the posters in the various rooms. The whole catechetical approach to teaching a specific belief system impressed me. Somehow I had missed that when I went to Sunday school as a child—probably because I wasn't paying attention, but wondering what my mother was fixing for lunch. I had enjoyed the

Mass very much, particularly the congregational response to the priest's petitions.

By the time I left the church that day, I no longer doubted the existence of God, and I felt strangely drawn to attend Mass several more times at a Catholic church near my home. After a few weeks, however, I decided not to go back. I didn't really understand why I was drawn to the church, but I did not want to get involved with an organization with so many rules. Nor had my opinion of Jesus changed, and I instinctively felt that because I did not see the need to end my prayers with "in Jesus' name I pray," a Christian church was no place to hang out.

It took another nine years for God to get my attention in such a way that I began living from Sunday to Sunday, when I could attend the Divine Liturgy at Annunciation Greek Orthodox Cathedral in Atlanta, Georgia. I had found a home—where I was meant to be. It was as if I had been born Orthodox in my heart; it just took thirty-three years for my mind and body to catch up.

ST. GOLINDUC: A DIVINE DREAM

One of the first sets of books I bought after joining the Orthodox Church was on the lives of the saints. Christianity began during the time of the Roman Empire, when most people were either pagans or Jews. Many who became Christians did so after being taught, as we see in the letters of St. Paul. As Christianity gained followers, more and more of those who became saints were born to Christian parents, but conversions of those who started their lives as pagans continued. These were the stories that interested me most. I considered myself a pagan before I came to the Church, because I had never been baptized and had consciously rejected Christianity in my teens. Some of the conversions from paganism to Christianity were because of encounters with Christians. Curiosity or admiration led some to seek out the Church. Some searched for meaning and found Christianity. But some experienced miraculous conversions. They encountered angels who taught them, or had dreams that led them to the Church. To me, these are the most interesting, because they relate to my own experience.

One of the saints who was converted in a dream was St. Golinduc (baptized Mary), who lived in Persia in the late sixth century. She was either the wife[1] or the daughter[2] of the chief magician of the empire and assisted him in his feats of magic. One night as she slept, she had a divine visitation, which showed her the horrors of hell reserved for sinners and the beauty of heaven accessible through Jesus Christ. She became an instant convert and sought out the local Christian community, in which she received instruction and then baptism.[3] She made no attempt to hide her new faith and abandoned her life as the magician's assistant. This ultimately led to imprisonment, with a sentence to last as long as she clung to her Christian faith.[4] After many years in prison, an ambassador from the Byzantine Empire was allowed to visit her and taught her to sing the Psalms. When he left, the emperor ordered her into his presence, where she was subjected to many tortures, from which she suffered no harm. Finally he ordered her beheaded, but "the Lord sheltered her from the hand of the executioner and brought her to Christians living in concealment."[5] Eventually the persecution of Christians ceased in Persia, and Golinduc was able to preach the Christian faith openly. At the end of her life, she made a pilgrimage to Jerusalem and then set out for Constantinople.[6] She died en route to the church of the holy martyr Sergius in Nisibis.[7]

ST. CHRISTINA: A DIVINE VISITOR

There are two popular saints who were raised as pagans, confined in towers by their fathers, and only allowed contact with immediate family and trusted servants. St. Christina of Tyre was the first, followed by St. Barbara. St. Barbara's story is told in another chapter in this volume, so I will focus here on St. Christina's miraculous conversion. She was born in the seaport city of Tyre around 200 AD, during the reign of the Roman emperor Septimius Severus. In 202 the emperor enacted a law against the further spread of both Christianity and Judaism, which brought about violent persecutions.[8] Christina was destined to be caught up in this frenzy of hatred, and to give her life for Christ.

The daughter of Urbanos—a wealthy man, a general, and a high-ranking Roman official[9]—she was a beautiful child who promised to be an even more beautiful woman. Wanting to protect her from the world and from the advances of men, her father took the rather extreme measure of sequestering her in a specially constructed tower. Christina's "prison" was lavishly furnished and contained numerous gold and silver idols for her to worship. Many servants were appointed to wait upon her and provide for her every need and desire. For many years she seemed to be content with her life, but as she grew up she observed from her tower window the beauty of the earth and the sea, and the variety of living creatures. She began to ponder how all of these things came into being, and she came to the conclusion that the idols she had been worshipping could not have created anything, because they themselves had been created by human hands.[10]

As a result of this curiosity, and her strong desire to know about the Creator of all things, she was visited by an angel, who taught her all that she wanted to know, especially about Christianity.[11] Christina began to pray and fast, and her faith grew, as did her love of God and all creation. This eventually led her to destroy the gold and silver idols and distribute the pieces to the poor.[12] On his next visit to the tower, her father discovered that the idols were missing and questioned the servants (no doubt suspecting that they had stolen the priceless treasure). The servants replied that his daughter had destroyed them and "cast the pieces out the window."[13]

Although Urbanos was sorrowful that the daughter he loved so much had betrayed all that he believed, his sorrow was far surpassed by his rage. At first he tried having her beaten to regain her submission, but when that failed he had her thrown into prison. There she was visited by her mother, who begged Christina to come to her senses and give up the worship of this "foreign God," lest her father slay her. When she remained immovable her father sent soldiers to bring her before the governor, at which point he disowned her.[14] At her father's direction, and in his presence, she was subjected to a series of tortures, including being flayed alive, tied to a torture wheel over a fire, starved, and bound to a large rock and thrown into the sea. Through all this Christina prayed aloud and spoke to her tormentors about Jesus Christ, and she was nourished and healed by God. Her father viewed her repeated miraculous escapes from certain death as the result of sorcery, and finally ordered that she die the following day. Instead, he died a tormented death that night.[15]

Christina remained in prison but was left alone until her father's successor, Dion, arrived. He tried to sway her with flattery and offers of marriage to a great ruler, but to no avail. Once again she was subjected to unspeakable tortures, which only resulted in the seemingly supernatural destruction of the statue of Apollo, which Dion had commanded her to worship. Although thousands of bystanders at this event were converted to Christianity, the magistrate remained speechless and died from "vexation and distress."[16]

A third leader was brought to Tyre, one Julianos, who tried her with five days in a fiery furnace, from which she stepped unscathed. Once again she testified to the help she received from God, and once again her escape was deemed sorcery.[17] Julianos tried other tortures, which backfired and resulted in his own physical blindness. During her imprisonment, between bouts of torture, she was attended by many women, who were brought to Christianity by her teaching.[18] Christina was finally released from torture and imprisonment and died by the sword on July 24, 234. As with her first two persecutors, Julianos died in great torment immediately afterwards.[19] The saint was buried in a church constructed by some of her relatives, who had come to believe in Christ through witnessing her ordeals.[20]

A great many of the saints were subjected to unspeakable tortures, while loudly proclaiming Christian teachings and glorifying God. Most, like Christina, ultimately perished at the hands of their tormentors, after converting many to the faith by their teaching and fortitude. A smaller number, like St. Golinduc, were released and continued to proclaim their Christian faith and bring many converts into the Church. The thing that strikes me about these two young women is that they did not gain the knowledge they passed on to so many others by conventional means—they did not go through a systematic course of catechism. Although Golinduc was taught by a Christian clergyman, it was after she had accepted Christianity because of divine visitation in a dream. Her instruction served only to enlighten her about the finer points of what she already believed in her heart. St. Christina, on the other hand, was instructed in a miraculous way by an angel sent from God. Both women lived lives of prayer, through which their faith and knowledge grew, and by which their bodies were strengthened to withstand the tortures to which they were subjected.[21]

A PERSONAL LABYRINTH

My own conversion to Christianity was not as dramatic as either that of St. Golinduc or that of St. Christina, which I have talked about here, but I believe it was miraculous. I wasn't visited by a vision in a dream, but I believe I encountered at least one angel (on the telephone!) along the way. In the mid 1970s I was experiencing a great deal of dissatisfaction with my life. As one begins to seek meaning in life, certain things (like sex, drugs, and alcohol) start to get old. I decided that what I needed was some new friends, but, being shy, I didn't know how to go about meeting new people.

In the summer of 1977, a former girlfriend of the man I was dating joined our circle of friends. One day, while talking about places we had been on vacation, we discovered a mutual desire to go to Greece. The more we talked about it, the more determined we became to make this dream a reality, which we did in August 1978. I fell in love with the country and the people, but was frustrated by the language barrier and wanted to learn to speak Greek before I went back.

Since I frequently passed the Hellenic Community Center, I decided to call there to find out how to locate a Greek language class. The man who answered the phone told me there was a class starting soon at the church, so I immediately called to sign up. That was in September, and I continued to attend classes until the end of May. Over the summer I had no place to use the Greek I was learning, and I began to get frustrated. I couldn't afford to go back to Greece that summer, and I decided not to continue with the lessons. When my teacher called me early in September to tell me the classes would start the following week, I intended to tell her that I would not be continuing, but what came out of my mouth was, "I'll see you Tuesday." Again, I planned to tell her that I wouldn't be continuing on the night of the first lesson, but instead I wrote her a check for the next ten lessons. It seemed that my sub-conscious had other plans, and thus my Greek lessons continued.

Shortly after the semester started, I did tell her that I had considered not returning because I had no place to practice what I was learning, and she invited me to come to the church on Sunday. She explained that the Greek used in the services was an older form of Greek than what we were learning, but said it sounded the same and I would be able to practice reading by following the service in the book. I assured her that if I came into her church "the dome would fall down." But a seed had been planted, and I began to think that if I started going to this church, I might be able to make some new friends. The others in my class were members of the church and often talked about the social events they attended, which were sponsored by the community. So one Sunday morning in the early fall of 1979, when the

10 a.m. movie on television was something I didn't want to see, I decided to check out the church.

The cathedral in Atlanta has a sloping floor, so that it is fairly easy to see, even from the back. But at that time the pews didn't extend all the way to the door. There is a flat surface under the choir loft where they had set up folding chairs. I sat in one of those, from which I had a clear view of the pulpit and the chanter's stand, but not much else. The service is intoned rather than said, and the acoustics where I was sitting are not very good. Being unaccustomed to the chanting, I had difficulty catching individual words. Occasionally I would recognize a word of English, but for the most part the service was in Greek, and there were no service books in that section to which I could refer.

When the priest came to the pulpit, however, he spoke in English. I don't remember what the sermon was about, but I was struck by the way he spoke about Christ—as if he were talking about a friend—and I thought, "This man could answer all my questions." This thought came as a shock, because I was not aware that I *had* any questions until that moment. I wasn't sure when the service ended, because the chanting was still going on, but people began to come up the aisle, so I got up and left. As I was going out a side door, I passed a bulletin board with a banner across the top: "Orthodox? Is that Christian?" It was in that moment that I realized I had become a Christian and I thought, "I don't know what these people believe, but whatever it is, they're right." Like St. Golinduc, I needed to find someone to teach me the tenets of my new faith.

The first place I went to learn something about Greek Orthodoxy was the main branch of the Atlanta Public Library. This was before computers, so I had to use a card catalog. I tried looking up "Greek Orthodox," but found no references. Then I tried "Orthodox, Greek," but again found no help. I did see "Orthodox, Eastern," but I didn't know it was the same thing. I left the library thinking that if the whole Atlanta library system had nothing on this church, it must be a pretty obscure religion, but I was not dissuaded from my absolute conviction that I must become Greek Orthodox.

At my Greek lesson that week I asked my teacher if she could recommend a book. She didn't know of one written for adults but suggested that I come back the following Sunday and she would sit with me and help me with the service. I did as she suggested, sitting very close to the front, but she was unexpectedly called to teach Sunday school that day and wasn't able to join me in church. At the end of the service, as the pews were emptying, people were filing past the priest and receiving small squares of bread. I finally leaned over to the woman sitting next to me and asked what was going on. She explained the practice of receiving a piece of blessed bread from the priest (not to be confused with Communion) and invited me to the coffee hour. In the hall, she took me over to introduce me to someone who could recommend a book, and he turned out to be a friend of my parents, whom I had met once or twice before. He recommended *The Orthodox Church* by Timothy Ware (now Metropolitan Kallistos Ware) and said I could get it from the church office.

I bought the book that week, and I wasn't too far into it when I read something I had never known before—Jesus is God! I had always thought of him as a "nice man, kind of like Moses," and couldn't understand why prayers ended with "in Jesus' name we pray." I was so excited I could hardly contain myself. I started pacing around my apartment exclaiming out loud, "Why didn't anyone ever tell me this? How could I have missed it in Sunday school?" I finally calmed down enough to finish the book that day, and I wanted to become a member of the Church immediately, though I suspected that some catechism would be required.

It was about six weeks before I was able to make an appointment with the priest, but I continued to attend church every Sunday, and became good at following along in the book. Often during that time it seemed like I had a little devil on one shoulder and a little angel on the other. The little devil would nag at me that I didn't approve of organized religion, and that churches have rules, which I didn't like. The little angel replied that the rules would give me guidelines and help me know how to live a good, Christian life. This was a completely new way of thinking for me. I remember clearly the day I got rid of the little devil. I was sitting at a traffic light and the usual argument was going on in my head, when I shouted out loud, "Leave me alone! I'm happier than I've ever been in my life! The future used to look dark and gloomy; now I feel like the whole world is full of light!"

When I finally did start meeting with the priest and began to read the Bible, I discovered that Christ is "the light of the world." Because I had experienced this before I knew anything about it, there was proof that I was on the right track. In my catechism class there would sometimes be another person, someone who was converting because she was marrying a Greek Orthodox man, but often I was the only one, and it was a wonderful opportunity to ask questions. After almost six months Fr. Homer said I should probably be giving some thought to whether or not I wanted to join the Church, to which I responded that I had wanted to join for a long time before I started meeting with him but was waiting until he told me I had learned enough. He replied that there was no test to pass, and we set the date for my baptism. On June 11, 1980, I was baptized and chrismated with the name Eleni.[22] As my godparents I chose my Greek teacher, Jean; and Pete, the man who had suggested the Timothy Ware book.

I continued to meet with the priest for several months after my baptism, as it was a wonderful opportunity to further explore my new faith. Orthodoxy "fit me like a glove." I firmly believe that the reason I was never comfortable in any of the churches I attended in my youth is that I was not where I belonged.

God did not speak to me out loud, but I felt that he was guiding me. Every time I told someone how I had found out about the Greek classes, that person was puzzled. The Hellenic Center did not have a staff, and the only people there in the daytime during the week were some elderly Greek men, who met to play cards or backgammon. Nobody could imagine that any of them would know about the language classes at the church. Also, they all spoke English with a very heavy Greek accent, whereas the man I spoke to had no difficulty expressing himself clearly in English. I am convinced that the man was an angel.

When I started attending church regularly, I completely forgot that my original reason for going was to try to make some friends and enjoy some of the social activities at the church. After church I usually went into the hall for coffee, but if no one came up to me and started a conversation, I would take my coffee and leave. I didn't attend a social event until more than a year after my baptism, but I started meeting people fairly quickly because of my future godfather, and because I began attending an adult Sunday school class. Our church's national clergy-laity conference took place in Atlanta about a month after my baptism, and I spent several evenings volunteering. I met a few members of the choir and was encouraged to join that August.

Gradually, I got more and more involved with the various ministries in my parish, but I felt that the miraculous nature of my conversion called for some sort of more defined ministry. This led me to leave my job as an accountant and enroll at Holy Cross Greek Orthodox School of Theology in Brookline, Massachusetts. Nine years of study there, where I was mentored by several extraordinary clergymen, helped me to define my ministry as one of education through writing. Because I am not comfortable speaking to groups of strangers, writing seems a good way to educate others.

Psalm 46:10 says, "Be still and know that I am God." St. Christina made an unconscious choice to ponder the source of all the wonders of the world outside her tower window. Her quiet pondering led to the angelic visitation that enlightened her about God and Jesus. When I entered the Orthodox church that first Sunday, I made an unconscious choice to open my heart, and when I did Jesus Christ slipped quietly inside. Both Christina and I made an unconscious choice, which led to a conscious choice to act on God's revelation. For Christina this led to immediate action: excitedly telling her father the good news. From that point on, all of her choices led to her eventual death, but not before she converted many by her testimony, both verbal and non-verbal. My own action was not as dramatic. I sought to learn about Christianity and to join the Orthodox Church. My next conscious choice was to exercise my free will by offering my life to God. I have spent many hours in prayer and quiet contemplation since then trying to discern God's will for me.

One of the things that stands out about those who have experienced miraculous conversions is a compulsion to tell others. Over the centuries this has often led to death, or at the very least to imprisonment and torture. Because I live in the United States, I have not been faced with either. What slows down my compulsion is my shyness—even writing is difficult because I have to get up the nerve to give what I write to someone for possible publication. But God has taken care of that. He has given me the talent to write and tell His story, the blessing to have had the opportunity to learn much about His saints, and the wonderful gift of St. Catherine's Vision as the vehicle by which I may use both.

Notes

1. "Martyr Golinduc, in Holy Baptism Mary, of Persia," Orthodox Church in America, *Feasts & Saints*, http://ocafs.oca.org/FeastSaintsViewer.asp?SID=4&ID=1&FSID=102013.

2. George Poulos, *Orthodox Saints*, vol. 3 (Brookline, MA: Holy Cross Orthodox Press, 1976), 89.

3. Ibid., 90.

4. Ibid.

5. "Martyr Golinduc."

6. Poulos, *Orthodox Saints*, 90.

7. "Martyr Golinduc."

8. *The Lives of the Holy Women Martyrs*, translated and compiled from the Greek of *The Great Synaxaristes of the Orthodox Church* (Buena Vista, CO: Holy Apostles Convent, 1991), 281.

9. "Martyr Christina of Tyre," Orthodox Church in America, *Feasts & Saints*, http://ocafs.oca.org/FeastSaintsViewerasp?SID=4&ID=1&FSID= 102084.

10. *Lives of the Holy Women Martyrs*, 285.

11. "Martyr Christina of Tyre."

12. *Lives of the Holy Women Martyrs*, 286.

13. Ibid.

14. Ibid., 286–87.

15. Ibid., 289–90.

16. Ibid., 291–92.

17. Ibid., 292–93.

18. Ibid., 294.

19. Ibid., 295.

20. Ibid. Another source specifies her uncle as the one who erected the chapel: see Christina Shaheen Reimann, "A Reflection on Saint Christina," *St. Nina Quarterly* 2, no. 3 (Summer 1999), available online at http://www. stnina.org/print-journal/volume-2/volume-2-no-3-summer-1998/reflection-saint-christina, posted July 23, 2005.

21. Frequently modern scholars will downplay the stories of saints, especially those from the early centuries of Christianity, and I was curious about what they might say about St. Golinduc and St. Christina. I could find nothing on the Internet about St. Golinduc except Orthodox sources, but the following is typical of the scholarly approach to St. Christina: "There are two claimants to this title who have come to share the same Acts: Christina of Tyre (Phoenicia) and Christina of Bolsena in Tuscany. It would seem that the former never existed . . . Both Eastern and Western churches had a cult of Christina on 24 July; the Legend which does duty for both made her the heroine of a series of unlikely tortures endured for refusing to sacrifice to the pagan gods . . . The Legend seems to be a conflation of those of Barbara, Catherine of Alexandria, and Ursula" ("Saint Christina," from the *Oxford Dictionary of Saints*, Answers. com, www.answers.com/topic/saint-christina). In the final analysis, whether one believes that these two saints lived the lives recounted in the histories passed down within the Church is a matter of faith rather than of scholarship.

22. It is customary in the Orthodox Church to take the name of a saint at baptism. The feast day of the saint (usually celebrated on the date of his

or her death) becomes the person's "name day." In many places in the world a person's name day is celebrated instead of his or her birthday as the most important date in his or her life every year. This is a custom not only among Orthodox, but especially among many Roman Catholics in Central and South America.

REFLECTION AND DISCUSSION QUESTIONS

1. Have you ever experienced a defining, connecting moment with Christ?

2. a. Before reading this chapter, what were your impressions regarding how God speaks with people?
   b. Have your thoughts changed as a result of reading this chapter? If yes, how?

3. What tests of faith have you experienced? How have these experiences affected your relationship with God and with others?

4. We sometimes hear or read about people receiving messages in dreams. Has this ever happened to you or to someone close to you? Whatever your response may be, what do you think about this phenomenon?

5. a. When you hear people say that God has called them to serve Him, do you wonder about the way God "spoke" to them?
   b. What makes a person so sure it was God and not some other phenomenon occurring?
   c. Has there ever been a time when you may have misunderstood something that concerned God's will for you? How?

6. Beginning by describing herself as someone who "vehemently rejected all 'organized' religion," the author, in an inviting and graceful manner, shares the story of her own gradual conversion to Orthodox Christianity.
   a. Do you know of persons who experienced this kind of gradual conversion process? Please discuss this.
   b. What are other ways by which people join the Church are you aware of?
   c. Is it possible to be born into the Church and still be a "convert"? Please discuss this.

7. The author relates how it seems as if she were "born Orthodox in [her] heart—it just took thirty-three years for [her] mind and body to catch up."
   a. How did you feel when you first read this? Responses, understandably, may be diverse here; please discuss them.
   b. What do you suppose may be happening spiritually under these types of circumstances?

8. In a more subtle manner than the examples of the saints she identified, the author shares how an "angel" directed her to the Orthodox Church.
   a. What do you think about this? Please discuss this.
   b. How could angels be working among us now?

9. How do you think God may be speaking to you, today?

A Desert Mother: Discovering the Treasure of Salvation in the Wilderness

Hilary Chala

EVANGELIST, MARTYR, AND EQUAL TO THE APOSTLES: OUR *MAR TAKLA* (ST. THEKLA)

*I*n December 2004 I traveled to Syria. While in Damascus, the group with which I was traveling was to make a pilgrimage to the small town of Ma'aloula to venerate the relics of a woman named Thekla (*Takla* in Arabic). I was told the monastery we were about to visit is the oldest surviving monastic community in Christian history. I didn't know who Thekla was, even though her name was read in the Church's commemorations and intercessions with a litany of others, all described as "the great women martyrs." Her name was always first, which gave it a sort of prominence: "Thekla, Barbara, Anastasia, Catherine, Kyriaki, Fotini . . ." The name drew my attention because it was so foreign to me. I knew who all the other women were, but who was Thekla?

THE TREASURE HUNT: PILGRIMAGE TO MA'ALOULA, SYRIA

As we bumped along in our minibus between Damascus and Ma'aloula, we saw nothing alive; we stared through the windows at rock. The Syrian desert is brutal even in the cold winter. One of the priests traveling with

---

Hilary Chala has a master of divinity from Holy Cross Greek Orthodox School of Theology. She is in the process of completing a master of theology, also from Holy Cross. She has completed eight units of Clinical Pastoral Education in the Texas Medical Center Hospital System, Houston, Texas. She also serves on the Board of St. Catherine's Vision.

us commented that the very landscape "desolates the soul." The large amount of rock and light from the sun makes the landscape blinding.

As we approached the monastery, we were at the bottom of a mountain that was as sharp as a cliff. In one spot on the mountain wall, we saw something green growing. This tree or bush stands out sharply, as it is the only visible living thing on the horizon.

The people in Ma'aloula speak Aramaic, an otherwise dead language that was spoken at the time of Christ. Other than the few homes we passed entering the village, there were only some small shops that sold their items to pilgrims who came to the monastery.

The Monastery of St. Thekla is the heart of the village. At the monastery the nuns run an orphanage for girls. The sisters live a simple life and devote their days to God through prayer and ministry. Their ministry is the care they give to the orphan girls, as well as the hospitality and spiritual care they give to the many pilgrims who come seeking spiritual and physical healing.

The sisters led our group around the monastery. Then they gathered us into a small chapel, and one of them taught us the story of Mother Thekla. This kind of story is an example of hagiography—that is, the accounts of the lives of the saints.

Thekla lived during the first century in Iconium, Greece. She was a beautiful young woman, and consequently her parents kept her locked away in her home. In 45 AD St. Paul was preaching in the streets of her city, and she could hear him from a window. Three nights in a row this happened, with the words of the Resurrection of Christ stirring her soul. She would ask her pagan family questions about St. Paul's teachings, but their answers never satisfied her.

As was appropriate for her time, Thekla's parents engaged her to be married. It became known to her betrothed that in her heart she was a Christian. Because of this, she was brought before a tribunal, which condemned her to death. First they tried to drown her in a large basin of water full of deadly animals. Instead, Thekla baptized herself in the waters, and all the animals in the water died. Convinced she was a sorceress, the tribunal tried to burn her, but the flames would not touch her; instead, they died out.

After this they let her go. She fled Iconium, eventually ending up in Ma'aloula, where she dwelt in a cave. God provided her with a little water to sustain her, and this water exists to this day. Eventually other young women came and lived with her, and a monastic community was formed. She was pious, humble, and righteous before God. Word spread that persons who visited her would be healed.

Later in her life, as the knowledge of Thekla's influence spread beyond Ma'aloula, the pagans in the area became increasingly jealous of her. They believed that her healing powers were the result of her virginity, so young men were sent to rape her, even in her extreme old age. When Thekla saw her pursuers, she fled to the mountain behind her cave. At the base of the mountain, the earth suddenly split apart, creating a very narrow opening. After she slipped into the crevice, water began to pour out from it. The men could not follow and had to give up chasing her.

Thekla continued to dwell in her cave and died peacefully around the year 100 AD.

The nun telling us about her life also told us stories of healing that continue to happen to this day at the monastery. Many of the pilgrims who come are ill or physically handicapped and need assistance to climb the flights of stairs to her cave. Most of the people who experience physical healing stay in the cave all night praying to Thekla for intercession for God's grace in their lives and drink the holy water from the spring in her cave. The morning following their all-night vigil, they experience healing as they walk down the steps from the cave.

After talking with us, the sister encouraged us to go up to her cave to see where Thekla lived and where so many people continue to find her. We had to climb up steps hewn into the mountain to get to the cave, which is somewhat like a large, three-sided room. In the deepest part, about twenty feet back from where the sunlight can reach, we saw a tree growing. Its branches hit the cave ceiling and ran towards the sunlight, all the way to the cave's opening. This was the tree we had seen as we approached the village in the minibus. It looked as though a beautiful hanging garden had been cultivated inside the cave. Nearby was the spring of holy water that God had provided for Thekla. This spring is still running after all these centuries and has no source to replenish it other than the One who gave it. It is a sort of well now, and there is a metal cup so that people can drink from it. Like so many before us, we drank too . . .

At the furthest part of the cave from the entrance is the chapel and tomb of Thekla, where pilgrims spend their time praying for healing. As we passed through this space, I saw a stack of crutches and canes, some of metal, others wood; there was even something that looked like a prosthetic leg. All of these had been discarded by people who, by God's grace, were made well through faith.

The priests in our pilgrimage group led us in prayers, and we were anointed with oil from the vigil lamp in her tomb before being led back down from her cave. Last of all, we were taken back outside the monastery walls to the base of the mountain and to the gap in the cliff that had miraculously opened for Thekla so that she could make her escape. Even now there is water running on the floor of the crevice. The gap is wide enough for people to pass through. The priests ran ahead, and I followed the other girls. We disappeared inside the mountain.

The ravine we were following would wax and wane in size, with the widest point not more than eight feet across. For stretches we were able to walk side by side on the floor of the gap on either side of the running water. Sometimes the water flowed more strongly, and the only foothold was a ledge in the stone that had not worn away from the constant flow of water. At some points this ledge was so narrow that we had to completely press our bodies and faces against the side of the cliff. I remember the cool feeling of the cliff against my cheek. Without being able to see, we would feel our hands over the rock until a hole would appear, soft and oiled over from the many hands that had rested there. We would use these to hold our balance as we slipped over. The feeling of the coarse cliff stone would wear away to something smooth, and we would find there a handhold to grasp, and then would reach our legs around and find a foothold to take a step forward.

For over nineteen hundred years people have been making this same journey. All of us pilgrims are either consciously or unconsciously thirsting for God and hoping to ease the thirst in our soul with water from the monastery at Ma'aloula.

My time in this village was magnificent, beautiful. It was also overwhelming because it seemed so otherworldly. This is everyday existence for the few hundred people who live there, but for us it was like stepping into a fairy tale consisting of an ancient hanging garden, water appearing from desert rock, and a mountain splitting in two. But most of all, it was the place where people who were bound by physical and spiritual illness experienced healing.

By encountering Thekla at her tomb, I discovered a treasure of living history. This image of godliness is for us Orthodox Christians a window into heaven.

THE DISCOVERED TREASURE

How St. Thekla's Life Is Preserved by the Orthodox Church

The Church[1] honors St. Thekla with these two special distinctions: "Equal to the Apostles" and "Martyr." The Orthodox have long affirmed that "Saint Takla was called the First Martyr because she was the first Christian woman who was exposed to torture and persecution for the sake of God."[2] Although many people will hear the word "martyr" and assume Thekla died a tragic death, she did not. This distinction of "martyr" is in the sense of her *witnessing* to Christianity by her preaching, for the word "martyr" means literally "one who offers testimony" or "one who bears witness." She is also honored as Equal to the Apostles "because she carried on preaching, calling and teaching as if she were one of the Twelve Apostles."[3] Being given a title that demonstrates her to be revered as one of the apostles recognizes the evangelical work she accomplished during her lifetime.

There are many issues surrounding the person of Thekla. For example, the most popular ancient portrayal of her life is the apocryphal work the *Acts of Paul and Thekla*,[4] which recounts her participation with St. Paul the Apostle in his ministry of evangelism before she retreated to her cave at Ma'aloula.

Also, Thekla is, in fact, one of the women saints who donned men's clothing[5] to participate anonymously in activities that typically were reserved for men, or that women participated in separately.[6] In fact, the title *"Mar"* in *Mar Takla*, although it is commonly translated as "saint," carries a greater significance: *mar* is an Aramaic word that is only used in reference to male saints. St. Thekla, however, "was awarded this name due to her similarity to [the] apostles through her performance of baptism."[7]

The Person of Thekla in My Life

There are two different reasons why I chose to write about Thekla. First, I am very concerned about the declining presence of Christians in Syria, as well as in other regions in the Middle East and Africa. My own family fled Syria because of religious persecutions over a hundred years ago. Thekla is for me a buried treasure in our times. In almost the same manner by which she fled into the crevice in the rock and disappeared, so too has her story, along with those of other Christians, seemingly disappeared underneath centuries of Islamic domination in the Middle East. For example, as Orthodox Christians we place icons of Christ and saints of the Church inside our homes and in churches. These serve as visual reminders of who God is, and the many unique and differing paths we can take to reach our salvation. It was disturbing to me that every Christian building we entered in Syria had a photograph of the country's president above the icons of Christ. This was something I visually experienced that demonstrated how Christians in Muslim nations live under a sort of house arrest and exist at the will of the state, as members of a second class citizenry known as "protected" ones.[8]

I asked one of the priests why Ma'aloula still exists if Muslims do not like it. He said it depends on who is governing Syria, but also that many people, Muslim and Christian alike, make pilgrimages to Ma'aloula for healing, and Muslims as well as Christians have been healed. I began to think deeply within my heart about his words. It reminded me of something I had read from the highly venerated contemporary ascetic Elder Paisios the Athonite: "In our days, everybody suffers from three things: cancer, mental illnesses and divorce."[9] He was describing the physical, mental, and relational afflictions from which people suffer. People bring all their tragedies to the feet of the Church, and here at Ma'aloula they ask for Thekla's intercession before God. The sort of ministry these pilgrims of Thekla receive in the bosom of her monastery carries on from one generation of pilgrims to the next. So the monastery remains as a testament of the faith of the people, Christian and Muslim alike.

The second reason why I chose to write about Thekla is that I wanted to share the life of a person who had the special and rare calling of building her relationship with Christ in the wilderness, in her case the desert. We can understand this calling as one that impels persons who follow it to work at purifying their hearts and souls, uniting themselves with God through prayer, fasting, contrition, and repentance. Many people desire solitude to be able to concentrate on purifying their hearts. To find this solitude they go into the wilderness—into the desert.

During my chaplain's residency at the Texas Medical Center, I was asked to read a book about Orthodox Christian desert spirituality written by someone who did not practice the Orthodox Christian faith. Reading this book was very disturbing, as the author had been introduced to, and subsequently misunderstood, Orthodox Christian "desert spirituality."

The author declared that one could have the same experience as the Desert Fathers and Mothers by going on a camping trip, perhaps bringing along chocolate chip cookies. She further suggested that if going into the desert was not possible, one could re-create the desert experience by going into a closet and putting one's hand in a box of sand. As Orthodox Christians, we understand that sin, in the broad sense, is "missing the mark" (the "mark" being obedience to our loving Lord and God; see Luke 11:28). Sadly, this writer, so confident that the experience of the desert monastics could so easily be reproduced, completely missed the mark.

It is tempting to delude myself into believing I can have my salvation through chocolate chip cookies and weekend getaways. And there is something spiritually arousing in being told that one can have a secret rendezvous with God in a closet with a box of sand. This has been taught by some as a healthy form of spiritual direction. It is not. Rather, it is a dangerous and misguided effort that can lead away from God, and toward spiritual seduction. It is extremely dangerous to participate in anything of such a nature.

As an Orthodox Christian, reading this book and recognizing the attitude it represented made me feel that my mother (the Church) had been wronged. I felt angry that someone had taken more than two thousand years of godly presence, holy Tradition, and obedience to God and reduced it to putting a hand in dirt. I felt that Orthodox Christianity had been misrepresented, slandered, and even violated by someone unrightfully claiming authoritative knowledge about desert Christian spirituality and speaking on our behalf.

I wanted to defend the Church. I wanted to right the wrong by correctly speaking the truth of what it is to acquire salvation in the wilderness. My way of doing this is by sharing the life of a woman saint who did achieve her salvation in the wilderness. Thekla, who fulfilled her call in the desert, has such a life that if someone asks the question, "How is it that a person might find Christ in the desert?" they may find an authentic answer in the life of Thekla, instead of a faux experience. Her primary hymn, or troparion, presents her as an early Church heroine:

> You were enlightened by the words of Paul,
> O Bride of God, Thekla,
> And your faith was confirmed by Peter, O Chosen One of God.
> You became the first sufferer and martyr among women,
> By entering into the flames as into a place of gladness.

For when you accepted the Cross of Christ,
The demonic powers were frightened away.
O all-praised One, intercede before Christ God
that our souls may be saved.[10]

CONCLUSION: INVESTING IN THE TREASURE

Today, images from St. Thekla's life and the pilgrimage to Ma'aloula have the power to transform intense experiences or even memories of the most difficult and joyful periods of my life. Still, there are many things I must continue to think about and learn from regarding this journey through Syria and with Thekla. She heard St. Paul preach the good news of the Resurrection of Christ, and she embraced it. This was her choice: to allow the Word of God to transform her and to perfect her over her lifetime. This is one lesson I learn from Thekla: to be open to and listen for God; He will guide our lives in ways we ourselves would never foresee. I do not want my personal relationship with Thekla to become dry. I can keep it alive by being with God in prayer, participating in the sacraments of the Church, and allowing my heart to be open to building a relationship with Thekla, who is alive in Christ. If I do this, if I invite Thekla or any saint more fully into my life, I may experience the same relationship she has with God. I will feel peace and love inside of me, inside my soul. I think this is what it feels like to grow in God's love. I also believe that this is what He wants for me, too.

NOTES

1. It is worth pointing out that in the Orthodox Christian Tradition the voice of the "Church" is spoken by all the people, not just the hierarchy. For example, it is the people of the Church, the "people of God" (the "*laos tou Theou*" in Greek), who *together* offer the prayers of consecration, which is why a service of consecration must be performed with at least two people.

2. Greek Orthodox Patriarchate of Antioch and All the East, *The Oldest Christian Sacred Sepulchre of the First Christian Century: Saint Takla, the Patron Saint of the Monastery of Mar Takla at Ma'aloula*, 10–11. Booklet obtained at the Monastery of St. Thekla.

3. Ibid.

4. *New World Encyclopedia* (online), s.v. "Acts of Paul and Thekla," accessed July 8, 2009, http://www.newworldencyclopedia.org/entry/Thekla#Cult_of_Saint_Thecla. By "apocryphal," I mean that the authenticity

of the work is somewhat doubtful, even though the document dates from 190 AD. The apocryphal work is available in its entirety on the Internet.

5. Stephen J. Davis, *The Cult of Saint Thecla: A Tradition of Women's Piety in Late Antiquity* (New York: Oxford University Press, 2001), 7.

6. It is important to be aware that at the time of Thekla, and today in the East, men and women remain on separate sides of their place of worship.

7. Greek Orthodox Patriarchate of Antioch, *Oldest Christian Sacred Sepulchre*, 10–11.

8. John L. Esposito, *Islam: The Straight Path* (New York: Oxford University Press, 1998), 39.

9. Priestmonk Christodoulos, *Elder Paisios of the Holy Mountain* (Holy Mountain, Greece, 1998), 19.

10. Troparion of St. Thekla, tone 4.

REFLECTION AND DISCUSSION QUESTIONS

1. Who are the female role models, mentors, and "mothers" in your life? What have they taught you about God?

2. Who are some of the female role models, mentors, and "mothers" in the Church today? How have you benefited from them?

3. The author describes St. Thekla's life as a buried treasure. Are there any people you know whose lives you would consider buried treasure as well (meaning that they are remarkable but unknown to the world around them)?

4. In what ways can we find ourselves acting as mothers or fathers in our lives to persons who are not our biological or adopted children? What do you believe the Church teaches about this?

5. The author offers an example of Orthodox Christian spirituality being misunderstood and hence misrepresented. Why do you think the misunderstanding occurs?

6. Have you ever been misrepresented in your life, and how did you respond? In what way could you have possibly responded better?

7. The author describes persons who seek God in the wilderness as a way to focus on their relationship with God away from the distractions of the everyday world. How does holding onto our "stuff" keep us from moving closer to God?

8. In what ways are we fulfilling our vocations to become saints in our present context?

St. Juliana and Women Who Weep

Susan Arida

*A*while ago, I agreed to teach an eight-week course to twenty women. Most, but not all, were women of color. My job was to help prepare them for jobs in a health-care facility. To be accepted, an applicant had to be a legal resident, a high school graduate, and a TANF recipient—in other words, a welfare mom.[1] I am a white woman who had been teaching similar classes for ten years, but I had never confronted race, class, and poverty in the way that I would in the coming weeks. In this classroom, I was not the program director or the seasoned mother or the priest's wife. Entering the empty classroom, I waited for the women to arrive, hoping for a successful class, anxious about the prospects of a new challenge . . .

A Chorus of Tears

What experience had taught me was that most of the students would enter the class with expectations and with some "attitude," feelings of hope and uncertainty. This class, however, would be different from any I previously encountered. On the first day everyone was quiet

Susan Arida attended St. Vladimir's Seminary in Crestwood, New York, from 1975–1977. After leaving St. Vladimir's, she and her husband taught at St. Herman's Seminary in Kodiak, Alaska. Deeply involved in parish life since 1981, when her husband, Robert, was ordained to the priesthood, she has taught English for Speakers of Other Languages (ESOL) courses at Hellenic College, Brookline, Massachusetts, and other institutions. Presently, she is the Director of the YMCA International Learning Center, a community-based ESOL institute in Boston, and serves on the Board of St. Catherine's Vision.

and watchful, but by the second class an undercurrent had developed that was aggressive, defensive, and vulnerable, all at the same time. It turned out that their being there involved a struggle that I couldn't imagine. The expectations of this class and the program, which was supposed to lead to a job, a stable income, benefits, and ultimately a better life, was yet another worry for these mothers. They seemed smart and determined, yet they lacked the experience of success needed to succeed. I felt I was teasing them with a goal just out of reach, offering them an opportunity that would lead to another failure.

By 8:30 a.m. of the fourth class, no one was in her seat at the scheduled start time, and only half had arrived by 9:00 a.m. When I remarked on the importance of punctuality, a tired woman informed me that most of the women in the class didn't live near the school, and even those that did had to use public transportation to get their kids to day care and then make their way to class. "We have to get ourselves and the kids up before five in order to be in class by eight thirty," I was told. The message: don't expect punctuality. "Oh . . ." I said.

The first weeks passed. During the fourth week, when I asked the class to quiet down so we could begin, a woman in the front row said my way of asking them to quiet down showed I didn't respect them. Another agreed saying, "Yeah, she's probably never taught people like us."

The discord was clear. Something was broken, and I didn't know how to fix it. I wanted to believe that we had been brought together to achieve a goal and that there was something I could do to make this happen. We were all women, all of us were moms, struggling to raise our children and to keep our lives together, but in reality, the barriers that faced these women were not familiar to me, and their struggle was a world apart from mine.

There was a difference between us that I didn't want to acknowledge. The hard edges of their lives made each day a fight between life and death. I had never thought of myself as having a privileged life. Married to an Orthodox priest, I had lived at times near poverty level with five kids and a husband who was often occupied with parish work, but I had always been respected, safe in my role at home, in the Church, and in the classroom. Suddenly, I was face to face with women whose lives were defined by race, class, and poverty, and whether I wanted to admit it or not, a great gulf separated us, which made me shrink from them, and them from me.

Slowly, the facts of their lives began to emerge. All twenty women were victims of domestic violence. All had been forced to go to shelters because home had become a nightmare. Those who had been fortunate enough to move into housing were living in apartments that had mold and mildew, with poor heating and ventilation, and this led to high rates of asthma and other chronic diseases, especially among their children. Upon coming in late for class one morning, one mom simply stated she had been at the emergency room the night before with her baby, who couldn't breathe. I tried to imagine a panicked visit to the emergency room in the middle of the night; I tried to listen, tried to sympathize, but I couldn't reach her. The same day, I found out that another woman was still mourning the loss, over a year before, of her infant daughter.

Near the end of the course, a guest speaker was invited to address the class. The speaker was a man who had grown up as the son of a single mother who had also been the victim of domestic violence. I felt I should hear what he had to say. Maybe he could help me understand.

After speaking about the struggle his own mother faced in living her life and raising him, he spoke about his life and his encounters with violence. Then he spoke about falling in love with a woman who had given him a reason to change and who had brought him to God. At some point, the monologue became a conversation. Some began to respond when he asked them to say what they could about their lives and what they needed to do to finish the course. There was some hesitation. Several spoke up, saying they were there for their kids. But it went further. One woman stood up and talked about spending a night in jail, away from her son, and how in that most desperate moment, she turned to God for help. She said she knew the only way to go on was to thank Him for what she had, and to move forward knowing that, whatever happened, she would be thankful for what she had received. In the morning the charges were dropped, and she was able to get back to her son. In my presence and before others, she spoke, without shame or pretense, of God's love and of how God had given her hope in her darkest moments. Her story silenced the room, except for the quiet tears of mourning that began to flow. I still see several of the women weeping, their voices like the chorus in an ancient Greek tragedy:

—*We don't have to be this way because society is this way.*
—*Walking away doesn't solve anything.*
—*How can we release the pain and bitterness?*

—Through tears running down both sides of our bodies . . .
—What are we holding on to?
—Let the chains go. Open the window and step out on the ledge . . .

I was deeply moved by these women, who had put their hands in the hand of God when there was nothing left, women who cried out to God from the deepest pit. That moment touched my heart in a way that both challenged and confirmed my faith.

THE LAMENTATIONS OF RACHEL

The sorrow of the women in my class brought me to Rachel and the mothers of Ramah mourning the loss of their children: "A voice was heard in Ramah, sobbing and loudly lamenting: it was Rachel weeping for her children, refusing to be comforted because they were no more" (Matt 2:18).

The weeping and loud lamentation was for the children slain by Herod, a great king who was threatened and enraged when three Persian kings told him they were following a star that they believed was the sign of new king. These children are the Holy Innocents, who were slain by Herod's soldiers in order to eliminate a challenge to the status quo. Read every year in the Orthodox Church on the first Sunday after the Nativity of our Lord, the story is always a shocking contrast to the pleasures and parties that mark the Christmas season.

In her lament, Rachel's words are mingled with the voices of women who know grief. They are like the voices of the women in my class. They, like Rachel and the mothers in Ramah, were unable to protect their children from the horrors of a life limited by the powerful forces of society. Like the stories told by the women in my class, the hardness of this reality remains and confronts us with the unpredictable and fragile nature of life in the fallen world where the birth of Jesus Christ takes place—He who, like the Innocents, is Himself marked for death.

Only St. Matthew's Gospel records the story of these innocent children and the sorrows of their mothers. By invoking the name of Rachel, a woman who is considered the mother of all Israel, he links the death of the Holy Innocents to earlier tragedies in salvation history. Rachel, the love of Jacob's life—who could not be his first wife because of the deceit of her father, Laban—was unable to become pregnant for many years. Believing that not having a child is a curse, she begs Jacob,

"Give me children, or I shall die" (Gen 30:1). Ironically, Rachel dies in childbirth in Ephratha, near the town of Bethlehem, after delivering her second son, Benjamin. Her tomb, marked by Jacob, can still be visited today.[2]

St. Matthew quotes the Prophet Jeremiah (Jer 31:15) in order to link Rachel to this tragedy of the Holy Innocents. In the Old Testament tradition, Rachel is the mother of all, the woman who, along with her sister Leah, "built up the house of Israel" (Ruth 4:11). Being in this position, she is inextricably tied to the tragedies that befall the people of God. And yet the prophet, while speaking of the horror and injustice of Israel's capture by the Babylonians and acknowledging the deaths and the ultimate deportation of thousands, nevertheless promises consolation. Speaking through the voice of the prophet, God expresses the sorrow and grief that defies understanding yet consoles with hope: "Thus says the Lord, 'Now I will restore the tents of Jacob and take pity on his dwelling . . . Stop your weeping, dry your eyes, your hardships will be redressed . . . There is hope for your descendants,' says the Lord" (Jer 30:18; 31:16–17).

Rachel's grief embraces the mothers weeping for their children everywhere, and with them, she laments a lost promise. The prophet says to "stop [our] weeping," but isn't it too much to ask a mother to keep her eyes from tears? Or is it these shared tears that enable us as women to share our grief and that bring us to a place where comfort and hope may be found? One woman asked, "How can I release the pain and bitterness?" Another replied, "Through tears running down both sides of your body."

St. Juliana: Weeping and Witness

Merciful Juliana, a sixteenth-century Orthodox saint, experienced thirteen pregnancies and suffered the death of six of those children. Like other women, she struggled with how to cope with her grief. Following the death of one of her children, she nearly left her husband and remaining children to enter a monastery, but Juliana was not destined for monastic life. Instead she was called to live in the world and to care for those around her. In her life, with God's help, she was able to prevent the deaths of hundreds of starving people by offering all that she had to feed them.[3]

The kontakion sung in honor of St. Juliana places us in the midst of sorrow and hardship, yet consoles, offering hope to the moms in my class, to the mothers in Ramah, and to all who seek it:

> All of us amid misfortune and pain hymn the holy Juliana as a helper, quick to hear; For she lived a God-pleasing life in the world and gave countless alms to the poor. Wherefore, she has found the grace of miracles at the command of God. (Tone 8)

St. Juliana is often described as an ordinary "middle class" (white) woman, a housewife and a mother. She lived, however, at a time and in a society where cruelty was not limited by class or race, but rather constituted the daily reality for many Russians. Juliana was born in 1530 and died in 1604, and so her life coincidentally corresponds almost exactly to that of Queen Elizabeth I of England. Their lives, however, could not have been more different.

St. Juliana lived during the reign of Ivan IV (1533–1584), also known as Ivan the Terrible. Like King Herod, Tsar Ivan was a great builder, having in his earlier and more rational period ordered the construction in Red Square, Moscow, of the well-known Cathedral of the Intercession, also known as St. Basil's after the fool for Christ. Ivan's later rule, however, was no less paranoid and cruel than Herod's brutal treatment of his fellow Jews.

Born in Moscow, St. Juliana lived in the vicinity of the city all of her life, so it is possible that she beheld the magnificent domes atop the ornate new cathedral. Her parents—Justin and Stephanida Nedyurev, known for their pious virtue—were boyars, or members of the merchant class who served at the tsar's court. When Juliana was only six years old, her mother died. Because of her father's obligation to the court, he was unable to care for Juliana, so she was sent to Murom to live with her maternal grandmother, who, according to popular sources, continued to raise Juliana in the Orthodox Christian faith. With her grandmother, Juliana attended the divine services and learned Church practices and customs. When she was twelve, her grandmother died, and Juliana was again uprooted. She was sent to live with her aunt, who, along with her children, was impatient with Juliana's efforts to pray and fast, and with her sensitivity to the needs of the poor.

When Juliana was sixteen, she married Yurii Osorgin, the wealthy landowner of Lazarev, with whom she had ten sons and three daughters. Four sons and two daughters died as children, and in her grief she sought to enter a monastery. In one writing on the life of St. Juliana, her husband is said to have quoted one of the Fathers to her, hoping to bring some clarity to her heart by saying, "Children, orphaned, will often weep . . . saying: 'Wherefore, having given birth to us, hast thou left us in tribulation and suffering?' If it is commanded to feed the orphans of others, it follows that one ought not to starve one's own children."[4]

Eventually, Juliana agreed to stay with her husband and raise her other children. We can imagine that her memories of her own child- hood after the loss of her mother may have contributed to her decision. Though Juliana remained in the world, she spent her nights praying af- ter everyone else was in bed and then attended Church services in the morning. Her husband, Yuri, who must have loved her very much, agreed after the death of two of their sons that he and she would live together as brother and sister. He comforted the illiterate Juliana by reading the lives of the saints to her. In time, Juliana became well known in the sur- rounding regions for her kindness and charitable works. Her husband was required to serve in the tsar's army and was at times away for more than a year, leaving Juliana alone to cope with the affairs of daily life without him. But Juliana's kindness and hospitality endeared her to her husband's parents and family, and ultimately led them to ignore the cus- tomary subservient relationship with a daughter-in-law by entrusting her with the management of the family estate.

At that time, in Russia and in most other cultures, controlling and restricting the activities of women in their relationships and in their daily lives was considered essential for family life, and provided order within the society and country. This assumption sometimes presup- posed that women could not be trusted to remain faithful to their hus- bands, homes, and rulers if they were educated or exposed to outside influences. As a result, Russian boyar women were isolated in *terems*, living places for women, which kept them separate from men before marriage and served as a place for "unclean" (menstruating and post- partum) women. Privileged women were "imprisoned," secluded and unable to do much without their husband's permission. According to Eve Levin in her book *Sex and Society in the World of Orthodox Slavs, 900–1700*, a sixteenth-century German traveler reported that "Russian women were locked up in their houses with no control over their lives." Levin also comments that Russian society disregarded women's rights and focused only on their responsibilities and obligations. Women who did not properly fulfill their role as "wife" could be beaten and raped with no real opportunity for recourse. Divorce was possible, but rarely granted.[5]

During the lifetime of Juliana, around the 1550s, a manual for domestic life, called the *Domostroi*—translated as the "Homebuilder" or "House Order"—was written.[6] It is an authoritative manual that documents the rules for the proper management of a Russian household. The *Domostroi* was quite comprehensive, containing recipes, directions for domestic tasks, traditions, and descriptions of model behavior. It was probably written by a Kremlin monk who used Orthodox Christianity to frame the work. Known especially among the boyar class, the *Domostroi* became a unifying reference for Russian society by ensuring that the proper standard for a Russian household was understood and observed. Because it was not usual for women of that era to have an education, it was left to men to read, or at least to know its tenets, and to use it to manage their household, including family members and servants.

Furthermore, the *Domostroi* held men responsible for the heavenly salvation of the family, and so they were given the right to correct those in their care. Because this duty could be interpreted to justify the beating of both women and children, families could be trapped in abuse, with both women and men convinced that a woman's behavior is only properly controlled and corrected through violence. On the other hand, the rules of the *Domostroi* were also understood as a way to keep women safe. Given the instability of the government and the continuous reality of foreign invasion, unprotected women faced certain danger outside the home. Ironically, therefore, the culture of the *Domostroi*, while subjecting women to the authority of their husbands and fathers, also protected them from bands of vagrants, robbers, and foreign invaders roaming the countryside.

What is interesting in the *vita* of Juliana the Merciful is that, although she was indeed a "pious wife," her piety does not seem to be the result of her or her husband's conformity to the harshness of the *Domostroi*. To the contrary, rather than a prisoner, Juliana appears to have been the mistress of the estate, having the freedom to express her love for God through generous almsgiving. Instead of being trapped in abuse, Juliana sanctified her home through her charity and mercy. Her relationship with her husband was not formed by beatings, but by his reading to her, trusting her with his sizable estate, and apparently convincing her to remain with him and their children without brutally demanding that she submit to his will. All of this seems to testify to their mutual love and respect in a society where patriarchal control was valued and where marriage was often transacted on the basis of a family's vested interest in consolidating property, in increasing its rank, or in gaining a title.

Although Juliana and her family may not have been directly affected by the brutality of the tsar's rule, the Russian Church and society were driven by fear and were often victims of his cruel authority. Juliana may have indeed exhibited courage by reaching out to people fleeing the tsar's injustice, putting herself in danger.

During the so-called Time of Troubles (1598–1613), the country was destabilized when Russian leadership was called into question and when the Moscow region experienced several years of unusually cold summer temperatures, causing crop failure and leading to widespread hunger and disease.[7] The government's attempt to distribute food in the cities brought hundreds of hungry, homeless people from the countryside, hoping for anything to eat. Dedicated to almsgiving, Juliana became known as "the merciful," because she deprived herself of food and clothing so that she could use her means to feed the hungry. Juliana's sensitivity to the poor only increased as she grew older.

In the ten years that followed her husband's death, Juliana gave away or sold almost all that she owned to provide food for the poor, especially caring for poverty-stricken women and children. She supervised the distribution of food during a famine, making sure that nothing was kept back, that nothing was taken from others, and that clothing, household furniture, and goods were sold for money that could buy more food. It was said that no one left her house hungry.[8]

As the famine continued, Juliana moved what was left of her household east to Nizhegorod. Desperate, she had the servants gather pigweed and the bark from a certain type of elm tree. From this she made flour, praying as she mixed the ingredients with water and kneaded the dough. The hundreds who were nourished by the bread spoke about its unusual sweetness, saying that even bread of the best wheat was not as tasty. Others who had food for themselves nevertheless demanded some of Juliana's pigweed and elm bark bread, which she shared without question.[9]

Juliana was ill for six days before she died, staying in bed during the day but praying through the night. When she was chided for spending the night praying, she responded that the Lord expects everyone to pray, "even the sick." On the day of her death, Juliana received Holy Communion from her spiritual father, the priest Athanasius, and then called her children to her bedside and told them how she had wanted to enter monastic life, but that God in his wisdom had not taken her on that path. Then, after earnestly telling her children to do good works, she gave them a last kiss, called for a censer, and put incense in it.[10] Finally, it is written, she lay down in bed, made the sign of the cross three times, and offered herself to God, saying, "Glory to God for all things! Into your hands, O Lord, do I commit my spirit."[11]

After her death, a light in the form of a crown was seen around her head, and her body is said to have emitted a sweet fragrance. She appeared to several female servants and asked that her body be buried next to her husband's in Lazerevo. When a church dedicated to the Archangel Michael was built over her grave, her coffin was opened by village women and found to contain thick, fragrant myrrh.[12] The myrrh was removed, and the faithful anointed themselves with it. People from the surrounding areas began coming to Juliana's grave, seeking and receiving healing of many different illnesses. The sand under her grave was also sanctified and provided miraculous healings for those who rubbed it on infections or paralyzed limbs. The blind received their sight and the sick were restored to health by praying that she intercede on their behalf.

The church built over Juliana's grave was probably destroyed by fire in 1811. Like the graves of other saints, such as that of St. Herman of Alaska (whose burial site I have visited), Juliana's grave was said to be of warm, sweet-smelling earth, which comforted and healed many.

ON FACING THE NEW DAY

There is something about Rachel and St. Juliana that brings me back to the women in my class. For me, their voices are bound to the lamenting Rachel and the Merciful Juliana. Is there something that together they witness to? All endured great sorrows and loss, all wept with tears that well from a place deep inside the soul, but it is not that which binds them together, nor is it living with cruelty and injustice. Rather, it is their capacity to face the new day, to discern what is real and trust that God will not abandon them. Today, when so much emphasis is placed on power and empowering women, I am deeply struck by the stories of the women in my class, by Rachel, and by St. Juliana, powerless in their societies, and yet in their weakness—emptied of all pretense—they trusted in God, who gave them strength.

My grandchild was baptized on the Sunday of the Holy Innocents, and on that day, when Rachel's lamentations are remembered, I wept with joy at the new life rising from the baptismal font, knowing that, through no act of my own, I have been delivered from the horrors that Rachel and countless women faced in the past and continue to endure today. Their tears have watered the earth that I enjoy. Not having faced their struggle makes it easy for me to think that I trust in God, and yet I do trust that from the baptismal waters new life emerges and that in God, the impossible becomes possible. "Open the window and step out on the ledge," said one of the women in my class. To some it may sound reckless or rash, but it is an imperative that underscores the risk, even the danger, we know we will face if we trust in God. To trust means to give up control. To trust means to be in a place where God is all that is left. This trust is a gift from God. It is what enabled Rachel to stand before God, protesting the injustice of death. It is what enabled Juliana to show mercy to the poor. It is what enabled the women in my class to get up every morning and to thank God for his blessings. It is what brings God to live and dwell among us.

NOTES

1. Under the welfare reform legislation of 1996, Temporary Aid for Needy Families (TANF) replaced entitlement assistance. The Department of Health and Human Services' mission statement defines the TANF bureau as providing assistance and work opportunities to needy families by granting states, territories, and tribes federal funds and wide flexibility to develop and implement their own welfare programs. The goal of TANF is to help needy families gain self-sufficiency. To qualify for TANF, a single parent and two children must be living on less than $9,000 per year.

2. Living in a time of polygamy, Rachel is interesting because she is said to have built up the house of Israel, even though of the twelve sons of Jacob (Israel), her only sons were Joseph and Benjamin. She married Jacob to become his second wife while he was still married to her older sister, Leah. In addition, Jacob fathered children with the maids of his wives, Bilhah and Zilpah. For Rachel's story, see Genesis 28–35:20.

3. The *vita* of St. Juliana the Merciful can be found online at http://stjulianalazarevo.org/the_saints_life.html. This online text comes from: "The Life of the Holy & Righteous Juliana of Lazarevo," trans. Isaac E. Lambertsen, 1991, from *The Lives of the Saints in the Russian Language, As Set Forth in the Menology of Saint Dmitri of Rostov*, supplemental vol. 2 (January–April) of *The Lives of the Russian Saints* (Moscow: Synodal Press, 1916), 5–18.

4. "Life of the Holy & Righteous Juliana."

5. Eve Levin, *Sex and Society in the World of the Orthodox Slavs, 900–1700* (Ithica, NY: Cornell University Press, 1989), 236.

6. For more information on the *Domostroi*, see *The* Domostroi: *Rules for Russian Households in the Time of Ivan the Terrible*, ed. and trans. Carolyn Johnston Pouncy (Ithica, NY: Cornell University Press, 1994).

7. Dmitri Pospielovksy, *The Orthodox Church in the History of Russia* (Crestwood, NY: St. Vladimir's Seminary Press, 1998), 64–67.

8. "Life of the Holy & Righteous Juliana."

9. "Life of the Holy & Righteous Juliana."

10. In Orthodox Christian practice, the faithful offer incense in both communal and private prayer. We pray the words from Psalm 141: "Lord, I call upon you, hear me . . . Let my prayer arise in your sight as incense, and let the lifting up of my hands be an evening sacrifice. Hear me, O Lord." Incense is a symbol of prayer ascending to God.

11. "Life of the Holy & Righteous Juliana." Juliana's final prayer was spoken in Russian; this English translation incorporates the modern second-person possessive adjective "your" rather than "thy," the archaic form.

12. "Life of the Holy & Righteous Juliana." In Orthodox Christian Tradition, the bones or other relics of saints are sometimes known to exude myrrh. A prominent example of this phenomenon is that of the well-known saint Nicholas of Myra, whose relics are said to exude myrrh. Myrrh is a fragrant reddish-brown resin tapped from trees found in East Africa. In ancient times it was valued as a perfume and for anointing the dead. The Magi brought myrrh to Jesus' manger, and women brought myrrh to anoint Jesus' body after His Crucifixion. Relics that exude myrrh are understood to contrast with a decomposing, corrupted corpse. Such relics are fragrant, a sign of sanctification and of a person's communion with God.

Reflection and Discussion Questions

1. The author shares that she "lived at times near poverty level with five kids and a husband who was often occupied." Despite prevailing over numerous challenges, the author realized that she was profoundly unaware of the stark difference between her experience as a white, middle-class woman and the experiences of her students.

   a. Reflect on and discuss what this experience may have been like for her.

   b. How do you imagine that Orthodox Christians (and other persons of good will) should respond to such extreme divergences of human life and experience?

2. The author powerfully describes Rachel's weeping and the slaying of the Holy Innocents, remembered during the Christmas season and offering a stark "contrast to the pleasures and parties" of the secular Christmas period. Consider and discuss how this contrast affects: (a) our personal daily lives, (b) relationships within the family, (c) relationships in society, and (d) parish and greater Church life.

3. With the above in mind, how can Christians better respond to these challenges?

4. The manual for domestic life mentioned by the author, the *Domostroi,* clearly held husbands responsible for "controlling" their wives and children. This manual was interpreted as justifying violence against both women and children. The author notes that "families could be trapped in abuse, with both women and men convinced that a women's behavior is only properly controlled and corrected through violence." Compare and contrast the attitudes regarding family life that society has held during both St. Juliana's life and ours today.

5. Despite the apparent dominance of the attitudes espoused by the *Domostroi* across Russian society of the time, the relationship that St. Juliana enjoyed with her husband, Yuri, is reported to have been extremely different. In the face of heartbreaking parental grief, their marital relationship was built on a foundation of mutual sacrificial love and trust. In part, it was this sacrificial love

and trust that enabled St. Juliana to "[exhibit] courage by reaching out to people." What does this mean for you?

6. What do you imagine may be the "something" that attracted the author to write about these very different women spanning space and time?

7. How can disparate Christian experiences find commonality? Are Orthodox believers willing to see Christ in all believers, regardless of race, class, culture, and liturgical practice?

8. a. In what ways do you imagine the author could have been encountering women of faith? How did she know?

   b. The author also states, "To trust means to give up control . . . It is what brings God to live and dwell among us." Consider and discuss some of the implications of this statement.

SS. Perpetua and Felicitas: Motherhood and Martyrdom

Valerie A. Karras

While we were still under arrest . . . my father out of love for me was trying to persuade me and shake my resolution. "Father," said I, "do you see this vase here, for example, or water-pot or whatever?"

"Yes, I do," said he.

And I told him: "Could it be called by any other name than what it is?"

And he said: "No."

"Well, so too I cannot be called anything other than what I am, a Christian."

(*Passio Sanctarum Perpetuae et Felicitatis*, 3.1–2)

INTRODUCTION

The tension between a father and daughter who love each other deeply yet find themselves at odds is paradigmatic of the *Passion of SS. Perpetua and Felicitas*,[1] an eyewitness, autobiographical account of imprisonment

Valerie A. Karras is Assistant Professor of Church History at Southern Methodist University's Perkins School of Theology. She has earned doctorates in patristic theology and Church history from the Aristotle University of Thessaloniki and the Catholic University of America, respectively, and has a Master of Theological Studies degree from Holy Cross Greek Orthodox School of Theology and a diploma in Byzantine chant from Greece. Dr. Karras has held leadership positions in several academic organizations and has published a number of articles in academic, peer-reviewed journals. She is currently completing revisions to her forthcoming book, *Women in the Byzantine Liturgy*, which will be published by Oxford University Press.

and martyrdom in early Christianity. Issues of race, class, and gender are stirred into a recurring theme of love and conflict: the love of two young mothers for their infants, the love between a father and daughter, the love between a husband and wife, and the conflict between the demands of faith and society and the demands of faith and family, especially faith and motherhood.

This fascinating early Christian document, often known by the short form of its Latin title as the *Passio Perpetuae* ("Passion of Perpetua"), describes the incarceration, visions, and grisly martyrdom of two North African Christian women and several of their fellow Christians, thrown to wild beasts in the arena at Carthage at the beginning of the third century. Perhaps because they lived in the Latin West, they are not well known among Orthodox Christians. But they *should* be known and studied. With Perpetua's prison diary at its core,[2] the *Passio Perpetuae* is one of the only writings to come to us from the pen of an early Christian woman, and the anonymous final chapters provide one of the Church's earliest martyrdom accounts. But the *Passion of SS. Perpetua and Felicitas* is more than an interesting historical piece. Almost two thousand years later, this story continues to resonate with—or disquiet—many people with its overt praise of two young women who demonstrated a willful disregard for the familial, cultural, and social expectations made of them on account of their class and sex, as they remained faithful to Christ at the cost of their lives and of perhaps an even greater treasure: their motherhood.

TRANSCENDING RACE AND CLASS

Felicitas and a man named Revocatus are the first martyrs listed by the anonymous author of the introduction and martyrdom sections of the *Passio*, who then names two other men and finally Perpetua. Perpetua is described as a twenty-two-year-old, newly married Roman matron— that is, as a married woman of the middle or upper class—of respectable birth (that is, probably of the upper class),[3] with a father, a mother, and two brothers, one of whom was a catechumen like Perpetua (we also learn later that another brother had died as a child), whereas Felicitas is simply named as a fellow servant or fellow slave of Revocatus.[4]

However, despite the vast gulf between them in social status, there is a strong affinity between these two women. In part, the bond between Perpetua and Felicitas may be due to a similarity in their predicaments:

Perpetua was nursing her infant son when she and the other Christians were arrested—in fact, she kept him with her during the first part of her imprisonment[5]—and Felicitas was pregnant at the time of their arrest. Because the Roman authorities would not execute her until she delivered her child (in order not to be responsible for the death of the unborn infant), Perpetua and the other Christian prisoners prayed that God would grant Felicitas' desire to be martyred together with them. Their prayer was granted: Felicitas gave birth to a baby girl shortly before the prisoners were due to face the wild beasts in the arena.[6] Thus, the postpartum woman faced martyrdom "side by side"[7] with the recently lactating mother and her other companions, "going from one blood bath to another, from the midwife to the gladiator, ready to wash after childbirth in a second baptism."[8]

But it is not simply that the shared maternity and faith of Perpetua and Felicitas created bonds that transcended the gulf in their social status. The anonymous authors of the introduction and of the martyrdom account ignore or leave ambiguous some elements of social status. For example, although we know that Felicitas is a slave or servant (the Latin word *servus/serva*, similar to its Greek counterpart *doulos/doulē*, has the double meaning of "servant" and "slave"),[9] we do not know for *whom* she works.[10] Is it for a pagan, or for another Christian? Did her master have anything to do with her arrest? On the one hand, we might hypothesize that, precisely because of her low social status, the author would not be concerned with Felicitas' biography. Yet, he or she demonstrates great concern for Felicitas' ability to be martyred with her fellow Christians. So, the *Passio*'s authors chose not to describe Felicitas' personal background but devoted considerable space to describing her premature childbearing and her martyrdom in the arena.[11]

In fact, one of the things I find so fascinating about this martyrdom account is its complete subversion of late antique cultural mores regarding what differentiates persons from each other, and what social, cultural, and civil expectations are made of persons. Repeatedly, the *Passio Perpetuae* ignores class differences as apparently unimportant to Perpetua and her fellow martyrs, while emphasizing their courage and an intensity of devotion to their Christian faith that leads to conflicts with family, society, and the state.

In her seminal work, *In Memory of Her*, Elisabeth Schüssler Fiorenza advocates the necessity of "reading the silences" in order to recover the

missing voices of women: women were generally not considered important in male-dominated ancient societies and so tended to be ignored in
their literature, especially their histories. In the case of the *Passio Perpetuae*, the silences are similarly instructive, although because of an in-
verted set of priorities. Unlike the predominantly pagan Roman society
of the early third century, race, class, and sex are unimportant for the
North African Christian community. Instead, constancy and courage in
the face of persecution and impending martyrdom is the priority, regardless of the sex, marital status, or social class of the martyr. In other
words, Felicitas' courage as a martyr for Christ is developed; everything
else is extraneous. As Elizabeth Castelli, Thomas Heffernan, and Ross
Kraemer, among other scholars, have pointed out, there is a patent rhetorical purpose to this text: encouraging and strengthening the persecuted Christian community by an account of the courage and heroism
of these martyrs.

Another example of the *Passio*'s inversion of the traditional social
structures and priorities of Roman society is the lack of importance it
attaches to ethnicity and race (with one exception). Carthage was a Roman—formerly Punic—city set amid the Berbers and other indigenous
peoples of North Africa. Perpetua, an upper class matron, was of European extraction. Felicitas, however, may not have been. It should be
noted that race was not conceived of in the ancient world in the same
way as in contemporary American society. Slavery, for instance, was
not based on race and carried with it no cultural belief in intellectual
or other inferiority: slaves came generally from conquered peoples of
whatever race, and some were highly educated as doctors, scribes, and
accountants. Nevertheless, late antique Roman society was not color-
blind, and, not unlike contemporary American society, white Europeans
dominated economically and socially.

Access to Roman citizenship was greatly expanded to diverse ethnic
groups in the early Christian era (for example, the Apostle Paul proudly
proclaimed his own citizenship), but those of Roman and other Italian
descent living in North Africa were still more likely to be citizens than
were the Berbers and other indigenous peoples.[12] Hence Perpetua was
most likely a native Latin speaker of European descent.

We can also assume Perpetua was a white European because of her
dream of wrestling in the arena with an "Egyptian,"[13] whom she clearly
differentiates from herself and whom, as Gay Byron has noted in her

work on symbolic blackness in early Christianity, Perpetua interprets as representing the devil.[14] However, as Byron also observes, the rhetorical demonization in early Christian literature of black ethnic groups such as Egyptians and Ethiopians cannot be understood as simple racism; rather, blackness serves to denote "the other"—the extreme—in senses both negative and positive (for example, the Ethiopian eunuch in Acts 8:27, or the desert ascetic Moses the Ethiopian).[15] Thus it is telling that the race of none of the Christians is mentioned. Felicitas and Revocatus, as slaves or servants, may have been of European descent, but, conversely, they may well have been from one of the indigenous peoples in the region of Carthage. Their Latin names cannot be understood as indicative of their ethnicity because they are clearly Christian baptismal names ("blessedness" and "renunciation," respectively), given within a church that was Latin-speaking. So, the *Passio*'s editor ignores Felicitas' ethnic and racial identity precisely because Felicitas is *not* "other": she is a fellow Christian.

CONTEMPORARY REFLECTIONS 1

The editor's obliviousness to the race or ethnicity of Felicitas and the other Christians incarcerated with her seems odd to us today, when we regularly are expected to identify ourselves racially or ethnically on various documents and forms, and when our neighbors and friends are usually of our same race. It does remind me, however, of a couple of examples seared in my memory of Orthodox who identified with or, conversely, differentiated themselves from those not of the same race. The first is a negative memory from attending Liturgy at a Greek Orthodox church in downtown Philadelphia several years ago. I had seated myself near the center aisle toward the front of the church and was engrossed in the service. Therefore, it took me a little time to process in my mind what I had seen out of the corner of my eye: an Ethiopian or Eritrean woman, in traditional dress, who had come into the row in front of mine but was stopped by a Greek woman in that row. They conversed briefly (I could not hear what they said), then the African woman left the row.

When I realized what had happened, and confirmed it by looking around and seeing the woman seated at the back of the church, I confronted the woman in the row ahead of me. "What did you say to that woman?" I asked accusingly. She responded to the effect that the front rows were "reserved" and that the African woman knew where she was supposed to sit. I heatedly answered back that there were no "reserved" signs, that no one had stopped *me*, and that she had no right to say what she had to the other woman. The Greek woman gave me a disgusted look and turned back to the front, ignoring me. I was so shaken that I could think of nothing else for the rest of the service. Every time that I see in the back of a church Ethiopians, Eritreans, or others who appear visibly "different" from the majority of the congregation, my "Jim Crow" experience in that Philadelphia church rises like bile in my mouth. How frequently do we Orthodox see someone not as a fellow Orthodox Christian, as a fellow Christian, or as a fellow human being, but rather as black/yellow/brown . . . as too ethnic, not ethnic enough, or not the "right" kind of ethnic?

My other set of memories, fortunately, is positive, centered around a modern Orthodox hierarch who self-identified—as an oppressed Christian—with those who did not share either his Greek ethnicity or his Orthodox faith. I have in my office a copy of the issue of *Life* magazine whose cover photograph shows the late Archbishop Iakovos standing beside the late Martin Luther King, Jr., in preparation for the historic march on Selma. Iakovos, an ethnic Greek born and raised on the tiny Turkish island of Imvros, recalled well the oppression of ethnic Greeks by the Turkish government and so was sensitive to the oppression of and discrimination against African-Americans in his adopted country. I freely admit that I was critical of many of the actions and attitudes of the late archbishop of the Greek Orthodox Archdiocese, but his marching beside King was something for which I always respected and admired him—because it was something he did out of faith and conviction, not to further his own authority or ego.

Archbishop Iakovos received a great deal of criticism and hate mail—most of it from other Orthodox—for his public act of solidarity in the civil rights movement. I think that, from our vantage point now, well over forty years later, many of us fail to realize how prophetic and courageous Iakovos' actions were in the early 1960s. The reminiscences about Iakovos that I heard decades later from two other people bring that forcefully home. The first occurred in the mid-1990s when I attended a dinner in Atlanta inaugurating an endowment in Iakovos' name to benefit the Faith and Order Commissions of both the National Council of

Churches and the World Council of Churches. Coretta Scott King, widow of the slain civil rights leader, described how Iakovos had been a close family friend from the day of that march, when he was the only head of a major national church to respond affirmatively to King's request for their participation in the civil rights demonstration. Secondly, I remember my cousin, Fr. Steven Tsichlis, who had served briefly on an ad hoc basis as Iakovos' deacon more than two decades ago, talking to his congregation, just after Iakovos' death, about his own personal experiences with the late archbishop. My cousin described how, when he accompanied the archbishop on a pastoral visit to Atlanta, they were escorted by Secret Service agents out a back exit of the airport because Iakovos was still receiving death threats some twenty years after the historic march. How many of us, in our middle-class comfort and overwhelming whiteness, are willing—at such personal risk—to identify so vocally and so visibly with those who do not share our ethnicity, our race, our faith?

TRANSCENDING SEX, MARRIAGE, AND MOTHERHOOD

But class, race, and ethnicity are not the only things that Perpetua and her co-authors ignore. Except for Perpetua's family members, who play important roles in her diary, familial connections and other personal characteristics are not mentioned either for Felicitas or, for that matter, for any of the other Christians incarcerated with her. This is particularly striking given that Perpetua has a breastfeeding son with her in prison and Felicitas is advanced in her pregnancy—yet husbands are not mentioned for either woman. The *Passio*'s strong emphasis on pregnancy, childbirth, and breastfeeding, combined with its apparently deliberate omission of information on husbands for either woman, subverts both the later Christian tendency to exalt virginity and celibacy over marriage and family and, simultaneously, the late antique norm of identifying women through the men—especially the husbands—who have authority over them.

It is possible that the father of Felicitas' child was the master of the household in which she worked. Slaves and servants had no rights over their own bodies. Under Roman law, it was perfectly lawful—and Roman society considered it perfectly normal—for the master of a household (the Latin legal term is *paterfamilias*) to make sexual use of his female and young male slaves and servants. That Felicitas gave her newborn daughter to another Christian (a "sister"), who raised her as her own, indicates that there was no father who could—or would—exercise his normal parental role.

Alternatively, her child's father could have been a fellow slave to whom she was married, informally if not formally. If he were also a Christian who was not part of the group to be martyred, then the *Passio*'s editor may have wished to keep his identity secret for the husband's own protection. Conversely, it is possible that Felicitas' husband was indeed one of the other Christian prisoners, in which case it would most likely have been Revocatus, the fellow servant named with Felicitas in the introduction. The impending martyrdom of both parents would then explain why the infant girl was given over to another Christian woman, apparently not a relative, to raise.[16] Nevertheless, it is odd that, if Felicitas was married, her husband is nowhere mentioned.

Moreover, not only is no mention made of Felicitas' husband, but none is made of Perpetua's spouse either, despite her being described as a "newly married" matron.[17] This has puzzled most scholars, although Carolyn Osiek has provided a convincing solution: fellow prisoner and martyr Saturus is actually Perpetua's husband.[18] Osiek bases her conclusion on the closeness between the two and on their central roles in each other's visions.[19] If Saturus were Perpetua's husband, and if his family had disowned him because of his embrace of Christianity, it would explain why Perpetua initially turned her child over to her mother and then, after she received permission to keep the child in prison, her father took him away.[20] As Osiek notes, under Roman law, even in the case of a marriage *sine manu* (the most common type of marriage by that time, in which the wife remained under the authority of her father as opposed to her husband), the husband and his family would have guardianship of any children from the marriage.[21]

Of course, the question still remains of why Saturus is not specifically identified as Perpetua's husband. Osiek hypothesizes that there may have been something embarrassing about Saturus' absence from the original group arrested. She may well be correct, because it is puzzling that, while Perpetua is under house arrest but before she is imprisoned, she makes no mention of Saturus. Furthermore, Perpetua seems to be defending Saturus when she describes him as "the builder of our strength, although he was not there when we were arrested."[22]

Nevertheless, given the attention devoted to Saturus in the *Passio*, it makes little sense that he is not identified as Perpetua's husband simply out of embarrassment. Rather, the lack of explicit mention of husbands for *both* Felicitas and Perpetua is probably deliberate. Rex Butler has suggested that the omission may be related to the Montanism that appears to underlie the *Passio*. Montanism, also called the "New Prophecy," was a charismatic movement that originated in Asia Minor in the second century and found a strong foothold in North African Christianity. It was characterized by speaking in tongues, prophesying in worship, and anticipation of Christ's imminent Second Coming; the asceticism associated with this eschatological focus included the idea that marriage ceases after receiving the Holy Spirit. Much like the modern Pentecostal movement, the New Prophecy sought to retrieve what it believed to be the lost charismatic spirituality of the apostolic Church. The editor's emphasis on new prophecies and visions has led Herbert Musurillo to theorize that "the *Passio* is ultimately a proto-Montanist document, originating perhaps in the first decade of the third century from the Montanist circle of Tertullian himself."[23]

Rex Butler points out that, because of his focus on eschatology, Montanus, the movement's second-century founder, "'taught the dissolution of marriages,' particularly in the cases of Priscilla and Maximilla, the 'foremost prophetesses,' who, 'once they were filled with the Spirit, abandoned their husbands.' Later, Priscilla even received the title 'virgin.'"[24] Although the next generation of Montanists generally abandoned such extremism, Butler suggests that "the absence of Perpetua's and Felicitas' husbands from the *Passio* suggests that Priscilla's and Maximilla's abandonment of their husbands may not have been an aberration among Montanist women. Indeed the reappearance of both husbands in the liturgical *Acts of Perpetua* indicates Catholic concern about an ongoing Montanist practice."[25]

Butler is probably right that the orthodox, catholic Church was uncomfortable with the *Passio*'s failure to mention Perpetua's and Felicitas' spouses. However, I don't believe that the omission indicates an abandonment of marital or familial ties for the two women. After all, Perpetua is specifically described as recently wed and has a young child whom she is still breastfeeding. She is clearly concerned about her infant son,[26] and, assuming that Carolyn Osiek is correct, she is strongly connected to her husband, Saturus, who is a principal character in one of her dreams.

Moreover, her affection for and strong ties to her family are evident in their frequent visits to her, despite the tensions these visits generate.

So why are these two young women described as young mothers, married even, but without reference to their husbands? Beyond any Montanist influence, I believe this was done in order to focus on their transcendence of the cultural stereotypes and restrictions of young married women in Roman society. They are indeed wives and mothers, but these relationships ultimately do not define them, important though they are. Maureen Tilley, for example, observes that Perpetua seems to begin "in a situation of dependency . . . defined by her relationship with these males [father, brother, judge, executioner]. Her faith, however, enabled her to transform each relationship. She strove for a self-definition against these men."[27]

Similarly, David Scholer, noting how Perpetua moves from feeling anxious about her infant son and about her father's keeping him from her to a sense of calm and relief upon learning that he no longer needs to be breastfed, comments that "in some sense she has left behind the traditional limiting role of motherhood, which in that culture would never give a woman an opportunity to be an empowered leader."[28] Characteristic especially of Montanism, which had restored the apostolic Church's practice[29] of giving women leadership roles in areas such as preaching,[30] the *Passio* depicts Perpetua and Felicitas as women who are strong enough in their faith to put nothing before Christ, even their own maternal roles. Both Perpetua's father and the Roman governor who judges her at her trial argue that she should recant her Christian faith out of concern for her infant son, but she refuses.[31] Felicitas and her Christian colleagues are so distressed at the thought that Felicitas might not be martyred with them that she, in answer to their fervent prayers, delivers her newborn daughter a month prematurely, allowing her to die in the arena with Perpetua and the others after giving up her daughter to another Christian woman to raise.[32]

I believe that a spiritual calling to transcend the gender-driven conventions of Roman society also explains one of the most radical elements in the *Passio*. In a dream she had shortly before she was martyred, Perpetua imagined herself as a man stripped down for contest in the arena.[33] Marie-Louise von Franz, in her Jungian analysis of Perpetua's dreams, interprets Perpetua's transformation into a man as her adoption of "the strong, masculine, aggressive spirit of the believer [throwing] herself actively into the spiritual battle."[34] Similarly, David Scholer, lifting up some examples of women being depicted as "becoming male" or "being male" in early Christian literature, opines that Perpetua's transformation represents her "new identity in that context—by which she transcends her own limiting sexuality to become an empowered leader in the church."[35] Indeed, the use of the Greek noun and related verb *andreia* and *andrizo* (literally, "manliness" and "being manly," that is, "courage" and "courageous") and similar phrases was common in patristic literature, for example, in St. Basil's homily on St. Julitta the martyr and in St. Gregory of Nyssa's description of his and Basil's older sister, St. Macrina.[36] It was based on the widespread metaphorical use of gendered language that assigned positive characteristics such as strength, courage, virtue, and intelligence to the masculine gender and negative characteristics such as weakness, passion, and emotionalism to the female gender. (These assessments are, unfortunately, still prevalent in our culture.) Early Christian writers, while acknowledging the force of these cultural gender stereotypes, simultaneously subverted them by describing courageous, virtuous women as "male," thereby denying the spiritual reality of such stereotypes. Therefore, I do not in any way interpret Perpetua's dream as her denial of her femininity. It is, rather, her recognition of the strictures placed upon her by Roman society's denial of full *humanity* to her *because of* her femininity. Perpetua "becomes a man" at the point in the dream when she is being stripped and oiled for combat (perhaps an association with baptism and chrismation[37]) by her male attendants. Gladiatorial-style combat in the arena was a strictly male activity. Rather than shying from such an image altogether because of her sex, Perpetua in her subconscious simply becomes externally male in order for her to engage the devil (the "Egyptian") in a wrestling match, which she wins. She does not, however, see herself as becoming truly a man, for, as Maureen Tilley notes, the giant trainer or "referee" in her vision refers to "her."[38] In other words, she *acts* as a man, but does not really see herself as having become a man. As Felicidad Oberholzer notes, "She puts on the masculine body as a person might put on armor for a battle."[39]

Her vision of herself in the arena fighting an Egyptian is actually one of two dreams that Perpetua has that involve the devil. The other is her first vision while imprisoned, in which she dreams that Saturus encourages her and precedes her up a narrow and dangerous ladder (from earth to heaven?).[40] As in her match with the Egyptian in the arena, Perpetua steps on the head of the devil-*cum*-dragon or Egyptian wrestler. The resonance with God's prophecy in Genesis 3:15—that Eve, or her offspring, would bruise the serpent's head— is unmistakable.[41] So, not only does Perpetua break from cultural stereotype by envisioning herself, a lactating mother, as strong and combative, but she also identifies herself in this sense as Eve's offspring conquering the devil.

CONTEMPORARY REFLECTIONS 2

This insistence of both women on martyrdom, at the cost of abandoning their own infants, is troubling to many people. As a Church history and theology professor, I have often given this account of the martyrdom of Perpetua and Felicitas to my students, both undergraduate (at my former university) and graduate. I usually find a number of devout women—Catholic, Orthodox, and Protestant alike—distressed that Perpetua and Felicitas would be willing to die while leaving their children for others to raise. For my students, as for Perpetua's father, the Carthaginian governor, and so many others both then and now, Perpetua and Felicitas had a primary responsibility to their children—and thus, by consequence, *not* to Christ. Some students would become uncomfortable upon realizing this logical consequence and argue that, even if these women denied Christ publicly, they would still have been able to fulfill their commitment to him by raising their children as Christians. But, of course, it appears that the children will be raised Christian in any case: Felicitas' child is explicitly turned over to another Christian, and in Perpetua's case, even though her parents (her father, at least) appear not to be Christian, her brother is a catechumen, and so she may assume that he will impart their faith to her orphaned son.

I find it interesting that I never hear arguments against martyrdom on the basis of martyrs' *fatherhood* (in fact, male martyrs' marital and familial situations are rarely even mentioned), just as, in contemporary discussions about women in the armed forces, women's familial responsibilities are raised as an argument against their participation, whereas such commitments are considered irrelevant with respect to their male counterparts. Perpetua and Felicitas, however, refuse to be judged under a different standard because they are women—because they are wives and mothers. As Scholer, Tilley, and others have observed, they are women who are most definitely identified as women through the most sexually stereotypical role possible, yet they insist on the priority of their role as Christians over their role as mothers.

Although I am unmarried and have no children, I identify with Perpetua's and Felicitas' refusal to be identified primarily as women and, consequently, to be restricted as women in a way that denies their full capacity to act and live as Christians first. I, too, have experienced—too many times to count—an attitude by many within the Orthodox Church, both clergy and lay, that because I am a woman it is improper, or even inconceivable, for me to assume certain roles: as a chanter, as a theology professor at an Orthodox seminary, as a theologian generally. I am also acutely aware that, even though I do not feel called to it personally, ordained ministry in the Orthodox Church—especially to the three "major orders"—is closed off to every Orthodox woman simply because of her sex.

The specific reasons given for such restrictions vary. A priest years ago forbade me to chant because he claimed that my female voice sounded like a "mewling kitten," although the well-known and accomplished head chanter was excited at my ability to read Byzantine music and eager for me to join him.

When I was on the faculty at Holy Cross Greek Orthodox School of Theology (the seminary of the Greek Orthodox Archdiocese of America), some seminarians felt it improper for a woman to teach theology, although they would usually couch it in code—for example, that "*priests should be teaching future priests.*" These students, and others who share(d) their opinion, were blithely oblivious to their inconsistency, given that *male* lay faculty had taught at the seminary from its inception and that most of the faculty at the theological schools in Thessaloniki and Athens are likewise laymen (I should add that a woman faculty member who preceded me fell victim to this same mentality).

In fact, many among our laity seem unable to comprehend that a woman could even *be* a theologian. I remember several instances when laity assumed that a priest, because of his clerical status, must be more authoritative than I, even though I have two doctorates in theology and might have had him as my student. One particularly humorous and, simultaneously, painful memory is of my first Christmas back home with my family after beginning my teaching at Holy Cross. When a fellow parishioner asked where I had been and I responded, the person asked if I was teaching high school! (A fellow choir member in my home parish wryly commented to me once that most of the congregation just thought of me as "that woman who chants.")

This attitude is particularly lamentable given the historical importance of lay theologians in Orthodoxy, from the charismatic prophets and prophetesses of the apostolic Church; through the Desert Mothers and Fathers of the fourth century, the Byzantine missionary Constantine/Cyril, and the liturgical mystic Nicholas Cabasilas (the latter two both tonsured as monks only a few months before their deaths); to the lay men and women on the theological faculties of the Greek universities. The sin of clericalism that seems to have infected Orthodoxy in America is particularly damaging to the participation of women in the Church precisely because of our exclusion from all the major ordained orders, including our contemporary exclusion from the diaconate. However, beyond that, such clericalism is damaging to the Church because it denigrates the importance of the *charismata* (spiritual gifts) that the Holy Spirit bestows on lay men and women and that they are called to use to build up the body of Christ.

CHALLENGING AUTHORITY

As striking to me as Perpetua's willful transcendence of her culture's sexual restrictions and gender stereotypes is her continual challenge to (male) authority, both familial and civil. Women in the ancient world were always under the legal authority of a man, whether it be their fathers or, later, their husbands. As mentioned previously, Perpetua was apparently in a marriage *sine manu*, that is, the type of arrangement in which legal authority over the woman (and her property) was not transferred to her husband, but instead remained with her father (or, if he were deceased, with his surrogate within the family, typically a brother or uncle). Perpetua's father was able to take custody of her infant son from her,[42] to her initial distress, but was frustrated by his inability to force her to recant her faith in order to save her life.

We see this from the very beginning of Perpetua's diary, when she had just been placed under house arrest.[43] Her father visited her to try to convince her to recant; when she refused (her response prefaces this article), he "was so angered by the word 'Christian' that he moved toward me as though he would pluck my eyes out."[44] Her mother and brothers also visited her, and Perpetua's father attempted to dissuade her at least

two more times, but she remained unmoved, despite his literally dragging her from the podium where she appeared before the governor, who
added his own support to her father's pleas.[45]

What makes her refusal so poignant is that it was not simply an act
of defiance against parental and civil authority. Perpetua and her father
clearly loved one another deeply; her father even admitted that she was
his favorite child.[46] He wanted nothing more than that his daughter be
safe and happy, yet she seemed, to his mind, intent on destroying herself
and her family.

CONTEMPORARY REFLECTIONS 3

As I reflect on their relationship, I find myself identifying with their
strong bond of love, yet grateful that my father and mother always gave
me unflagging support for whatever life decision I made, no matter how
much they may have disagreed. I am reminded of this most strongly
when I remember the conversation we had when I decided—shortly after
graduating from college with a degree in political science—that, instead
of going to law school (as I had planned to do from the age of thirteen), I
would enroll in seminary. My new intent was to obtain a master's degree
in theology as preparation for a career within the Church, working with
choirs and Church music at the diocesan or archdiocesan level. My parents were astounded at my dramatic change in career goals and were also
concerned about the challenges I was likely to face in my new chosen
field. My mother, who rarely made any kind of political or social critique,
cried out, "But, why do you want to bang your head against a brick wall
fighting those sexist men in the Church? You would have been such a
good lawyer!" (I have to say, I think she was right, on both counts.)

Nevertheless, my parents, out of a love for me based not on what
they thought would make me happy but rather what *actually* made me
happy, supported my decision: they drove me halfway across the country to Boston, helped me find an apartment (and even co-signed the
lease, the only time I ever needed them to do so), and sent me care
packages. Likewise, they supported my decision to go on for doctoral
work, and even helped me move my belongings back from Washington, DC, where I did my coursework for my doctorate from Catholic
University, to be stored in their basement for years while I pursued another doctorate at the University of Thessaloniki. (My family, including

my two sisters, was invaluable in most of my moves.) After my father's death during my first year in Greece, my mother continued her unstinting and uncritical support.

My family's support was also crucial to me during a time when I challenged ecclesiastical authorities at the highest level. Just before I planned to take a sabbatical from Holy Cross in order to complete my Catholic University doctoral dissertation, Spyridon, former archbishop of the Greek Orthodox Archdiocese, fired one of the seminary's most senior professors, Fr. Theodore Stylianopoulos. Fr. Ted, the school's tenured, full professor of New Testament, had chaired a disciplinary committee that had recommended expulsion for a Greek archimandrite who had persistently sexually harassed an undergraduate male student at a party and lesser disciplinary actions for the party's host and a couple of other students (all archimandrites). When the theological school's dean threw out the disciplinary actions, the committee appealed to the school's president, Fr. Alkiviadis Calivas. A week after firing Fr. Ted, the archbishop fired Fr. Calivas and the two other priests on the disciplinary committee, former college dean Fr. Emmanuel Clapsis and school librarian Fr. George Papademetriou.

I was appalled by the firings because of their injustice both to the fired academic clergy and to the harassed student (and all our students). I realized that it was unlikely that anything would be done to reverse these actions unless they became widely known, both among the laity and beyond the Orthodox community. So, I informed the press. The story made the online edition of the *Chronicle of Higher Education* the next day and the *Boston Globe* a couple of days later; the following week Gustav Niebuhr of the *New York Times* visited the campus to investigate.

Soon after this, I filed formal complaints with the seminary's two accreditation agencies and with the Massachusetts Attorney General's office. A connection to computer programmer and analyst Harry Coin through a mutual friend, my dentist Dr. George Stevens, led to Harry's creation of the website *Voithia*,[47] which became indispensable in providing reliable information as well as opinion pieces to combat the spin, half-truths, and sometimes outright lies emanating from officials within the Archdiocese during that time.

I also became one of the founding members of a short-lived group named GOAL (Greek Orthodox American Leaders), organized and led by Dr. Thomas Lelon, former president of Hellenic College/Holy Cross

Greek Orthodox School of Theology, who brought together concerned lay leaders from various Church organizations, including the Archdiocesan Council, Philoptochos, Leadership 100, and Orthodox Christian Laity (OCL). The group disbanded after the election of Archbishop Demetrios, who immediately restored the fired clergy at the seminary after his installation.

Needless to say, my activities made me anathema to many within the Church. The archimandrite who acted on Archbishop Spyridon's behalf at the seminary accused me of always having hated him and anyone else in a collar. The dean who had thrown out the disciplinary committee's decisions barred me from the *analogion* (the chanter's stand) when he celebrated Liturgy at the seminary chapel and even refused me communion (the only time I cried for myself during this two-year tumult within the Archdiocese). So, I feel a certain kinship with Perpetua in her confrontations with the Carthaginian governor and the military tribune.[48] As I responded to the archbishop's representative at the time, I had no trouble sleeping at night because I knew I had done the right thing. Abusive authorities do not understand that those who challenge them object not to their authority, but to their *abuse* of their authority.

Nevertheless, despite a certain level of identification with Perpetua, I know that my own defiance of Church authorities was much easier for me than was Perpetua's defiance of the Roman state. I had the strong and loving support of my family, I had no spouse or children to consider, and it was only my career that I was jeopardizing. Perpetua, on the other hand, had to battle her own family as well as the civil authorities, she agonized over the infant son she loved, and it was her very life that was on the line. Would I be able to act so confidently against authority figures if the stakes were that high?

CONCLUSION

The lives of Perpetua and Felicitas, two Christian women living in Roman North Africa in the early third century and persecuted by their government for their faith, seem so distant and different from our own. Yet, on closer examination, we see how similar they are, as women, to most of us: women trying to live normal lives of work, marriage, and motherhood, with families who love and care about us. They are also like us in that, despite our good intentions, some of our decisions create conflict in our lives because they challenge familial or societal expectations. We may have families who don't understand us, or we may feel called to paths in life that are unusual for women in our culture or in our Church.

Perpetua and Felicitas show us that, ultimately, we may not always be able to convince others of the truth or correctness of our actions and decisions, and we may have to pay a very high price because of that. Although we cannot control those around us, including those who have authority over us, we *can* control how we respond to those around us. We always have within our power the choice of challenging others' expectations rather than bowing to them, of paying the price for following our calling, and of paying that price with courage and conviction. Two young women, new mothers, followed Christ's call at the cost of their own lives, meeting their deaths with a steely grace and transcendent joy that we can only hope to emulate in the lesser challenges of our own lives.

Notes

1. Note that the word "passion" in the title of the martyrdom account refers to the original meaning of its Latin root, *passio*, as "suffering" (for example, the movie *The Passion of the Christ*). The most recent critical edition of the original Latin text is in *Passion de Perpétue et de Félicité suivi des Actes*, ed. and trans. Jacqueline Amat, Sources Chrétiennes 417 (Paris: Éditions du Cerf, 1996). A side-by-side Latin text and English translation are in Herbert Musurillo, ed. and trans., *The Acts of the Christian Martyrs* (Oxford: Clarendon Press, 1972), 106–31. In addition, there are a number of English translations of part of the text, primarily in collections of early Christian sources.

The text includes (1) Perpetua's diary of her imprisonment and her visions and dreams while jailed (chaps. 3–10); (2) a lengthy description (probably written by Saturus himself) of the vision of Saturus, her fellow prisoner and companion, and perhaps husband, in chapters 11 through 13 (see Carolyn Osiek, "Perpetua's Husband," *Journal of Early Christian Studies* 10, no. 2 (2002): 287–90); and (3) an introduction (chaps. 1 and 2), as well as the story of Felicitas' childbearing, an account of the actual events of the martyrdoms, and a conclusion (chaps. 14–21), written by an anonymous editor who may also have edited part of the diary.

2. A good overview of nineteenth- and twentieth-century scholarly hypotheses regarding the *Passio*'s original language and authorship may be found in Rex D. Butler, *The New Prophecy and New Visions: Evidence of Montanism in The Passion of Perpetua and Felicitas* (Washington, DC: Catholic University of America Press, 2006), 44–57 (chap. 2). Thomas J.

Heffernan, "Philology and Authorship in the *Passio Sanctarum Perpetuae et Felictatis*," *Traditio* 50 (1995): 315–25, has used, primarily, textual analysis to challenge the older scholarly view that the central section of the *Martyrdom of Perpetua* was written by Perpetua herself. His doubts have been seconded by Ross Kraemer in Ross S. Kraemer, *Women's Religions in the Greco-Roman World*, rev. ed. (New York: Oxford University Press, 2004), 5–6 and 356–57; and Ross S. Kraemer and Shira L. Lander, "Perpetua and Felictas," in *The Early Christian World*, vol. 2, ed. Philip F. Esler (New York: Routledge, 2000), 1048–68, at 1051–58. Erin Ronsse, "Rhetoric of Martyrs: Listening to Saints Perpetua and Felicitas," *Journal of Early Christian Studies* 14, no. 3 (2006): 283–327, agrees that the text displays a conscious and deliberate rhetorical style but simultaneously allows for the possibility that such rhetoric could have been authored by Perpetua herself. Elizabeth A. Castelli, *Martyrdom and Memory: Early Christian Culture Making* (New York: Columbia University Press, 2004), 235n29, notes the recent questions regarding authorship but sidesteps making her own assessment. In any case, as Butler has noted, "Heffernan did not deny the veracity of the events reported in Perpetua's narratives; instead he suggested that Perpetua orally transmitted her stories to the editor . . ." The arguments against Perpetua's authorship are unconvincing, however, because they assume that she could not have used a rhetorical style herself, although she appears to have come from a wealthy family and so was probably well educated. Moreover, both Maureen A. Tilley, "The Passion of Perpetua and Felicity," in *Searching the Scriptures*, vol. 2, *A Feminist Commentary*, ed. Elisabeth Schüssler Fiorenza (New York: Crossroad, 1994), 829–58, at 829–30; and Sara Maitland, in *The Martyrdom of Perpetua*, intro. and comm. Sara Maitland, trans. W. H. Shewring (Evesham, England: Arthur James Ltd., 1996), 39–43 (in Maitland's short but insightful commentary), note the *Passio*'s unusual emphasis on maternal bodily functions; this would also lend weight to the argument for the authenticity of the contents of the account. Given that the textual evidence evinces three authors, that Perpetua's portion shows a level of biographical specificity unmatched by the other two, and that there is no mention of a scribe visiting her, I see no reason to question the first editor's own statement (*Passio* 2) that "the entire account of her [Perpetua's] ordeal is her own, according to her own ideas and *in the way that she herself wrote it down*" (Musurillo, *Acts*, 109, emphasis added).

    3. "Inter hos et Vibia Perpetua, honeste nata, liberaliter instituta, matronaliter nupta . . ." (*Passio* 2.1).
    4. *Passio* 2.
    5. *Passio* 3.
    6. *Passio* 15.
    7. *Passio* 20.
    8. *Passio* 18.3; Musurillo, *Acts*, 127.

9. The Latin text simply identifies Felicitas as *conserva eius*, that is, "his [Revocatus'] fellow servant/slave" (*Passio* 2.1). Greek and Latin used the same word for "slave" and "servant" because the practical differences between enslavement and servitude were few; in most respects, the master of the household (*paterfamilias*) had complete authority over both.

10. Although many (e.g., David M. Scholer, "And I Was a Man: The Power and Problem of Perpetua," *Daughters of Sarah* 15, no. 5 [September/October 1989]: 10–14, at 10) have assumed that Felicitas was Perpetua's servant, the *Passio* nowhere states or implies this.

11. *Passio* 15 and 18–21, respectively.

12. For more on ethnicity and race in Roman North Africa, see L. C. Brown, "Color in Northern Africa," in *Color and Race*, ed. John Hope Franklin (Boston: Houghton Mifflin, 1968), 186–204.

13. *Passio* 10.

14. Gay L. Byron, *Symbolic Blackness and Ethnic Difference in Early Christian Literature* (London: Routledge, 2002), 45. See also Butler, *The New Prophecy*, 73–75; Joyce E. Salisbury, *Perpetua's Passion: The Death and Memory of a Young Roman Woman* (New York: Routledge, 1997), 110; and Tilley, "The Passion of Perpetua and Felicity," 845.

15. Byron, *Symbolic Blackness*, 1ff. and 29–51.

16. *Passio* 15.33.

17. "*matronaliter nupta*" (*Passio* 2; Musurillo, *Acts*, 108–9).

18. Osiek, "Perpetua's Husband."

19. See *Passio* 4 for Perpetua's vision with Saturus, and *Passio* 11–13 for Saturus' vision with Perpetua.

20. *Passio* 3 and 6, respectively.

21. Osiek, "Perpetua's Husband," 288. For more on Roman marriages *cum manu* and *sine manu*, see Susan Treggiari, *Roman Marriage: Iusti Coniuges from the Time of Cicero to the Time of Ulpian* (Oxford: Clarendon, 1991), 28–36.

22. Musurillo, *Acts*, 110–11.

23. Musurillo, *Acts*, xxvi. Tertullian was the first major Latin Christian theologian; later in his career, he became associated with Montanism. Studies of the Montanist element in the *Passio Perpetuae* include Butler, *The New Prophecy*; Cecil M. Robeck, Jr., *Prophecy in Carthage: Perpetua, Tertullian, and Cyprian* (Cleveland, OH: Pilgrim Press, 1992); and Andrzej Wypustek, "Magic, Montanism, Perpetua, and the Severan Persecution," *Vigiliae Christianae* 51, no. 3 (August 1997): 276–97. Maureen Tilley, "The Passion of Perpetua and Felicity," 832–36, is one of the few scholars who denies Montanist, and particularly Tertullian's, authorship of the text (this seems to be, at least in part, because of her concern that identifying it with the New Prophecy movement allows the dominant patriarchal authorities within the Church to marginalize its emphasis on women's courage and wisdom). Butler (49–57)

reviews the question of Montanist, and specifically Tertullianist, authorship and essentially concurs with Musurillo's hypothesis, as do I.

24. Butler, *The New Prophecy*, 39. The embedded quotes are attributed to Apollonius by the fourth-century bishop Eusebius of Caesarea in his *Historia ecclesiastica* [Ecclesiastical history], 5, 18, 2–3.

25. Butler, *The New Prophecy*, 130. The *Acts of Perpetua and Felicitas* is a revised and abridged version of the earlier, original *Passio*; it adds a non-Christian husband who attends Perpetua's trial and, like her father, attempts to dissuade her from her persistence in confessing her Christian faith.

26. "Then I got permission for my baby to stay with me in prison. At once I recovered my health, relieved as I was of my worry and anxiety over the child. My prison had suddenly become a palace, so that I wanted to be there rather than anywhere else" (*Passio* 3; Musurillo, *Acts*, 110–11).

27. Tilley, "The Passion of Perpetua and Felicity," 836.

28. Scholer, "And I Was a Man," 11.

29. See Acts 21:9 and 1 Cor 11:5.

30. "Prophesying," as that term is used in New Testament and other early Christian writings, refers to preaching.

31. *Passio* 5 and 6.

32. *Passio* 15.

33. *Passio* 10.

34. Marie-Louise von Franz, *The Passion of Perpetua*, trans. Elizabeth Welsh, Jungian Classics Series 3 (Irving, TX: Spring Publications, 1979), 56.

35. Scholer, "And I Was a Man," 11–12.

36. Basil of Caesarea, *Hom. de mart. Julitta* [Homily on the martyr Julitta], PG 31:237abc; Gregory of Nyssa, *De vita Macrinae* [Life of Macrina], GNO 8.1.371. For more on the metaphorical use of masculine language for female Christian models, see, for example, Elizabeth A. Clark, *Jerome, Chrysostom, and Friends: Essays and Translations*, in vol. 1 of Studies in Women and Religion (New York: Edwin Mellen Press, 1979); Gillian Cloke, *This Female Man of God: Women and Spiritual Power in the Patristic Age, AD 350–450* (London: Routledge, 1995); Verna A. E. Harrison, "Male and Female in Cappadocian Theology," *Journal of Theological Studies* 41, no. 2 (October 1990): 441–71, at 446ff.; and Tilley, "The Passion of Perpetua and Felicity," 844–45.

37. Salisbury, *Perpetua's Passion*, 109.

38. Tilley, "The Passion of Perpetua and Felicity," 845.

39. Felicidad Oberholzer, "Interpreting the Dreams of Perpetua: Psychology in the Service of Theology," in *Theology and the Social Sciences*, ed. Michael Horace Barnes, The Annual Publication of the College Theology Society, vol. 46 (2000) (Maryknoll, NY: Orbis Books, 2001), 293–312, at 309.

40. *Passio* 4.

41. I disagree with Oberholzer, "Interpreting the Dream of Perpetua," 299, who does not believe the resonance with Genesis could be true because

Perpetua came from a pagan background and so would be unfamiliar with Genesis. But, would not Genesis be a likely part of her catechism? Marie-Louise von Franz, *The Passion of Perpetua*, 21–25, interprets the dragon as "the symbol for an 'unconscious nature-spirit,' as 'the wisdom of the earth,'" which "represents at the same time the Pagan conception of the world in which experience of the Deity, or of the spirit, was projected into the material reality of the world" (von Franz, *The Passion of Perpetua*, 223). In other words, von Franz interprets the dragon not as evil, but as earthly and thereby impeding Perpetua's ascent to the heavenly realm.

42. *Passio* 5.

43. *Passio* 3.

44. Musurillo, *Acts*, 109.

45. *Passio* 6.

46. *Passio* 5.

47. *Voithia*, which was formally dismantled after Demetrios Trakatellis was installed to succeed Spyridon as archbishop of the Greek Orthodox Archdiocese, morphed into the Orthodox News website (www.orthodoxnews.org).

48. *Passio* 6 and 16, respectively.

REFLECTION AND DISCUSSION QUESTIONS

1. The story of these saints provokes us with the choice they made: Christ over motherhood. Discuss what this stirs in us.

2. What are other ways that we may incur the wrath of family members for the sake of the gospel?

3. Have you ever faced a highly charged and stressful situation that demanded an irreversible decision? What was the price you had to pay?

4. What are some of the gender-related stereotypes that may distance men and women from the gospel? How do we transcend these stereotypes?

5. The author powerfully describes examples of racism that she witnessed not too long ago.
   a. What have been your experiences concerning racism?
   b. What do you think about the author's example of an Orthodox Christian hierarch during the 1960s in the United States who displayed unprecedented heroism by defying the sin of racism?
   c. How do you imagine that Christ would have us be in these contexts?

6. This story also identifies the sin of clericalism: when ordained leaders exercise power inappropriately and/or abusively. This is a sin that the Church has always stood against.
   a. How would you describe this sin in your own words?
   b. How do you think clericalism affects others?
   c. How could this affect the Church's witness?

7. With the above in mind, the Church also equally stands against the sin of congregationalism, or "lay-ism": when members of the laity exercise power inappropriately and/or abusively.
   a. How would you describe this sin in your own words?
   b. How do you think congregationalism affects others?
   c. How could this affect the Church's witness?

8. The author shared poignantly about her parents' supporting her desire to leave home and study at an Orthodox theological seminary in order to be better able to serve the Church.
   a. How would you respond to your daughter if she, like the author, desired to serve the Church and attend seminary?

    b. How should Orthodox generally respond to their "daughters" who have attended, or are attending, an Orthodox theological seminary?

    c. Would this be different if "she" were a "he"?

The Search for Silence
and St. Anna the Prophetess

Nikki Stournaras

INTRODUCTION: SEEKING "THE ONE"

*B*lessed also is that Anna who hated her house and loved the Temple of her Lord.
She gazed intently at hidden beauty for eighty years but was not sated.
Blessed is her gaze that she concentrated on the One.[1]

Two holy women described within the Scriptures who have deeply influenced my life are Anna the Prophetess and St. Mary Magdalene. Both are persons of virtue who through the centuries have been held in high esteem by the Church for their perseverance, faith, courage, and love. Mary Magdalene, with her conviction of courage, stood by the foot of the Cross before the One she adored and loved. She suffered unspeakable sorrow while watching as they pounded nails into Him. The Prophetess Anna, with patience, humility, and prayer, spent eighty-four years waiting in anticipation in the temple to behold the Messiah.

They both have a good deal to offer modern-day society. Their love, humility, and daring to endure what the vast majority of people in any

Nikki Stournaras serves as Administrator of the Deans of Hellenic College-Holy Cross Greek Orthodox School of Theology, where she also pursues studies in theology on a part-time basis. A past president of St. Demetrios Philoptochos in Weston, Massachusetts, and a former board member of the Metropolis of Boston Philoptochos, her personal interests include studies in Orthodox spirituality and pastoral care. She is the grandmother of "seven adorable cherubs" and also serves on the Board of St. Catherine's Vision.

age cannot endure were the vital building blocks of their spiritual receptivity. And it was this receptivity that enabled them to become filled with
God's grace, whereby each of them made an extraordinary and bold pronouncement. Anna announced to the world that the infant Jesus was going to redeem Jerusalem, and Mary Magdalene announced to the world
that Christ had risen. Both shared triumphant news with the people of
God.

In the previous volume of this series, I offered a chapter on St. Mary
Magdalene; in this book I am offering a meditation on the remarkable
story of the Prophetess Anna. What we know about her from the Bible
comes only from the verses of Luke 2:36–38. We may wish that more
were recorded regarding the Prophetess Anna, especially in the Scriptures. But what we can discern from the reliable, scholarly information
that is available—precious little though it may be—provides us with an
astounding witness.

Her story is an important component of a very remarkable event that
occurred in the temple of Jerusalem. This event took place while Mary
and Joseph were following the Jewish practice of bringing a male child to
the temple forty days after his birth in order to offer him to God (see Lev
12:2–4).[2] In Luke 2:22 we read: "And when the time came for their purification according to the law of Moses, they [Mary and Joseph] brought
him [the infant, Jesus] up to Jerusalem to present him to the Lord . . . and
they offered a sacrifice according to what is stated in the law of the Lord,
'a pair of turtle-doves or two young pigeons'" (vv. 22, 24). At this point a
unique encounter occurs with the elderly, devout Simeon, who was led
by the Holy Spirit of God to the temple in that moment; as "it had been
revealed to him by the Holy Spirit that he would not see death before he
had seen the Lord's Messiah" (v. 26). Simeon then gently took the Christ
Child into his arms and pronounced the following:

> Master, now you are dismissing your servant in peace,
> according to your word; for my eyes have seen your salvation,
> which you have prepared in the presence of all peoples,
> a light for revelation to the Gentiles and for glory to your
> people Israel. (Luke 2:29–32)

The account continues with Simeon offering other significant prophecies related both to the Child and His mother, after which Anna is introduced. Luke's witness makes it clear that Anna had already been in
the temple for decades, carefully preparing to meet the long-awaited

"Anointed One" (the "Messiah," or "Christ"). She "never left the temple" for eighty-four years, "but worshipped there with fasting and prayer night and day" (Luke 2:37). A more literal translation of this part of the verse from the original Greek reads: she was "petitioning (*deisesin*) God with fastings and worship (*latreuousa*)." The Greek nuance here for me points to some of the underlying motivation of her worship. The specific word for "worship" that was chosen hints strongly that her motivation was grounded in an overwhelming and compelling, loving devotion—a devotion that was wrought with toil directed solely toward the divine. It was this love that propelled her through the decades. She, too, perhaps not unlike the righteous Simeon, was waiting patiently for a response to her petitions. And in the very instant of their meeting in the temple, "at that moment," Anna "began to praise God and to speak about the child to all who were looking for the redemption of Jerusalem" (v. 38). Her silence and perseverance had been rewarded with an encounter with God and the privilege to share His "good news."

Within the greater context of this passage, we see that Simeon—a righteous, devout elder of the temple—and the Prophetess Anna are counterparts. Anna and Simeon are both advanced in age, yet righteous and devout. Both represent different stations in life, as well as diverse life histories. Still, by the standards of the world, each may have been considered a rather commonplace person. Yet these two ordinary, elderly people represent an extraordinary symbol: that of a bridge connecting the Old Testament with the New Testament. Eastern Orthodox Christians celebrate this historic moment annually on February 2; it is commemorated as the "*Hypapante*," which translates as the "Meeting" or the "Encounter with the Lord." This day is commemorated forty days after the celebration of the birth of Christ and concludes the Christmas/Epiphany season. In the Roman Catholic Church, this celebration is known as the "Purification of Mary" or "Candelmas."

God Calls Anna

Call to me and I will answer you, and will tell you great
and hidden things which you have not known. (Jer 33:3)

The verses in Luke's Gospel (vv. 36–38) give us only the most basic information about Anna. The evangelist refers to her as a "prophet" (*profetis* in the biblical Greek); he states that she was married for seven years and, as a widow, spent eighty-four years in the temple. Luke also tells us that she was the daughter of Phanuel and a member of the tribe of Asher. The account of the entire event at the temple ends with Luke describing how she "gave thanks to God, and spoke of him to all who were looking for the redemption of Jerusalem."

Anna's name, also written as Hannah, means "graced by God" or "God's favor." This was not a common name in Jewish tradition. Only two other women in the Greek Old Testament (Septuagint) had the same name: the mother of Samuel (1 Sam 1:2), and the mother of Tobias (Tob 1:9).[3] In both Eastern Orthodox and Roman Catholic traditions, Anna was also the name of the mother of the Theotokos (that is, of Mary, the Mother of God—Christ's mother).[4]

Phanuel is the name of Anna's father mentioned in Luke (2:36). The name Phanuel is the Greek form of Penuel or Penial, which in the Hebrew means "the face of God." The name only appears in the Old Testament genealogies in 1 Chronicles 4:4 and 8:25. In the Old Testament the phenomenon of the "face of God" is used as a metaphor to show God's favor or disfavor. The Lord showed favor on Anna, who through the many years persevered in faithfulness to him. He bestowed favor on her by allowing her to recognize the face of God in the Christ Child.

That Anna specifically is named as a member of the tribe of Asher should not be overlooked. She is the only character in the New Testament who does not belong to the tribe of Judah, Benjamin, or Levi; her tribe is one of the northern tribes of Israel.[5] This point is an unusual one. It implies that most likely she had to travel from her distant, pagan-dominated homeland in the north to the "heartland" of the Jewish faith, where she would spend her time in the temple worshipping, praying, and fasting.[6] This is another indication of her overwhelming, loving devotion, which enabled her to prefigure obedience to our Lord's essential directive to "hear the word of God and do it" (Luke 8:21; 11:28).

Perhaps one of the most striking pieces of information about Anna is that through her preparation for her inspired identification of this Christ Child, she is designated as a prophetess (Luke 2:36).[7] Although this appellation applied to Anna in the biblical record may seem unusual to the general reader, Anna does not come to us out of the blue as a prophetess; she is not the only female prophet identified in the Bible. Anna is preceded by several female Old Testament prophets, including Miriam, the sister of Moses (Exod 15:20); Deborah (Judg 4:4); and Isaiah's wife

(Isa 8:3).[8] Anna is also compared to Judith, who was a devout, elderly widow (see Jth 16:21–24).

There are some other things we can say related to Anna that may help us learn more about her vocation of loving service to the Lord. The Hebrew word for "prophet" is *nabi*, which means to "call out" or "be summoned by God." The English word "prophet," according to Mackenzie's entry in the *Dictionary of the Bible*, is derived from the Greek term for "one who speaks before others"; in addition, "the Greek word almost always denotes one who communicates divine revelation."[9] Anna makes a riveting statement to the people of God about the One who will bring redemption to those in Jerusalem. As a result of her willingness to persevere, to wait faithfully through the decades, she was granted the gift of discernment in order to recognize that the Christ Child was not just an ordinary baby, but an extraordinary Baby, and in order to spread hope to others with this good news.

The spiritual Tradition of the Church indicates to us that both the Prophetess Anna and the holy elder Simeon were granted the privilege of meeting the Christ that day because they shared in common a heavenly gift: their hearts were purified. St. Gregory Palamas, in his homily on the Transfiguration of Christ, writes that Simeon and Anna were granted spiritual lenses that enabled them to recognize the divine.[10] Strangely enough, although Simeon's prophecy is recorded, why does the evangelist keep silent about Anna's prophetic acclamation? Some will contend that she was made invisible because of her gender. Though we are blessed to receive Simeon's prophecy through the recorded word, why wasn't there more recorded about *Anna's* prophecy?

Through silence, St. Anna demonstrates at least two differing dynamics of silence at work. The first dynamic of silence concerns the humble, persevering witness of the saint. Throughout the decades, we know of no peer who offered her human encouragement or consolation as she waited for the Lord. In some ways, she prefigures the "wise maidens" in the parable told by Jesus (Matt 25:1–13). Here, He urges his hearers to emulate these maidens who courageously and unconditionally persevered, waiting even into the darkest, loneliest, and coldest hours of the night for their Bridegroom. Anna demonstrates a powerful witness through an astonishing silence; so much so that some of us, pondering deeply into the reality of what it must have been like for her to live this way, may experience a deep spiritual or psychological reaction; the effects can be deafening. The second dynamic of silence refers to an interesting fact: in their commentaries on this passage, many Fathers of the Church, such as Cyril of Alexandria, do *not* offer any observations on the section of the text where the Prophetess Anna is mentioned.

Nevertheless, Anna did not wait in vain. Night and day, for eighty-four years, she was preparing to meet her—and our—Lord and Savior. The Prophetess Anna chose the life of stillness, of prayer, fasting, and serving in the temple in a solitary manner. Wrapped in silence, she stood on the holy ground and announced to the world the "good news."

PERSONAL REFLECTIONS

How can it be that an opportunity like this was given to such a hidden, humble lady? She wasn't royalty. She did not have any academic degrees, nor any fancy letters after her name. She never wrote, so that her scholarly works would be assessed by her peers and others, nor was she a CEO, nor a rabbi. She was just an ordinary person with an extraordinary pronouncement. As a matter of fact, there were no airs, no narcissistic and grandiose traits, no sense of self-serving urgency, no frenetic energy— only an ordinary and poor widow who prayed and fasted. How contrary this is to our own society. Her witness directs us to inward stillness, humility, and patience in a world that incessantly proclaims that business and doing are of utmost importance.

A modern man who had a very busy life but understood the importance of quiet and stillness was Dag Hammarskjöld, Secretary General of the United Nations in the late 1950s. Metropolitan Kallistos Ware quoted him as follows: "One understands through the stillness, one acts out of the stillness, and one conquers in the stillness. So, we, too, can understand through the stillness, act out of the stillness, and conquer in the stillness."[11] Anna not only "[conquered] in the stillness," but, even more importantly, this stillness led her to the eternal source of joy. We find the stillness and joy of Anna's life reflected in the poetic words of Psalm 84:

> How lovely is your dwelling place, O Lord of hosts!
> My soul longs, indeed it faints for the courts of the Lord;
> my heart and my flesh sing for joy to the living God.
> Even the sparrow finds a home,
> and the swallow a nest for herself, where she may lay her young,
> at your altars, O Lord of hosts, my King and my God.

Happy are those who live in your house . . .
(Ps 84:1–4)

*Acquire inner peace and thousands around you will find their
   salvation. – St. Seraphim of Sarov*

We live in a noisy world. Our society bombards us with all sorts of sounds
from television, MP3 players, telephones, Internet, and radios—constant noise. Even though we may be alone, we are surrounded by a society filled with noise pollution; this noise pollution pervades our work,
homes, and even our play.

As far back as 1927, noise was identified as a slow agent of death.
Today, the medical profession links our hearing problems, high blood
pressure, heart disease, and ulcers to our exposure to noise pollution.
James Truslow Adams, an American historian, said that "Perhaps it
would be a good idea, fantastic as it sounds, to muffle every telephone,
stop every motor and halt all activity for an hour some day to give people
a chance to ponder for a few minutes on what it is all about, why they are
living and what they really want."[12] Søren Kierkegaard, the great Danish philosopher, emphasized the urgency for attaining genuine silence
when he stated: "The present state of the world and the whole of life is
diseased. If I were a doctor and were asked for my advice, I should reply:
Create silence! Bring human beings to silence. The Word of God cannot
be heard in the noisy world of today. And even if it were blazoned forth
with all the panoply of noise so that it could be heard in the midst of all
the other noise, then it would no longer be the Word of God. Therefore,
create silence."[13]

Jesus calls us from a place filled with noise and distraction to a place
of solitude in His presence. His own earthly life was exemplary of how to
keep one's heart in solitude. Richard J. Foster, in his book *Celebration of
Discipline*, writes beautifully on this issue. He reminds us that "solitude
is more a state of mind and heart than it is a place . . . Whether alone
or among people, we always carry with us a portable sanctuary of the
heart."[14]

This type of solitude is vital. Scripture offers us many examples in
which the Lord went out to pray alone. At the beginning of His ministry, He spent forty days in the desert, where He was tempted to do
the devil's will instead of the will of God, and to choose earthly power

over divine. The devil used Scripture to put Jesus to the test. Jesus, of course, did not submit to the will of the devil, but through prayer and fasting committed Himself to do the will of the Father (Matt 4:1–11). Subsequently, even before Jesus chose His twelve disciples, He went out to the desert to be alone and pray. We read: "Now during those days he went out to the mountain to pray; and he spent the night in prayer to God" (Luke 6:12).

The Lord also encouraged solitude in His disciples. After the miraculous feeding of the five thousand and the death of John the Baptist, Jesus directed His disciples to board a boat and go before Him to the other side, while He sent the multitudes away. "And after he had dismissed the crowds, he went up the mountain by himself to pray. When evening came, he was there alone" (Matt 14:23). With the three disciples, He sought the silence of a lonely mountain as the stage for the Transfiguration (Matt 17:1–9), and as He was preparing for the Passion he sought out the solitude of Gethsemane (Matt 26:36–46; Mark 14:32–42; John 18:1). Before His Crucifixion He poured out His soul in prayer in a lonely corner while His disciples slept.

In our society there appears to be an unconscious fear of silence, of being alone with oneself in the presence of the Other. There seems to be a confusion between loneliness (or isolation) and solitude. Foster writes,

> The fear of being left alone petrifies people. A new child in the neighborhood sobs to her mother, "No one ever plays with me." A college freshman yearns for his high school days when he was the center of attention . . . A business executive sits dejected in her office, powerful, yet alone . . . An old woman lies in a nursing home waiting to go "Home."[15]

Jesus calls us from this life of loneliness, too often filled with noise, to a place of solitude in His presence. We need that time of quiet. We need a time to recollect. We need a time to be alone with God.

How is it that, on the one hand, we as people of God desire in the depths of our souls this time of quiet—a time to recollect, and a time to be alone in the presence of God—and, on the other hand, we work and play constantly? We become agitated as we expect things to be done for us instantly, at the speed of light. We are easily distracted. We jump the gun. We become disgruntled. We lose our tempers. Nevertheless, at the very same time, the deepest desire of our souls is to be with God. This is not only a contemporary need, a need of our generation. Writing in the fourth century, St. Augustine addressed this desire succinctly when he said: "You stir man to take pleasure in praising you, because you have made us for yourself, and our heart is restless until it rests in you."[16]

By your endurance you will gain your souls.
   (Luke 21:19)

Another symptom of unhealthy, noisy distractions is our constant rushing. We may often feel trapped in a frantic, senseless race through an endless maze, or tethered to the same old wearying treadmill. The words of the Prophet Isaiah, however, offer us an antidote by calling us to be renewed through God-centered waiting, which is perseverance, when he exclaims that "those who wait for the Lord shall renew their strength, they shall mount up with wings like eagles, they shall run and not be weary, they shall walk and not faint" (Isa 40:31).

The whole concept of waiting on the Lord is foreign to me. To be honest, I am totally impetuous and impatient. I don't wait; I expect. There is an important difference between the two words, "wait" and "expect." "Waiting" connotes remaining or standing fast with perseverance, whereas "expecting" connotes looking forward to something anticipated in a more active sense.

Waiting, from this perspective, is very difficult. Waiting demands unconditional acceptance. The waiting described in Isaiah implies accepting completely the whole context in which I find myself. It relies on genuine acceptance, which is not to deny, but rather to acknowledge, everything in the present moment. This is not easy! The more I monitor how I accept the circumstances of a given situation, the more I realize that the quality of my acceptance directly affects my ability to be all right with whatever is currently in front of me. I have to accept fully the reality that surrounds me; however, I do not have to endorse or like what is going on. "Acceptance" and "approval" are two very different concepts! Still, it seems that my serenity is a direct expression of my striving to wait before God; in fact, my serenity is proportional to my acceptance and inversely proportional to my expectations. As my acceptance increases, my serenity also increases. But as my expectations increase, my serenity decreases.

In my own spiritual journey, I find myself resonating in the deepest parts of my being with the words of Augustine in his *Confessions*: "[my] heart is restless until it rests in you." But my life is filled with so many responsibilities that at times everything is one loud noise. My mind is filled with noise pollution. I jump to conclusions. I rush. How often in my daily activities and relationships do I fail to recognize Christ in the other?

One thing that has helped me in my journey is spending time studying and reflecting on the life of St. Anna the Prophetess. She was a woman who knew how to wait for God through silence. She has become like a near and dear friend to me, a friend who speaks through silence. Through God's love, she mysteriously intercedes, helping me to slow down as I strive to attend to the "one thing necessary" (Luke 10:42). Through unspoken action she directs me to remain vigilant and aware that Christ is in our midst. Perhaps through silence, I, too, may come to recognize the Lord as I strive to "seek the Lord and his strength, seek his face continually" (1 Chron 16:11).

CONCLUSION: "SEEK THE LORD, AND HIS STRENGTH: SEEK HIS FACE EVERMORE" (PS 105:4)

What could have inspired Anna to seek God so intently and in the manner of a solitary, through prayer and fasting in the temple? Could it have been possible that the book of Tobit was a pattern for Anna's life, nurturing her piety and love for God? The book of Tobit narrates how Tobit sends his only son out alone to find a bride. In addition to the powerful theme of "going out on one's own," the story is about *returning* from the desert of exile through obedience to God, as well as seeking His face in the faces of strangers. Understood from this perspective, this story in its entirety is a foreshadowing of the faithful who prepared themselves for the coming of the Messiah, who was to redeem Israel.

Thus we see Tobit's theology and message fulfilled in Luke's spiritual description of Anna. She was a woman who prayed, worshipped, fasted, and waited patiently for the redemption of Jerusalem. She, too, invites us to "seek the Lord, and his strength: seek his face evermore." For us, Anna thus faithfully fulfills the joyful desire exclaimed in Psalm 27:

> One thing I asked of the Lord, that will I seek after:
> to live in the house of the Lord all the days of my life,
> to behold the beauty of the Lord, and to inquire in his temple.
> For he will hide me in his shelter . . .
> he will set me high on a rock. (vv. 4–5)

NOTES

The author would like to thank the Rev. Dr. Eugen Pentiuc for his assistance, advice, and support of both this chapter and St. Catherine's Vision as a whole.

1. *Hymn* 24 in *Ephrem the Syrian: Hymns*, trans. Kathleen E. McVey, preface by John Meyendorff (New York: Paulist Press, 1989), 367.

2. Even today, it is still the usual Orthodox custom for infants, whether male or female, to be brought to church in order to be blessed forty days after their birth.

3. Richard Bauckham, "Anna of the Tribe of Asher (Luke 2:36–38)," *Revue Biblique* 104 (1997): 161–91, at 161–62, 179. See also Margaret H. Williams, "Palestinian Jewish Personal Names in Acts," 79–113, chap. 4 of *The Book of Acts in Its First Century Setting*, vol. 4, *Palestinian Setting*, ed. Richard Bauckham (Grand Rapids, MI: Eerdmans, 1995). In this chapter, Williams presents an interesting point on the naming of children in the Jewish tradition: many Palestinian Jews were named Miriam (or Mary/Maria) not after Moses' sister, but after Herod's wife, the Hasmonean princess Miriamme (107).

4. "Protevangelium of James," in *The Other Gospels: Non-Canonical Gospel Texts*, ed. Ron Cameron (Louisville: Westminster John Knox Press, 1982), 110.

5. Richard Bauckham, *Gospel Women: Studies of the Named Women in the Gospels* (Grand Rapids, MI: Eerdmans, 2002), 77.

6. Ibid.

7. John Nolland, *Luke 1:1–9:20*, vol. 35a of *World Biblical Commentary* (Dallas: Word Books, 1989), Luke 2:36–38. Electronic edition online at Logos Bible Software, www.logos.com.

8. In the Church's infinite mercy and love, names of the prophetesses are remembered in the fourth-century ordination rite for woman deacons: "With the 'laying on of hands,' the bishop offers the following prayer: 'O Eternal God, the Father of Our Lord Jesus Christ, the Creator of man and woman, who did replenish with the Spirit of Miriam (Ex. 15:20–21) and Deborah (Jg. 4–5), and Anna (Lk 2:36) and Huldah (2 Kg. 22:14–20); and who did not disdain that your only-begotten Son should be born of woman; who also in the tabernacle of the testimony, and in the temple, did ordain women to be guardians of your holy gates; look down now upon this your servant, who is ordained for the diaconate . . . and grant her your Holy Spirit, cleanse her from all that can defile flesh or spirit, (2 Cor. 7:1) so that she may worthily accomplish the work which is committed to her to your glory, and the praise of your Christ, with whom glory and adoration be to you and the Holy Spirit for ever. Amen'" (Kyriaki Karidoyanes FitzGerald, *Women Deacons in the Orthodox Church: Called to Holiness and Ministry* [Brookline, MA: Holy Cross Orthodox Press, 1999], 59–60).

9. John L. Mackenzie, *Dictionary of the Bible* (New York: Macmillan, 1965), s.v. "prophet."

10. Gregory Palamas, *Homily 34*, in *The Homilies of Saint Gregory Palamas*, vol. 2, *Homilies 22–42*, ed. Christopher Veniamin (South Canaan, PA: St. Tikhon's Seminary Press, 2004), 142: "That is why the Virgin, who mysteriously conceived and bore Him, recognized her Child as God incarnate, as did Simeon, when he took Him up in his arms as an Infant, and the aged Anna, who came to meet Him (Luke 2:25ff)."

11. Metropolitan (then Bishop) Kallistos Ware quoted Dag Hammarskjöld in a presentation at St. Demetrios Greek Orthodox Church in Weston, Massachusetts, 2006.

12. Online at Living Life Fully, http://www.livinglifefully.com/perspective6.htm.

13. Søren Kierkgaard, *The Sickness unto Death* (Garden City, NY: Doubleday, 1954), 10, in George A. Maloney, *Abiding in the Indwelling Trinity* (Mahwah, NJ: Paulist Press), 2004, 13–14.

14. Richard J. Foster, *Celebration of Discipline: The Path to Spiritual Growth*, 3rd ed. (New York: HarperCollins, 1998), 96–97.

15. Foster, *Celebration of Discipline*, 96.

16. *Saint Augustine: Confessions*, trans. Henry Chadwick (New York: Oxford University Press, 1992), 3.

REFLECTION AND DISCUSSION QUESTIONS

1. a. What are some of the internal noises that may distract us?
   b. In what ways can these noises harm us?

2. a. How do you make time for silence in your day?
   b. What may get in the way of this?
   c. What can help correct such distractions?

3. a. How are you tempted to be constantly on the run?
   b. Do you easily "become disgruntled"? If so, how?
   c. Do you easily "jump the gun"? If so, how?

4. Consider and discuss the two dynamics of silence that are identified in Anna's story.

5. a. What speaks to you about Anna?
   b. Is there something in particular in her life that is nudging you to change? Discuss this as you are able.

6. a. What do you think it means to be invisible?
   b. How could this have occurred in Anna's day?
   c. How might one experience this today?

7. a. Has your view of the Meeting of Christ in the Temple changed as a result of reading this chapter?
   b. How?

8. a. What do you imagine that it really means to be able to see the divine?
   b. How do we prepare for this?
   c. What clues do you receive from this chapter (as well as others in this volume) about what this may mean for you?

9. a. Just for fun, using the biblical account to help supply some of the information, how old do you suppose that the holy Anna was on the day that she met the Lord in the temple?
   b. How may this speak to our own journeys in life?

St. Paula and the Order of Widows

Stefanie Yova Yazge

INTRODUCTION

*T*here seems to have been an energy in the Church during its formative years after Pentecost that we really cannot appreciate today. Those who embraced the one living God, whose Son had come so that they could have life, "and have it more abundantly" (John 10:10), established communities virtually lit up with the power of the Holy Spirit. In each new community (local church), Christians found ways to participate in this new and abundant life. St. Paul, writing to the believers in Corinth, reminds them that they are all part of the one body of Christ, but are given different gifts of the Spirit, "manifestations of the Spirit for the common good" (1 Cor 12:7). It becomes clear that everyone at every age and in every life situation has a gift to offer.

Jesus gave us the foundation for using our gifts in Christian life through his most basic teaching of two commandments that summarize all the rest: "Love the Lord your God with all your heart, with all your soul, with all your strength . . . and love your neighbor as yourself" (Luke 10:27; Matt 22:37–39).

Stefanie Yova Yazge is a graduate of St. Vladimir's Seminary and is presently completing her doctoral dissertation in interdisciplinary studies, specializing in theology, at Union Institute and University. Married to Fr. Anthony Yazge, a priest in the Antiochian Archdiocese, she is the mother of three. Professionally, she has taught for twelve years as a college instructor in theology, as well as an Assistant Professor at Saint Mary-of-the-Woods College (IN). Currently she serves on the adjunct faculty in theology at Seton Hill University, following the appointment of her husband as Director of Camping at the Antiochian Village in Ligonier, Pennsylvania. She also serves as Consultant to the Board of St. Catherine's Vision.

So how am I supposed to show love for my neighbor? St. Luke's Gospel answers that question with the story of the good Samaritan. The person who proved to be "neighbor" to the stripped and beaten man found on the side of the road was the one who showed him mercy. "Mercy" (*eleimosini*) is the word also used in Jesus' teaching (Matt 6:2–4) that we usually see translated as "almsgiving," as in the three components of Christian discipline: prayer, fasting, and almsgiving. We are called to use whatever gifts we have to do God's work, to *do mercy*, to actively show mercy just as God shows mercy, to our neighbor—and our neighbor is anyone whom we encounter who needs it. That includes the widest possible range of people: all people and every circumstance we encounter, from the proverbial little old lady who needs help crossing the street to the guy who cuts us off in traffic!

Showing mercy in caring for the weak and the vulnerable, however, was not a new teaching for God's people. In the Old Testament God told His people of their responsibility to care especially for widows and for orphans. Specific reference is made to widows, who under Jewish law (with rare exception) had no inheritance rights and were often left destitute. Jesus encountered such a widow at the temple, the one who gave the two copper coins: "she out of her poverty has put in everything she had, her whole living" (Mark 12:44). Just two copper coins. Such a widow had no way out of her poverty unless a "kinsman redeemer" married her, and then the widow was inherited with the property.[1] Therefore, God was very pointed in His charge about caring for widows: "Do not take advantage of a widow or an orphan. If you do and they cry out to me, I will certainly hear their cry. My anger will be aroused, and I will kill you with the sword; your wives will become widows and your children fatherless" (Exod 22:22–24). There were also other instructions, including to the harvesters to leave the overlooked sheaves of grain, so that the widows might come and glean, and have something to eat (Deut 24:19).

It was this very concern for widows that brought about one of the first dilemmas for the young Church. With the fast growth of the faith, how could the apostles minister to everyone? In Acts 6 we have members of the Church complaining that "their widows [are] being overlooked in the daily distribution of food" (v. 1). The solution: the apostles called for seven deacons (*diakonoi*), or "ministers," as servants to the widows and needy of the community.

Although the first deacons were men, the role of "minister" was not limited to men, because women deacons also emerged.[2] We must remember that the words "minister" and "deacon" simply mean "servant." Something dynamic, something revealing the "new creation" of the life in Christ, was growing in this young Church. And service in some manner was the hallmark of every Christian. As an identified group in the earliest days of New Testament Christianity, widows were no longer merely the ones who needed to be cared for by others. What has caught my attention and interest about this specific group is that widows now also became "ministers" to others, as women who served the Church in various and very public ways.

The lives of the Widows[3] as an Order in the Church have remained obscure, and so they are the subject of this chapter. Why? I have become interested in women in the life of the Church after having designed and taught a college course with a Western Christian colleague on holy women. This friend seemed to have an easier time finding resources on Western saints than I did locating in-depth Orthodox sources.

A more significant interest comes from a simple statistical reality: on average, women today outlive men by at least five years. This means a growing number of widows will be filling our parishes as the baby boomers age. How has the Church involved women who have survived the loss of their husbands, from its beginnings to today? What will be the role(s) of the widowed boomers today?

My own mother has now been a widow for over a dozen years. My father was a deacon who faithfully served the Church for thirty years. She helped and shared in aspects of his very active ministry, and she has continued a portion of that work as a widow. Could she be a living vestige of that ancient Order, if only informally? Shouldn't the Church somehow be acknowledging and blessing her and her work, and others like her? I wonder. But before we can have an enlightened conversation or make decisions pleasing to God about the possible revival of the Order of Widows, we need to know the history of the Order, and more about the women themselves.

THE ORDER OF WIDOWS IN THE NEW TESTAMENT

The First Letter to Timothy identifies Widows as more than simply women whose husbands have died. Widows are described as active members ministering to others. They appear to serve in an important role, one important enough to be listed as a position in the community. The Widow is pointed out as one who, finding herself alone, "trusts in God and continues in supplications and prayers night and day" (1 Tim 5:5). Her situation first turns her toward God, and then guides her in reaching out to and for others in a spiritual role. To be enrolled as a Widow, a woman had to be at least sixty years of age. In addition, this ministry was restricted to one who "has been faithful to her husband, and is well known for her good deeds, such as bringing up children, showing hospitality, washing the feet of the Lord's people, helping those in trouble and devoting herself to all kinds of good deeds" (1 Tim 5:9–10). This again points to the teaching that all of us at every stage and place in life have an ability to serve by offering our particular gifts.

As the Church grew among the Gentiles, the widow and Widows' service became more apparent because changes in Roman society now afforded women greater possibilities for a life outside the four walls of their homes, especially as widows. Widows began to gain access to the family estate, increasingly without the approval of a legally mandated "male guardian" who had to sanction any and all financial or legal transactions. Consequently, women could finally direct the use of their own material wealth. Their activity shows the sense of equality in Christ that allowed widows, particularly ones who had the means, to use their situation as a gift for "manifestations of the Spirit for the common good" (1 Cor 12:7).[4]

In trying to decide on a particular widow/saint as the subject of this writing, the research proved a bit daunting. In the New Testament, almost nothing identifies any woman specifically as a member of this group or records examples of widows and their work. In Acts 16 we meet Lydia, a seller of purple cloth, which was a valuable commodity for the wealthy. She is the one who opens her house in the city of Philippi to Paul and Silas, after choosing to be baptized and becoming Paul's first convert on European soil. We do not know for sure that she was a widow, but there is no mention of a husband. Therefore, the argument is made from silence that Lydia would have likely been a widow. Although some scholars speculate that she was a freed slave who worked hard for poor wages to make and sell the purple cloth, others maintain that she must have been a businesswoman of means (an emerging class in the Roman world[5]) because she has a "household" who are all baptized, and a house big enough for guests and a gathering of "the brothers" (Acts 16:15, 40). Her home becomes a place for the growing Christian community, which shows us that she has an active role and also suggests that she has the financial means to support it. If she is really not a well-to-do woman, as some suggest,[6] then offering what resources she does have as a single woman (widow or otherwise) makes her all the more a model of using one's gifts. She does what Jesus asks of all of us: offer what you have for the sake of God and neighbor.

There is also another perspective to examine in the New Testament writings. This one concerns the place of widows in the community. The First Epistle to Timothy gives us a sense of this emerging structure. St. Paul addresses the requirements for the overseer (*episcopos*), or "bishop," of a community. Then he speaks about the qualifications for deacons, including a specific section concerning "the women" (1 Tim 3:11). Historically, even from early patristic times, the Orthodox have understood this to refer to female deacons, or "deaconesses."[7]

From there, St. Paul addresses the duties of ministry and then speaks about widows and elders. Why is St. Paul's description and inclusion of Widows of any importance? The answer is: because there are scholars who point out that Widows are an ecclesiastical order and are officially listed as Church ministers. Tertullian's writings from the early third century provide evidence of how the role of the Widow developed and was lived out in the Church. He records the inclusion of the Widow in the *ordo*, or Church orders, which also included the bishops, priests, and deacons.

> How detrimental to faith, how obstructive to holiness, second marriages are, the discipline of the Church and the prescription of the apostle declare, when he does not let men married twice preside (over a Church) [1 Tim 2:2; Titus 1:6], when *he would not grant a widow admittance into the order* unless she had been "the wife of one man;" for it behooves God's altar [1 Tim 5:9–10] to be set forth pure.[8]

As one who vehemently held that women not be permitted to teach or perform a sacramental ministry, Tertullian surprises me because he not only admits the Widow as a member of those set apart (that is, the clergy), but he also indicates something of their function. The repenting sinners were to come before the assembly (the community gathered for worship) and "prostrate themselves before the widows and before the presbyters." The Widows also had seats reserved for them and were appointed to the office by the bishop.[9] As the Order continued to develop, we find that the *Testamentum Domini* ("Testament of our Lord") from the fifth century even shows that the Widows are instructed to stand opposite the deacons during the Eucharistic offering, and to receive communion after the deacons and before the subdeacons.[10]

So why has it been difficult to find a Widow-saint to write about? It is because the office seems to have faded from existence by the fourth century, being absorbed by the role of the female deacon. As local churches grew, the deaconess came to serve the needs of the women in the community, as the counterpart to the male deacon's work. Taking communion to the sick and working with catechumens were among the tasks of the deacons, male and female. In addition, the deaconess was responsible for overseeing the area of the church building itself where the women stood. The result was that the deaconess became a solid part of the Church's organizational structure. Another reason for the decline of the Widow was that many of the women who were inclined to the office of Widow became monastics as that vocation developed. Those widows seeking the life of prayer, according to what we read about them, usually embraced Christ and their new celibacy in the monastic life that blossomed in the desert with and after St. Anthony the Great.

However, there is also another type of monastic life that evolved. St. Macrina influenced her brother St. Basil as he developed the model of the monastic life in which Christian holiness—growing in the likeness of God—takes place not just in prayer, but in living in and through community, combined with service to and engagement with the world.[11] Simply on the level of human social contact, as persons created by God for communion with God and other people, it would make sense that widows would gravitate to this latter type of monastic life. They had enjoyed the communion of persons in married life in the world. Rather than seeing life as void of worth and meaning and purpose without a husband, they found their grief transfigured in the life dedicated to Christ with other women of like mind and intention. In this new community they would support, encourage, and sustain each other in finding and offering meaningful service to others in these growing women's monasteries. An excellent example of such a woman is St. Paula. As a widow, she chose a life in Christ, which took her on an amazing path. Her life and her work have not only been passed along to this day, but she herself still has things to teach us.

St. Paula: Patron Saint of Widows

Picture yourself in the place of a wealthy woman of society, well-bred and well-heeled, in one of the world's greatest cities. You have a husband and five children whom you love, and life is very good; very good, that is, until your husband dies and you find yourself a widow at the age of thirty-two. The love of your life is unexpectedly gone. Grief brings the realization that money is not everything, and you seek solace, meaning, and direction for your changed life, a life turned upside down. You find it in the Christ revealed by the Scriptures. And you choose to give your life and all its wealth over to Him. This, in brief, is the life of St. Paula of Rome and Bethlehem, whom the Church of Rome designated patron saint of widows.

Before the Cross

Born in 347 AD, from the renowned Scipios and Gracchi families, Paula was among the elite of patrician women in Rome. Most of what we know about her has come from a long letter written by St. Jerome to her daughter Eustochium after Paula's death in 404 AD, in addition to several other letters.[12] The relationship that the three of them shared included some important pieces of Christian history, not the least of which was the translation of the Bible into Latin. It was her life as a widow that allowed much of this to happen.

Coming from a prominent family, Paula was suitably married at the age of sixteen to the gentleman Toxotius, also of the patrician class. Life would have been comfortable given their wealth and place in Roman society. Their household was filled with children: four daughters and a son. However, in 379 Toxotius died. Jerome recounts that, "When he died, her grief was so great that she nearly died herself."

This would be a turning point in any woman's life. However, Jerome goes on to tell us, "Yet so completely did she then give herself to the service of the Lord, that it might have seemed that she had desired his death."[13] This is a rather striking statement to our ears, but it is a sign of Jerome's deep respect for the life in Christ that Paula made for herself after Toxotius' death. This new life began with her friendship with (St.) Marcella, a woman who grew up as an orphan and was herself a widow after only seven months of marriage, and with the group of patrician women Marcella formed in Rome for growth in their Christian faith.[14]

In 382 Marcella arranged for these faithful women to meet with Bishops Epiphanius of Cyprus and Paulinus of Antioch, who were accompanied by the priest Jerome, when the men were summoned to Rome by the emperor during one of the Christological controversies that was tearing Antioch apart. From her encounter with Jerome, who met for some time with the women and taught them the Scriptures, Paula's life took the road that led her deeply into her relationship with Christ. She and her daughter Eustochium began by learning Hebrew, so that they could read the Old Testament in the original language.

As her study and devotion continued, Paula also continued raising her family. She saw to it that her daughter Paulina was suitably married. Her daughter Blesilla also married, but was soon widowed herself. For Paula, the worst came in 384 when Blesilla died, and she again experienced an overwhelming grief. In the same year, Jerome also experienced a profound loss when Pope Damasus, who actively supported Jerome both personally and in his work translating the Hebrew Scriptures (Old Testament) into Latin, also died. The widow and the spiritual father were brought closer by their grief and were strengthened in their faith. From these shattering events came the monumental changes in Paula's life.

Turning to God, instead of fleeing from Him, Paula chose to consider the spiritual life. She may have already become familiar with the life in the desert as a spiritual seeker because of what Jerome perhaps shared concerning his own life in the desert. From 374 to 379, he was in the desert region some fifty miles southeast of Antioch. When he came back to Antioch from the desert, his ordination by Bishop Paulinus only occurred with the reassurance that Jerome would not be assigned to serve any specific church, because he felt called to the monastic life and to someday living in a monastic community.[15] Finding that destination began with their departure from Rome. Jerome returned to the East in August 385, and Paula and her daughter Eustochium joined him in Antioch a month later.

Paula left behind in Rome her son, Toxotius, who was probably about thirteen years old, and her grown daughter Rufina. Jerome describes the boy and his sister as pleading with her not to go as she boarded a boat at Portus; the daughter "with silent sobs besought her mother to wait till she should be married."[16] Maybe this was not desertion of her young son and unmarried daughter. After all, he was left with his grown sister, who was capable of caring for him, and he married only four years later.

I tried to justify Paula's decision in my own mind by recalling that "childhood" and its extension well into the teen years is a very Western and modern concept. Girls in Paula's time were married and became wives and mothers as soon as they were capable of having babies. Growing up was a rather quick process for the boys as well. Perhaps it wasn't really *that* traumatic for Toxotius that his mother chose to leave him, their family and friends, and the life of luxury for the Christian ascetical life.

As a mother, I cannot fathom doing what Paula did. My children have been one of life's greatest gifts. Despite those long days every mother has, I cannot imagine leaving them by choice, especially before they are grown. They have shown me the face of God in their smiling faces. They have shown me simple faith and total trust in God at times when I needed it. They have loved as God loves, unconditionally. How could a mother ever walk away from that? But lest we judge her too harshly as uncaring, we should be aware that apparently even for Paula her departure was not easy, as Jerome recounts:

> But still Paula's eyes were dry as she turned them heavenwards; and she overcame her love for her children by her love for God. She knew herself no more as a mother, that she might approve herself a handmaid of Christ. Yet her heart was torn apart within her, and she wrestled with her grief, as though she were being forcibly separated from parts of herself. The greatness of the affection she had to overcome made all admire her victory the more . . . But she turned away her eyes that she might not see what she could not behold without agony. No mother, it must be confessed, ever loved her children so dearly.[17]

The only way I can comprehend what she chose to do is by accepting that Paula had a faith and conviction that I lack in taking the words of Christ to heart: "He who loves father or mother more than Me is not worthy of Me. And he who loves son or daughter more than Me is not worthy of Me. And he who does not take his cross and follow after Me is not worthy of Me" (Matt 10:37–38). As a widow, feeling she had raised her children and was leaving her son in good hands, Paula felt an irresistible call to take up her cross and follow Christ.

Following the Cross

To begin her spiritual quest, Paula took advantage of her financial means, doing what many Christians were doing in that day. Although not nearly as well known as Egeria, the woman pilgrim who traveled to the Holy Land,[18] Paula also became a spiritual pilgrim, journeying through the Holy Land and Egypt for a year and a half. As a pilgrim, she chose not to enjoy the first-class accommodations offered by the proconsul of Palestine, who was a close family friend with a lavish home and connections to wealthy people throughout the region. Instead, Paula stayed in simple quarters and humble monastic cells.[19] Traveling to holy places and other sites of biblical importance in Palestine, Paula virtually connected with the people of God from Abraham to the New Testament Christians, and with the places where they had encountered God's presence. Because she had come to know the Scriptures, she knew the importance of the places she visited. One of her most deeply moving experiences was venerating the Cross and tomb of Christ, where "she threw herself down in adoration as though she beheld the Lord hanging upon it: and when she entered the tomb which was the scene of the Resurrection, she kissed the stone which the angel had rolled away from the door of the sepulcher."[20]

Another place she visited came to hold special importance in Paula's heart and life: Bethlehem, the place of Christ's birth. Seeing the inn made famous for its lack of a room and the stall where Jesus was born, Jerome says that she spoke of being able to see the babe in swaddling clothes, the wise men, the Virgin and Joseph, the shepherds, the star. All of this caused her to be filled with the opening lines of St. John's Gospel: "In the beginning was the Word" (v. 1) and "the Word was made flesh" (v. 14). Leaving Bethlehem, she continued her pilgrimage, which included spending time in Egypt to learn the ways of the desert monastics and their communities.

However, the impression made at Bethlehem shaped her to the end of her days. At the conclusion of her eighteen-month journey, taking inspiration from St. Melania, who established a monastery on the Mount of Olives,[21] and from what she had experienced in her visit to Egypt, she returned to Bethlehem and founded two monasteries. The monastery for women was built next to the cave of the Nativity. The other was for men, constructed nearby and directed by Jerome. However, Paula had to live for three years in a "miserable hostelry" while the monastery was being built. The construction could have been completed in less time, but Paula had insisted the monastery include a guest house for passing travelers, "where they might find the welcome that Mary and Joseph had missed."[22] The life of prayer in the desert formed the bedrock of her life of hospitality to pilgrims and service to the poor.

It wasn't unusual in that day for a woman like Paula to use her own money to build a monastery not only for herself and other women, but for a spiritual father like Jerome and males as well, and to be its patron. Ancient Greco-Roman society had developed the custom of patronage. Starving artists needing support are not something new! Wealthy people even several thousand years ago were patrons of artisans of all types. The arrangement usually meant that there was an exchange between the two parties involved. The patrons provided the financial means needed for the less wealthy artisan to use his artistic gifts to create works for the patrons, and sometimes for the community in general.

There was also a level of loyalty that developed toward the patron in return for the ongoing funding and goods supplied to the artisan. In this arrangement, a real relationship developed, but usually it was "asymmetrical" because of the social inequality of patron and artisan.[23] However, Paula lived an example of Christian patronage that she had learned directly from her friend Marcella. She had the gift of financial means to accomplish that work. But she and her daughter Eustochium were not simply "writing the checks," as uninvolved supporters. She and Jerome were equally engaged in their mutual spiritual work. Having learned Hebrew, both mother and daughter played an integral part in Jerome's work of translating the Bible into Latin (the Vulgate). He also taught them so well, and they learned so well, that they developed an intellectual respect for each other. The fruit of this was seen in the help the women gave him as sounding boards in his theological work dealing with the heresies of the day. Paula also receives credit as one of the few people who could handle Jerome and his "fiery personality," the polite way of referring to his infamous temper. They came to value each other as brother and sister in Christ, becoming so close that gossips in Rome started rumors about their relationship even before they left for Antioch.[24]

As her life progressed, Paula endured more hardship, with the deaths of both her daughter Rufina in 386 and her daughter Paulina in 395. Jerome recounts how she was crushed by their deaths, becoming physically weakened in ways that her severe fasting had never produced. In fact, fasting was a true source of spiritual strength for a woman who in her "worldly life" had never gone hungry: "Except on feast days she would scarcely ever take oil with her food; a fact from which may be judged what she thought of wine, sauce, fish, honey, milk, eggs, and other things agreeable to the palate."[25] Severe fasting caused both Paula and Jerome some negative physical consequences. Yet she was determined to subject herself to the strictest of disciplines, seeing it as a way to develop the Christian virtues in herself as a servant of Christ.

Following in the way of St. Basil's monastic rule, Paula withdrew from her worldly life to follow Christ, but in seeking and working at Christian perfection, she still stayed engaged with that life through acts of mercy. She did this by using her wealth to help anyone and everyone in need whom she encountered or who came to her. Her desire to assist the needy was unrelenting, as was her generosity. Jerome describes this generosity and how it expressed her understanding of Christ's teaching:

> Her liberality alone knew no bounds. Indeed, so anxious was she to turn no needy person away that she borrowed money at interest and often contracted new loans to pay off old ones. I was wrong, I admit; but when I saw her so profuse in giving, I reproved her alleging the apostle's words: "For I do not mean that others should be eased and you burdened; but by an equality, that now at this time your abundance may supply their lack, that their abundance also may supply your lack—that there may be equality." I quoted from the gospel the Savior's words: "He who has two tunics, let him give to him who has none; and he who has food, let him do likewise," and I warned her that she might not always have means to do as she would wish. Other arguments I adduced to the same purpose; but with admirable modesty and brevity she overruled them all. "God is my witness," she said, "that what I do, I do for His sake. My prayer is that I may die a beggar not leaving a penny to my daughter and indebted to strangers for my winding sheet." She then concluded with these words: "I, if I beg, shall find many to give to me; but if this beggar does not obtain help from me who by borrowing can give it to him, he will die; and if he dies, of whom will his soul be required?"

I wished her to be more careful managing her concerns, but she
with a faith more glowing than mine clung steadfastly to the Savior
with her whole heart and poor in spirit followed the Lord in His poverty, giving back to Him what she had received and becoming poor
for His sake.[26]

She gave and gave again to the poor and the destitute, borrowing more
and more money to do so. Then, in the winter of 404, she became very
ill. Her daughter, the nun Eustochium, cared for her mother and was
sincerely heartbroken at the thought of losing her to death, wishing that
she, too, would die so that they would not be separated. But Eustochium
would live, and was left with a financial debt so great that "only the mercy
of Christ can free her from it."[27]

In Paula's last days, she continued to pray the Psalms: "Lord, I have
loved the habitation of Your house, and the place where Your glory
dwells" (26:8) and "How lovely is Your tabernacle, O Lord of hosts! My
soul longs, yes, even faints for the courts of the Lord; My heart and my
flesh cry out for the living God" (84:1–2). Jerome recounts how, when he
asked why she didn't answer him or if she was in pain, she responded
"that she had no suffering and that all things are to her eyes calm and
tranquil." Then she went back to reciting Psalm verses, made the sign
of the cross upon her lips, and peacefully died at the age of fifty-six on
January 26, 404.

The Roman patrician woman, wife, and mother had given all of
herself as a widow to Christ. She embraced poverty with zeal—as well
as fasting, prayer, study, and theological work—by serving the poor
and training other young ascetics (including her own daughter) in
this way of the life in Christ. In the process she touched many people,
and they came to pray for her soul. Jerome recounts how there was
no weeping or lamentation in the monastery church after her death,
but the chanting of the Psalms in several languages, including Greek,
Latin, and Syriac. Not just the nuns and monks were present, many of
whom had come in from the desert, but the bishop of Jerusalem and
other bishops, priests, and deacons came to honor Paula, in their own
way acknowledging how "God is wondrous in His saints." The bishops
themselves laid her body on a bier and carried her to the cave in the
Church of the Nativity, placing her body in the middle of it. Because of
the renown that her holy work had gained, people came from across all
of Palestine for her funeral. At the end of the three days spent praying

for her soul and rejoicing in God for her life, she was buried beneath the church, close to the cave that she had held so dear.[28]

CONTEMPORARY REFLECTIONS AND DISCOVERIES

The Spirit blows where it wills, and it took me as a writer in a direction I had not anticipated when I started this project. At first I planned to write about a woman who had been a member of the Widows' institutional ministry. This led me into a deeper exploration of the history of this ministry. I came to a profound appreciation both of the Jewish and the early Christian attention to widows, particularly the ministry *to* them, as these practices also identify issues in our day.

This study led to my first discovery: a much deeper appreciation of the stark needs of the widowed in our own day. We live in a society that does not like to deal with death and grief. Whenever any of us suddenly experiences inexplicable, overwhelming bereavement, soon afterwards we are prodded in numerous ways to comply with certain assumptions held regarding death and loss. These essentially voice the same message: that we can and should swiftly "just get over it." Rather, the message should be that by the grace of God, we move *through* profound loss. This is because successfully moving through takes time, sometimes a lot of time. A widow, especially if she cared for her husband in illness for a very lengthy period, has endured the reality that the husband with whom she shared years of the good and bad has slipped out of her earthly life and into God's hands. If the two had become not just one flesh, but one mind (at least sometimes!) and one heart, such a tearing apart of a life shared can, and probably will, leave a widow feeling physically and emotionally destitute for a very long time.

This prompts me to ask how conscientious we are in offering mercy to our widowed neighbors. Do we think about widows in the weeks and months after the funeral? What are their needs? How do we care for them? These are not easy or simple questions, perhaps because we feel helpless or unequipped. Yet we forget that even the simplest gestures of authentic connection and acts of kindness would be most appreciated, reminding a widow that in the body of Christ, we journey together through joy and sorrow. Are we bold enough to offer material assistance for those in need of it? Are we ready to offer ourselves in genuine friend-

ship? As God allows, I hope to engage this concern more deeply in the
days and months ahead.

The second discovery focuses on the Order of Widows as an "institutional ministry." "Institutions" as ends in themselves are not "ministers"—real human persons, obedient to the Lord through the Holy
Spirit, are! I fear that far too many of us today have lost the sense of this
truth as our attitude and vision of the Church have become institution-
alized. The Church has been reduced, from this perspective, to a fallen
human institution, not unlike a business. The Church is reduced to a
building where we go to worship, to the organizations that do the work,
to the priest as the man in charge. Yes, this approach may produce types
of fruit; nevertheless, it leads essentially to a dead end.

As members of the Church, we are all called to humbly acknowledge our sins and shortcomings, which keep us from becoming what
God intends for us as His Church, collectively and personally. The following discipline helps set us right: acknowledging our shortcomings;
facing temptations to be less than the human persons that we were
created to be—persons in the image and likeness of God; and seeking the help of our merciful God through the life of the Church. This
discipline serves as both a foundation and vehicle for the love of the
living God.

Each one of us is called in some manner to share God's love with
a needy, love-starved world. The Order of Widows turned out to be
one of these godly institutions; it was comprised of persons who loved
and served the Lord and neighbor. They received not only opportunity, but also the Church's blessing, direction, and support to attend
to the needs of others. In this case, we are speaking about women who
endured the death of their husbands and who in some way or other
became "chipped" or even "broken" vessels through experiencing loss.
Yet the early Church afforded them the opportunity to be restored,
and refined, spiritually. Their pain and sorrow were transfigured into
joy. Those who had the material means gave to the Church for the
needs of their neighbors. The emptiness in their hearts was filled by
the love of God and by giving to others. So, instead of remaining only
persons to be cared for by their fellow Christians, these Widows became active ministers themselves.

This exploration led me to discover a woman of noble birth and even
more noble character. Paula embraced her patrician life in a godly way,

both as wife and mother in a Christian household. And when the death of her dearly loved husband left her a widow at only thirty-two, Paula did not let grief destroy her or render her life useless, nor did she bury herself in the self-absorption of material things that her wealth could purchase. To use the cliché, she didn't decide to "shop till she dropped." She chose instead to completely and totally embrace Christ, to allow Him to transform her grief. She showed mercy in giving all her financial means to those in need, she fasted until she *almost* dropped, and she prayed until her last breath. Paula lived out the two great commandments, bringing others with her on the journey to find the living God and a joy this world cannot know.

At the same time, I will admit that I wonder about St. Paula. Couldn't she have waited a few more years before leaving Rome, until her son was grown and her daughter married? What about her strict discipline in fasting? To deny oneself food to the point of ill health does not seem wise, even if trying to "repent" of one's former wealth and overabundant lifestyle. And why would someone go beyond giving all their earthly possessions to the poor and actually keep borrowing money in order to keep giving, while leaving her daughter to inherit that massive debt?

Or, maybe my questions should be those asked by Susan Arida on the first page of the first chapter of the first volume written by the members of St. Catherine's Vision: "Is it possible to know these women of antiquity? Or to put it more incisively, can we overcome the historical biases that affect the way we hear their stories and understand their relationship to God?" Maybe in my twenty-first-century world, it is really *my* problem. Part of me was hesitant to embrace such a woman and her story. It is a foreign concept in our society today for one to sell all that one has, give it to the poor, and follow Christ. In fact, even the *thought* of doing so seems foreign. To be honest, people like Paula, who are so obviously holy and Christ-like, make me nervous. They raise my awareness of the holiness I lack and of my shortcomings. Nonetheless, Paula drew me into her life, and there I discovered a brave and dedicated woman whose single-mindedness allowed her to love God and neighbor in ways I cannot begin to grasp. In a way that cannot be explained, I felt welcomed and embraced by her through the process. And her example encourages me. More importantly, I have come to love her as a sister in Christ.

WIDOWS AND THE NEEDS OF THE CHURCH TODAY

What can we say about St. Paula as a model for widows or for their place
in the Church today? I know widows who are in some way fulfilling the
same ministry that Paula did, quietly sharing their lives more fully with
God and with the whole Church. These generous persons choose to care
for others as they offer their grief and their futures to God. Their cumulative life experience, including their losses, makes them not just more
dedicated to Christ and His work, but more sensitive to the trials and
tribulations of others. Having endured enough of these themselves, they
seem to have an awareness of what is really important. Such awareness
can be the cornerstone of pastoral service. But we cannot ask or expect
this to come about without our support.

St. Ambrose of Milan (340–97) recognized this phenomenon quite
well in his day: "But there is no praise simply in widowhood, unless there
be added the virtues of widowhood."[29] Given the longevity we now enjoy,
I would hope and pray that we would come to call our widows together,
as Marcella did, for spiritual fellowship and learning, so that the depth
of their own spiritual life grows in virtue. Nurturing them spiritually
should be a part of our community life, and from it may come their personal service to Christ and the Church—just as it did for St. Paula.

Researching and reflecting on the ministry of Widows urges me today to be even more open to the ways each of us is called to offer his
or her gifts for the common good. We are obliged to encourage and remain open to what each of us has received, recognizing it as a gift and a
charism from God. This is equally important for all of us as individual
persons and as members of various "subgroups" that exist in the life of
the parish, such as teens, young adults who are single, young adults who
are married, single parents, and many others—including, of course, widows. We are called to consider the needs and spiritual gifts that are put
before us in various ways. This nudges us to "think outside the box" instead of remaining static and entrenched in an "institutional mindset."

As an example of creative openness to the Spirit, an entire 2005 edition of the journal *Christian Bioethics* examined what the ancient Order
of Widows could teach and offer us today, just in the area of health care.
Professor H. Tristram Engelhardt, an Orthodox Christian bioethicist who
wrote the issue's introduction, urges us to consider the thoughtful ideas
presented in the issue, many of which are from a Roman Catholic perspective. Using what these scholars offer as a starting point, we need to

allow the Spirit to guide us to a renewed vision of the Order of Widows. Widows could even serve in a manner that would theoretically coincide with some of the ministries of a rejuvenated diaconate, both male and female. Nevertheless, this specific Order of ministry would definitely have unique dimensions to its charism that deserve consideration. In the Apostle Paul's First Letter to Timothy, we see the ancient requirements and form of the office. But what would be appropriate today? I think we need to look at this question with an eye toward discerning what would be for the good of both the Church and the widow today.

It seems appropriate to prayerfully consider how the Church may publicly, officially, and liturgically recognize those who are willing to make such a commitment to Christ through this ministry. We may well discover that, in fact, many women are *already* conducting this kind of ministry, consciously or not. By making these women and their good works more visible, many opportunities may arise that will encourage even more people to actively become "a Christ"—an anointed one—in the Church and for the present day; in this way we will be contributing to "the building up of the body of Christ" (Eph 4:12). We really do need all the "manifestations of the Spirit for the common good" that God gives us as members of the body of Christ seeking the Kingdom today.

NOTES

1. For a prime example of all of this, read the short Old Testament book of Ruth. There was also the custom of Levirate marriage, in which, if the deceased husband had a brother, the surviving brother was to marry the widow and produce a child/heir for the dead brother (see Mark 12:18–27).

2. For more on women deacons, an excellent resource is *Women Deacons in the Orthodox Church: Called to Holiness and Ministry,* by Kyriaki Karidoyanes FitzGerald (Brookline, MA: Holy Cross Orthodox Press, 1999).

3. The capitalized "Widow" refers to the Office or Order and the women who are part of it, to differentiate between them and the generic term for a woman whose husband has died.

4. For a more in-depth historical review of the Widow, see Bonnie Bowman Thurston's book *The Widows: A Women's Ministry in the Early Church* (Minneapolis: Fortress Press, 1989).

5. Bruce W. Winter puts forth the proposition of a "new woman" in his book *Roman Wives, Roman Widows: The Appearance of New Women and the Pauline Communities* (Grand Rapids, MI: Eerdmans, 2003).

6. Ivoni Richter Reimer contends that as a *"pupurarii,"* Lydia may have been merely a freed slave who became an artisan making subsistence wages, like literally thousands of other small traders in those days (*Women in the Acts of the Apostles* [Minneapolis: Fortress Press, 1995], 100–112).

7. In addition to Kyriaki FitzGerald's *Women Deacons in the Orthodox Church*, Valerie Karras has written on the female deacons. See "The Liturgical Functions of Consecrated Women in the Byzantine Church," *Theological Studies* 66, no. 1 (March 2005): 96–116; and the soon-to-be-published book *Women in the Byzantine Liturgy*, Oxford University Press.

8. Tertullian, *Ante-Nicene Fathers*, vol. 4 (reprint, Grand Rapids, MI: Eerdmans), 43, in Roger Gryson, *The Ministry of Women in the Early Church*, trans. Jean LaPorte and Mary Louise Hall (Collegeville, MN: Liturgical Press, 1980), 21. The emphasis in the quote is mine.

9. Ibid., 21–22.

10. Grant Sperry-White has done work with this document: see *The Testamentum Domini: A Text for Students, with Introduction, Translation, and Notes*, vol. 19 of Joint Liturgical Studies (Cambridge: Grove, 1991).

11. See this article by Metr. Maximos of Pittsburgh for a brief account of the development of monasticism and its different forms: "Monasticism in the Orthodox Church," Greek Orthodox Archdiocese of America, http://www.goarch.org/ourfaith/ourfaith7103.

12. Jerome, *Letter* 108: *To Eustochium*, in vol. 6 of Nicene and Post-Nicene Fathers, Second Series, trans. W. H. Fremantle, eds. Philip Schaff and Henry Wace (reprint, Grand Rapids, MI: Eerdmans, 1980), 195–212. Other letters concerning Paula and/or members of her family include 22, 30, 31, 33, 38, 39, 66, and 107.

13. Ibid., § 5.

14. Jerome, *Letter* 127: *To Principia*. This letter is a memoir written to Marcella's closest friend, Principia, after Marcella's death.

15. "St. Jerome: Doctor of the Church," Catholic Online, http://www.catholic.org/saints/saint.php?saint_id=10.

16. Jerome, *Letter* 108.6.

17. Ibid.

18. John Wilkinson has produced a commendable edition of Egeria's writings that includes informative maps and diagrams: *Egeria's Travels*, 3rd ed. (Oxford: Aris & Phillips, 1999).

19. Jerome, *Letter* 108.9.

20. Ibid.

21. Hieromonk Makarios of Simonos Petra, "The Memory of St Paula of Rome," in vol. 3 of the *Synaxarion*, trans. C. Hookway (Mt. Athos: Holy Monastery of Simonos Petra, 2001), 319.

22. Jerome, *Letter* 108.14.

23. Carol Osiek and Margaret Y. MacDonald, *A Woman's Place: House Churches in Earliest Christianity* (Minneapolis: Augsburg Fortress Press, 2006), 195.

24. Jerome, *Letter* 45: *To Asella.*

25. Jerome, *Letter* 108.17.

26. Jerome, *Letter* 108.15.

27. Ibid.

28. Jerome, *Letter* 108.30.

29. Ambrose, *Concerning Widows* 1.3, in vol. 10 of Nicene and Post-Nicene Fathers, Second Series, trans. H. de Romestin, eds. Philip Schaff and Henry Wace (New York: Christian Literature Company, 1896), 391.

Reflection and Discussion Questions

1. a. What is the most difficult challenge that a widow faces in life after the death of her husband? How could the Church, your parish, or you personally be of help?

   b. Discuss the similarities and differences in the challenges, needs, and opportunities that widows and widowers may be facing today.

2. How do you respond to Jerome's statement that Paula threw herself into charitable work so completely after her husband's death that it was almost as if she willed him to die? Do you agree with his interpretation?

3. Read Matthew 10:37. In another chapter of this book, the life of St. Perpetua is highlighted. She, like St. Paula, wrestled with the issue of leaving her family in order to follow Christ. These saints' life situations were very different.

   a. Could they both have been obeying Christ, or was one person's choice justified and the other's not? Could they both have been mistaken? Discuss this.

   b. How could Matthew 10:37 apply to us today?

4. What unique gifts would a widow bring to ministry? How do you think the service of Widows might be made a viable and "official" ministry of the Church today? The author suggests some ways; add to or comment on these.

5. a. What do you think about anyone who would give all he or she owned to the poor and to the good works of the Church, and then go into debt to keep giving, leaving that debt for children to inherit?

   b. Why does such giving bother us? Are we overly cautious, or is a negative reaction a sign of a spiritual weakness?

6. a. Why should anyone have to wait until the death of a spouse, or a similar life crisis, before finding his or her relationship with God and discerning the gifts he or she has to offer? Why does this seem to happen?

   b. Have you ever seriously thought about what gifts you might have? How do we learn about them? Name at least one.

7. This chapter describes how St. Paula's deep grief was transformed.

a. Do you know of any other situations when something like this occurred? What happened?
b. How can we, as individual persons and as members of the Church, help others through this process?

Four Who Said "No"

Valerie Zahirsky

J esus Christ once answered a question the Pharisees put to Him
by telling them to "render to Caesar what is Caesar's and to God
what is God's." In doing this, He upset their craftily laid plans.
The Pharisees' intention was to make Him say the wrong thing, no matter what He said. So they had asked Him whether it was "lawful" to pay
taxes to Caesar. To advocate paying taxes to the hated Roman government would be offensive to many fellow Jews. But to counsel anyone *not*
to pay taxes was clearly an act of disloyalty to the empire. However, Jesus'
balanced answer made His interrogators marvel. He had evaded their
trap, and so they "left Him and went away" (Matt 22:22). They could ac-
cuse Him of nothing.

Christ's response to the Pharisees is more than a wonderfully con-
founding reply to ill-intentioned questioners. It is an acknowledgment of
the dignity of all human beings. We are God's creatures, made uniquely
in His image. We have the ability to discern and figure out correctly what
is Caesar's and what is God's.

Paul Achtemeier, in his book *Invitation to Mark*, makes the point
that when Jesus replies to the Pharisees by asking "whose image" is on
the coin, He knows that His Jewish listeners will immediately think of

Valerie Zahirsky holds a master's degree in English from the Claremont Graduate School in California and a master of divinity degree from St. Vladimir's Orthodox Theological Seminary in Crestwood, New York. She writes curriculum for Orthodox churches in the United States, Eastern Europe,
and the Middle East, and speaks and writes on topics concerning education and women in the
Church. Her husband, Fr. Michael, is a priest of the Orthodox Church in America. Their two grown
children are Barbara and Peter. Valerie also serves on the Board of St. Catherine's Vision.

the Genesis teaching that human beings are made "in God's image" (cf. Gen 1:26). They will understand that Jesus is saying that coins can be given to Caesar, whose image is on the coins, but that their deepest loyalty must be given to the One whose image is on *them*—that is, to God. They must be obedient to their true Master.[1]

In the long history of the Christian Church, many have stayed faithful to their "true Master" by saying "no" to authorities who wanted to usurp God's place. Among them are four women. Two lived in the time of the pharaohs, one led a women's monastery in fourth-century Antioch, and one died in a German concentration camp in 1945.

PUAH AND SHIPHRAH, MIDWIVES

Exodus 1:15–20 gives us the story of two women who defied a terrible order. They were Egyptian (not Hebrew) midwives who, like most women who served in their capacity, probably did not have families of their own. They had been appointed as midwives by the Egyptian government, and had long experience assisting Egyptian women who were having trouble giving birth. The all-powerful Pharaoh had every right to order them, as he would order any official, to carry out his wishes. In the Exodus story, his wishes were to murder male babies, and so Puah and Shiphrah were told to kill Hebrew boy babies as they were being delivered.

The two women were, in the words of one commentator, "caught between two fires."[2] Their decision to save the lives of children—and spare the Hebrew mothers untold grief—meant that they would have to find a plausible explanation to give to Pharaoh when he called them before him to explain why the male Hebrew children were continuing to live. We can almost picture them conferring in whispers as they hurried to answer the ruler's summons.

Their experience as midwives serving the Egyptian women helped them answer their ruler. They told Pharaoh (who goes unnamed throughout the story) that the "vigorous" Hebrew women gave birth easily and quickly, before the midwife even arrived. In this way, their explanation suggested, the Hebrews were different from the presumably more delicate women of Egypt.

Because of the courage of these two women, Hebrew boys—including Moses—continued to be born. Puah and Shiphrah were blessed with families themselves, and the nation grew strong.

What was it that gave these midwives the courage to disobey a ruler who had the power of life and death over them? Perhaps they simply would not kill innocent children. Having been among the oppressed Hebrew people, perhaps they had learned about the God of the Hebrews. They may have come to believe in this God who wanted His people to be merciful rather than bloodthirsty.

Like many stories in Scripture, this one has a certain moral ambiguity. Puah and Shiphrah, in defying their absolute monarch, told an out-and-out lie. They are among several scriptural characters who had to do something dishonest or questionable to bring about a greater good. It is an uncomfortable choice that often faces those who follow the narrow path of obedient faith. Puah and Shiphrah had to decide what is truly lawful (saving the lives of babies) and what is not (carrying out the wish of their murderous earthly ruler). They had to choose a master and take the risk that came with obeying him. Jesus would later challenge His listeners to make a similar choice, holding a Roman coin in His hand.

St. Poplia of Antioch

In Rome in the year 361, another man was assuming overwhelming power. This was the emperor Flavius Claudius Julianus, who would come to be known in history as Julian the Apostate.

Julian's upbringing was at least nominally Christian, though he was also tutored by pagan philosophers.[3] But his abiding hatred of Christianity seems not to have been engendered by what he was taught, but by the behavior of some who shaped his youth. Julian's unhappy childhood was filled with deceit and terror. He lost his mother very early, and carried loving, longing memories of her—though he had barely known her—for the rest of his life. In the next few years, several family members were murdered by power-hungry men. Julian specifically blamed his relative, Constantius. The result, as a scholar puts it, was that "Julian was driven to hate [Christianity] not by any philosophical or abstract reasons but by the fact that his murderous cousin was a Christian."[4]

As emperor, Julian did his best to undermine Christianity and its growing strength in the empire, and to "restore" the more ancient practice of paganism. He sometimes did this with violence and cruelty.

St. Ephrem the Syrian described the effects poetically: "The ugly, dead, all-gloomy winter robbed the beauty of the all-rejoicing spring./ Thorn-bushes and tares were disgorged and sprang up."[5]

But did Julian actually find paganism, which attracted him with its divinations and omens, superior to the Christian faith? An answer may be found in his own words. He wrote a description of what the ideal pagan priest should be and do. It reads like a list of qualities that a true Christian would possess: philanthropy to all, including one's enemies; avoidance of scurrilous literature and speech; and pious meditation. These were the values Julian recommended. As one writer notes,

> [Christian] norms had penetrated his soul and had been partially assimilated. He later believed that the gods had inspired him with them and they were consequently his own. He then set about in-troducing them into paganism like one attempting to transplant the palms of the fiery Sahara to the frozen wastes of the arctic.[6]

If this damaged man hated the Christian faith, it was in large part because of the disgraceful examples he had seen in his childhood. Yet he still found its ideals worthy of emulation, and well he might, since numerous historians attest that Christians practiced loving charity and moral self-discipline in a way that most pagans simply never had. But in his mind, Julian found it necessary to twist Christian teaching till it became "his own" and a gift of "the gods."

Julian's obsession with paganism did little to improve his character. Gregory Nazianzen (often called "the Theologian"), who had once been his schoolmate, expressed grave doubts about him.[7] And while Julian certainly had intelligence and ability, even these were not particularly outstanding. In his writings against Christianity, it is easy to find points that are not new insights, but merely ideas that have been and still are being expressed by others. For example, he writes: "But why do you [Christians] not cease to call Mary the mother of God, if Isaiah nowhere says that he that is born of the virgin is the 'only begotten Son of God' and the 'firstborn of all creation'?"[8] This, of course, has been debated from the time of the early Church to our own day; it is not a novel insight or challenge.

He also resorted to sarcasm, asking why Christians were not as pure in their diet as the Jews, who followed the law of Moses and ate, among the four-footed animals, only those that had cloven feet and chewed their cud. He went on to ridicule Peter's vision (Acts 10:9–16), in which the apostle is shown many foods, some considered unclean in the Old Testament, and is told by God to go ahead and eat them. Julian wrote that if the pig (an unclean animal in the Old Testament) were to suddenly begin chewing its cud, we should indeed feel free to eat it, for such a change would be "in very truth a miracle."[9] What proof is there, Julian wondered in his writing, that what God once considered abominable He has now made pure?

Julian's attitude toward the faith reminds us that many, like him, reject Christianity not because of what it is, but because they see it so badly practiced. We can only wonder how many powerful people who have persecuted the Christian Church might not have done so if they had had better examples and teaching.

Yet this emperor's apostasy cannot be completely blamed on the Christians around him, because he himself was not intellectually honest. He acknowledged the excellence of Christian teachings but convinced himself that they were his own ideas. Nor was he at all moderate in his practice of paganism. He devoted himself so thoroughly to blood sacrifice that he "drenched the altars with the blood of too great a number of victims."[10] This could include a hundred bulls at a time, plus other animals and birds. When he came to Antioch shortly before his Persian military campaign, "the city was suffering from a scarcity of provisions, but for the sacrifices there was an abundance of everything."[11]

Julian did not even seem to notice, or perhaps to care, that many people made fun of him as being more a slaughterer than a priest. He was apparently oblivious to the fact that they had no desire to take part in his offerings to the gods. "In the temples, after he had spent a long time with his tunic tucked up and sweating like a slave at quartering the victims, he would suddenly realize that all the spectators had quietly walked away."[12]

One Christian in Antioch was quite ready to confront Julian with the truth he had abandoned. Her name was Poplia (sometimes written as "Publia"). She had been widowed young and had taken upon herself the ministry of guiding other young women and widows. They gathered for prayer in her house, and gradually the group grew into a monastic community, with Poplia as its abbess. Her son, John, was deeply influenced by growing up in the home she made for him; he was ordained to the priesthood. Her bishop greatly admired her work and made her a deaconess.

What did Poplia know about the apostate emperor? She may not have been aware of the misery inflicted upon him in his childhood by other royals who were at least nominal Christians. But she did know that he had inflicted misery on Christians by his efforts to destroy the faith in the empire. She must certainly have been suspicious of his claim that he really found paganism to be nobler than Christianity. She could see that the virtues he wanted pagans to have were all "borrowed" from the Christian faith, and that he was willfully failing to recognize the real source of those virtues.

So it was that when Julian came through Antioch in formal procession and passed by Poplia's monastery, he distinctly heard the nuns and their abbess singing Psalm 115:

> Our God is in the heavens; he does whatever he pleases.
> Their [i.e., pagans'] idols are silver and gold, and the work of
> men's hands. They have mouths, but do not speak; eyes,
> but do not see.
> They have ears, but do not hear; noses, but do not smell.
> They have hands, but do not feel; feet, but do not walk;
> and they do not make a sound in their throat.
> Those who make them are like them; so are all who trust in
> them. (vv. 3–8)

Julian ordered the nuns to cease their singing, knowing very well that they were aiming the words at him. But later, as his retinue passed the monastery again on its way out of the city, he plainly heard the words of Psalm 68 being sung: "Let God arise, let his enemies be scattered; let those who hate him flee from before his face. As smoke is driven away, so drive them away; as wax melts before the fire, let the wicked perish before God!" (vv. 1–2).

This time the emperor ordered Poplia to be dragged out and beaten. He told her that when he returned from the Persian campaign, he would have her executed. But Julian never returned, dying during the campaign from a spear thrust deep into his chest by the Persian enemy or, some said, by one of his own legionaries. Still others said the assailant was a revenge-seeking Christian. History has never established certainty about this.

Like Puah and Shiphrah, Poplia and her sisters chose to defy a despotic earthly ruler and to proclaim the power and majesty of their true King, the God of heaven. Had he chosen to, Julian could have taken the scriptural words the nuns sang as a warning of the spiritually dangerous pride and error into which he had fallen. He had the chance to act on the warning and to change his life. He chose instead to treat the encounter with Poplia as a punishable offense, setting himself up as the only law. It was not long before he died a violent, early death, never having become reconciled with the faith into which he had been born.

Poplia, by contrast, lived on, and died a natural death. She was able to carry on her ministry to the Christian community, and to continue guiding her nuns in the life of Christian faith.

Jesus Christ said, "So every one who acknowledges me before men, I also will acknowledge before my Father who is in heaven" (Matt 10:32). Poplia shows us how it's done—how a person can acknowledge Him before men, even before unbelieving emperors. But her quieter, less dramatic witness as an abbess and deaconess over many years is also important. We are called to be faithful to God in the small day-to-day moments of life as well as in the big, remarkable ones. Poplia did both. She lived a daily life of faith that inspired others, and rose unforgettably to the occasion when that big, dramatic moment of confrontation with an enemy of the faith came her way.

MOTHER MARIA SKOBTSOVA

A book was once written about Mother Maria entitled *The Rebel Nun*.[13] When we learn that she was sometimes seen smoking while wearing her habit, often stayed up till all hours of the night, now and then skipped chapel services, and had two failed marriages, we might be tempted to believe that the book title tells us all we need to know about her. But there is infinitely more than "rebellion" to this woman, and very good reason why she is a saint of the Orthodox Church.

She was born Elizaveta (Elizabeth) Pilenko in 1891 in Latvia. Hers was a family of intellectuals, with roots in the Ukrainian aristocracy. She was encouraged to speak her mind and to think deeply about life and its meaning. Her parents valued their daughter's artistic talents of writing, drawing, painting, and embroidery. They were devout Orthodox Christians who instilled a love of God and the Church in Liza, as she was called.

But when her father died in her fourteenth year, the girl lost her faith and ceased to believe in God. Soon after this, the family moved to St. Petersburg, a city known not only for cultural greatness, but also for sheltering a variety of groups that openly discussed and advocated revolution and fundamental social change. Liza's eager mind, along with her rejection of her childhood faith, led her to become part of such a group. She spent long hours in deep discussion with such well-known poets and thinkers as Osip Mandelstam, Anna Akhmatova, and Alexander Blok. Their discussions often touched on theology, but in the same abstract and detached way as on other topics.

Before too long, Liza found that talking and proposing ideas did not fill her deep desire to *do* something, to be active in service to other people. Alexander Blok perceived the difference between what she wanted to do and what he and his friends were doing. He wrote a poem to her, which included these lines:

> And therefore I wish
> you could fall in love with someone straightforward
> a man who loves earth and sky
> more than rhymed and unrhymed
> talk of earth and sky.[14]

Slowly, Liza Pilenko was being drawn back to a different kind of love—the love of Christ and the Orthodox Church. She also chose to marry, with the sometimes unwise impetuousness that marked her whole life. A daughter, Gaiana, was born, and Liza loved the child with her whole passionate heart. But three years later she and her husband Dmitri were divorced.

She now began in earnest to consider a life of asceticism and service, and took on the physical discipline of wearing a lead belt under her clothes. She wrote, in her idiosyncratic, hurried style that sometimes ignored rules of punctuation, "I buy a thick lead pipe, quite a heavy one. I flatten it with a hammer and sew it into a rag. All this in order to acquire Christ. To compel him to reveal himself. To help me no simply to remind me that he exists."[15]

She also took on the management of the family estate at Anapa, a village by the Black Sea. In 1918 she was elected mayor of the village, but this did not protect her from being put on trial by leaders of the retreating White Army, who saw her as a danger because of her affiliation with the Socialist-Revolutionary Party. She was released, but later faced death at the hands of a sailor who took it upon himself to shoot her as an enemy of the revolution.

Quick thinking saved her. She insisted that the sailor send a telegram to officials in Moscow, with its first sentence to read, "Tell Krupskaia I am about to be shot." This totally invented closeness to the wife of Lenin, Nadezhda Krupskaia, was enough to convince the sailor to change his mind.[16] These incidents in Russia show how courageously and publicly she was already defying corrupt authorities.

Liza now came to believe with certainty that people needed God, not revolution. She also realized that to those who had seized the government she was an "enemy" and that this meant she could be killed and could lose her chance to serve God. Intending to save her family and continue her work, she decided to leave Russia and go to the West. By this time she had married a second time, and so her mother, her daughter Gaiana, and her husband Daniil made the arduous sea voyage with her. (She and Daniil would have two children: a daughter, Anastasia, and a son, Iura.)

In 1923 the family reached Paris, where they joined the largely impoverished and desperately needy thousands of other exiles who had left Russia behind. It had taken them three years of extreme hardship to make the journey. They had very little to live on or to eat.

The winter of 1925 was unusually severe, and the whole family contracted influenza. In March 1926, despite the efforts of doctors, little Anastasia died in a Paris hospital. In her terrible grief Liza ventured into some of Paris' worst slums to reach out like a mother to the most hopeless and degraded of the Russian émigrés. She helped them get the limited government care they were entitled to, aiding them in filling out forms in the alien French language. She spent many hours sitting and talking with them, treating each one as a living icon of the Lord Jesus Christ. Sometimes, when she had planned to give a formal talk to a group of exiles, she would find herself

> transformed from an official lecturer into a confessor . . . A queue would form by the door as if outside a confessional. There would be people wanting to pour out their hearts, to tell of some terrible grief which had burdened them for years, of pangs of conscience which gave them no peace. In such slums it is no use speaking of faith in God, of Christ or of the Church. What is needed here is not religious preaching but the simplest thing of all: compassion.[17]

By 1932 Liza knew she wanted to be a nun. Her bishop, Metropolitan Evlogy, invoked a Church law that allows for an ecclesiastical divorce if one partner wants to enter the monastic life. He also suggested that she do her work in the city, rather than retiring to a monastery, which he (perceptively) realized would never suit her. In March 1932 Liza was professed as a monastic. From that time on she would be known as Mother Maria.

During the following years, she established several residences for the homeless, the ill, tuberculosis patients, and those living on society's fringes. Relying on God to bring donors and gifts for the work, she managed with very little money. Dedicated advisors and assistants, including her children, Gaiana and Iura, helped her, but much of the work she did herself. One assistant described her routine at 77 rue de Lourmel, perhaps the best known of the residences:

> Well before dawn she would set out for Les Halles, then the central market of Paris . . . She brought a sack with her, and this was to be filled as daylight broke with all the odds and ends—particularly perishable goods—which were then sold off cheaply or simply donated to charities or to the poor. She was well known at Les Halles. Fish, bones, over-ripe fruit and vegetables past their prime were poured into her capacious container. This was eventually to be heaved onto her shoulders and taken via one of the early Metro trains to her kitchen. A wheelbarrow would be welcome, she remarked once: on the previous day fish had soaked the sack and she still carried the smell of it with her. A barrow would prevent that sort of thing.
>
> In this shabby nun "with the sleeve of her dusty cassock torn and well-worn men's shoes on her feet" it was difficult to recognize the poet, the intellectual, the once prosperous lady who in her youth had never been required to concern herself with where or how the servants bought the household's food.[18]

It was this daily work that sometimes kept her from attending chapel services. But Mother Maria built or created a chapel in every residence she established, and services were regular. Many witnesses have attested to the fact that when she was in church her face was radiant and her attention was given completely to worship.

The same assistant gives us a picture of her living conditions on the Rue de Lourmel:

> The room in which Mother Maria lives is under the stairs, between the kitchen and the hall . . . In it stands a large table, littered with books, manuscripts, letters, bills, and a quantity of utterly incongru-

ous objects. There is a basket of different coloured balls of wool, a bowl with some cold unfinished tea. A large portrait of Gaiana on the wall over the divan. Bookshelves, cupboards, an old armchair with its stuffing hanging out. The room is unheated. The door is always open. There are times when Mother [Maria] can no longer bear it, she locks the door, drops into the armchair and says, "I can't go on like this, I can't take anything in, I'm tired, I really am tired. There have been about forty people here today, each with his own sorrow and needs. After all, I can't chase them away." But locking the door is no solution. Persistent knocking begins. Mother opens the door and says to me, "There you are, that's how I live."[19]

Mother Maria wrote about her own understanding of her work:

Christ, in ascending to heaven, did not raise with himself the Church on earth. He did not halt the course of history. Christ left the Church in the world and the Church has remained as a small portion of the yeast which makes the entire dough rise. Put differently, within the limits of history, Christ has given the whole world to the Church and she has no right to refuse to spiritually lift the world, to transfigure it. And for this, the Church needs a powerful army, and this is monasticism.[20]

In 1935 Mother Maria's heart was pierced by the loss of another child. Gaiana had made the surprising decision to return to live in Moscow, and there died of typhus. Because there was no possibility of the family traveling to Russia for a funeral, a memorial service took place in Paris. Mother Maria prostrated herself in prayer throughout it.[21]

Both in marriage and parenthood, Mother Maria must have felt that she had failed. She obviously desired a good marriage but had two marriages end. She had lost two children. Of her son, Iura, one observer said: "[His] childhood [lacked] comfort . . . His mother lacked the time, his father the parental skills, to provide for him . . . It was a disturbing background. However with adolescence he was able to develop a positive attitude to it."[22]

The first part of this statement could certainly be seen as an indictment of Mother Maria, as could her marriages that did not last. Yet the second part shows us something else: the maturity of the son she raised, and the love his mother inspired in him despite her failings.

There were those, however, with whom Mother Maria simply could not find common ground. Some clergy were shocked and alienated by her unconventional form of monasticism. Nor was she ever able to form a community of nuns. Sisters came but did not stay. Mother Maria's strong and determined personality may well have been part of the reason. It overwhelmed some people and seriously offended others.

Mother Maria felt these judgments on her deficiencies keenly, and wrote about them in her poetry. The following lines give us an idea of her own apprehension and sadness about the future she foresaw and, despite her feelings, accepted:

> Not for me the sanguine dream
> of clever husband, life of normal bride.
> A dark cross weighs my shoulders down.
> My way grows straiter stride by stride.[23]

The "strait way" that she followed required her, like Puah and Shiphrah and Poplia before her, to decide what was truly lawful, and to which corrupt "law" she must say no. She wrote that, according to material laws, to give away a piece of bread is to become one piece of bread poorer. But the law of the Spirit teaches that the one who gives away receives in return; the person who becomes poorer becomes richer. She chose always to be governed by the law of the Spirit; this was the only "lawful law."

Mother Maria made it clear in many ways that she followed a law not of this material world. She had an extraordinary ability to go to the most profound truths about situations and people. Thus she wrote in a *Letter to Soldiers*: "Take care of the innermost self, which is subject to far greater dangers than the outer man . . . preserve the purity of your youth, do not treat war as something natural, do not mistake the sin and horror of life for life itself."[24]

In our day, when we are so conscious of the residual effects of war on soldiers' hearts and psyches, we can recognize that her concern for the "innermost self" was right on the mark. She comprehended what it really means for young people to be caught up in war, once they get beyond the patriotic feelings that may have brought them into it and actually face its horrible reality. This comprehension is reflected in her loving concern that they not mistake sin and horror, so much a part of war, for real life.

Another piece of clear evidence that this world's laws did not govern her is the description she bravely—and publicly—wrote of Hitler in 1941, saying that at the head of those who called themselves Europe's "master race" stood "a madman, a paranoiac, who ought to be confined to a madhouse, who needs a straitjacket and a cork-lined room so that his bestial wailing would not disturb the world at large."[25]

Writing these words for all to see was hardly discreet; it was another example of Mother Maria's sometimes rash nature. Yet it was courageous to say the things that so many were thinking but did not dare to express. And she gathered other brave people around her. One was a young priest, Father Dmitri Klepinin, who came to the house in Paris to share her work. He helped many families in need, and together he and Mother Maria began handing out false baptismal certificates to Jews. Mother Maria's ability to say "no" culminated in this refusal to comply with outrageous Nazi demands. The baptismal certificates probably saved many lives, but put her and Fr. Klepinin's own safety in peril.

Indeed, by 1943 their activities had become known to the authorities, and the savage worldly law of Nazism came down hard on the community at 77 rue de Lourmel. Iura Skobtsov was arrested while his mother was out of town. Later came the arrest of Fr. Klepinin, and finally that of Mother Maria herself. The house was closed, its good work put to an end.

Iura and Fr. Klepinin would die in the Dora concentration camp. For Mother Maria, the final destination was to be another camp, Ravensbrück. There are many accounts by survivors of her calm demeanor, unflagging smile, and constant efforts to raise others' spirits. She would pray, talk about the Church's teachings, and study Scripture with all who were interested. She shared her meager food rations. People lined up to speak with her and open their hearts to her, just as they had years earlier in the slums of Paris and outside the door of her basement room in the old house on the rue de Lourmel. But as she compassionately served others and kept her composure,[26] her health declined with alarming swiftness in the hideous conditions of life in the camp. One inmate remembered Mother Maria being part of an exhausted group that had to drag a heavy iron roller around the streets of the camp for twelve hours each day.[27]

March 31, 1945, was Holy Friday in the Orthodox Church calendar. As Mother Maria and others were going to meet their death in the gas chamber, the guns of the Russian armies, coming to liberate the camp, could be heard in the distance. She had foreseen her own "fiery death" in poetry, and had even managed, while a prisoner, to express her faith in an embroidered tapestry depicting the Mother of God with the crucified Child in her arms.[28] To the very last moment, according to several witnesses, she radiated the peace of Christ and helped others to face death more calmly.

Mother Maria's own peacefulness was hard won. She had not always gotten along with people, and had felt the loneliness of failing to do so. Her marriages did not last, and she lost her beloved children. Certainly she had endured the blackness of loss of faith, sharing the experience of a more recent Christian, Mother Teresa.

But she had much in common with Puah and Shiphrah, and with Poplia as well. Like them, she confronted an authority who wished to shut certain people out, to deny them compassion. Like Puah, Shiphrah, and Poplia, she gave a personal example of courage in refusing to bow to such an authority. Like them, she said a firm, resounding "no."

Perhaps her peacefulness was the result of knowing, finally, what is most important in life. Her words about this are especially important for Orthodox Christians:

> At the Last Judgement I shall not be asked whether I was success-
> ful in my ascetic exercises, how many bows and prostrations I made
> [in the course of prayer]. I shall be asked, Did I feed the hungry,
> clothe the naked, visit the sick and the prisoners. That is all I shall
> be asked.[29]

SOME PERSONAL REFLECTIONS

How does a person make the decision to stand up for what is right, especially when it is risky?

I truly admire Puah, Shiphrah, Poplia, and Mother Maria. They all stood up and took the risk involved. The two midwives and the saint of Antioch did it once that we know of; Mother Maria, about whom we have much more information, did it time and time again.

Did they think about the decisions they made, weigh the risks, consider the consequences, and think about the ramifications? Or did they simply "throw caution to the wind," and if so, is that a good thing or mere foolhardiness?

These questions are not easy for me to answer, especially in the case of Mother Maria. Caution, for me, can be a real problem. There always seem to be reasons not to do something: the car might break down, the weather might turn bad, the bishop might get upset with my priest husband, the kids' friends might make fun of them because of their mother, who does things that are so "out there."

I don't expect ever to do anything as "out there" as wearing a lead pipe in a cloth around my waist, as Mother Maria did for an ascetical discipline in her earlier years. Yet it is this image, coupled with another, that often strikes me when I think about her. The other image is of her carrying out the debilitating, pointless task of dragging a heavy iron roller around the Ravensbrück camp at the end of her life. I have wondered whether the terrible "job" with the roller, forced on her by others, made her think of the lead pipe, which she had worn of her own free will.

She wrote that she wore the pipe to "compel [Christ] to reveal himself." In the strength-sapping atmosphere of the camp, was she ever tempted—as I fear I might be—to see that iron roller as the mocking joke of a cruel world? She had asked, through a piece of metal, to have Christ reveal Himself. Did she believe that the taunting answer had now come, that there is no loving Christ, but only a piece of far heavier metal that would soon kill her through meaningless labor?

I am heartened by the firm conviction that she did not give in to such an ugly view of the world. She had once urged soldiers never to "mistake the sin and horror of life for life itself." From what witnesses tell us about her last days, she never made that mistake, even though she was so weakened and sick that she was near death even before she entered the gas chamber.

Mother Maria lovingly challenges me, and every Christian, not to lose heart and never to be despondent. Even for those of us who are unlikely to face the horrors she did, that is challenge enough. But Mother Maria also calls us not to be overly cautious. She would urge us to go ahead and *do* things, especially things for the benefit of others, without thinking too much about the consequences, without exerting too much self-protective caution.

It is hard to balance the desire to live and serve intensely, as Mother Maria did, with the cautiousness that keeps me from doing many things. Cautious people miss a lot of adventures in life, and their trust in God is sometimes far from perfect. Yet the loss of personal relationships was a price Mother Maria paid for her impetuosity. I would be reluctant to pay that high price.

So the struggle continues for me, as I think it does for many Christians. We try to balance trust that God's law will prevail with sensible but not paralyzing caution. Mother Maria's words can give us a nudge in the right direction: "We need to walk on the waters. The Apostle Peter did so, after all, and he didn't drown. Of course it is safer to go round by land, but you may never reach your destination."[30]

NOTES

1. Paul J. Achtemeier, *Invitation to Mark: A Commentary On the Gospel of Mark with Complete Text from The Jerusalem Bible* (Garden City, NY: Image Books, 1978), 173.

2. Herbert Lockyer, *All the Men of the Bible; All the Women of the Bible* (Grand Rapids, MI: Zondervan, 1996), 126.

3. G. W. Bowersock, *Julian the Apostate* (Cambridge, MA: Harvard University Press, 1997), 24.

4. Giuseppe Ricciotti, *Julian the Apostate*, trans. M. Joseph Costeloe (Milwaukee: Bruce Publishing, 1960), 42.

5. Ephrem the Syrian, *Hymn 1 against Julian*, in *Ephrem the Syrian: Hymns*, trans. Kathleen E. McVey (New York: Paulist Press, 1989), 229.

6. Ricciotti, *Julian the Apostate*, 22–23.

7. In the second of his two *Invectives against Julian*, Gregory describes his encounters with Julian when both men were students in Athens. He recalls "the inconsistency of [Julian's] behaviour and his extreme excitability . . . A sign of no good seemed to me to be his neck unsteady, his shoulders always in motion and shrugging up and down like a pair of scales, his eye rolling and glancing from side to side with a certain insane expression, his feet unsteady and stumbling, his nostrils breathing insolence and disdain, the gestures of his face ridiculous and expressing the same feelings, his bursts of laughter unrestrained and gusty, his nods of assent and dissent without any reason . . ." (*Oration 5.23: Second Invective against Julian the Emperor*, in *Julian the Emperor*, trans. C. W. King [London: George Bell and Sons, 1888]). Gregory concludes his early assessment of Julian by saying: "I saw the man *before* his actions exactly what I afterwards found him *in* his actions . . . I exclaimed as soon as I had observed these signs, 'What an evil the Roman world is breeding!'" (ibid., 5.24).

8. Julian the Apostate, *Against the Galileans*, book 1, in vol. 3 of *The Works of the Emperor Julian*, trans. Wilmer Cave Wright, Loeb Classical Library 157 (London: William Heinemann, 1923), 319–433.

9. Ibid.

10. Ricciotti, *Julian the Apostate*, 188.

11. Ibid.

12. Ibid., 189.

13. T. Stratton Smith, *The Rebel Nun: The Moving Story of Mother Maria of Paris* (Springfield, IL: Templegate, 1965).

14. Sergei Hackel, *Pearl of Great Price: The Life of Mother Maria Skobtsova, 1891–1945* (Crestwood, NY: St. Vladimir's Seminary Press, 1982), 84.

15. Ibid., 85.

16. Ibid., 92.

17. Ibid., 11.

18. Ibid., 37–38.

19. Ibid., 38–39.

20. Mother Maria, *Le sacrement du frère,* ed. and trans. Hélène Arjakovsky-Klépinine (Paris: Cerf, 1995), 126.

21. Hackel, *Pearl of Great Price,* 7.

22. Ibid., 117–18.

23. Ibid., 96.

24. Ibid., 102.

25. Ibid., 108.

26. Another of Mother Maria's courageous activities during the war is described in a children's book, *Silent as a Stone,* by Jim Forest (Crestwood, NY: St. Vladimir's Seminary Press, 2007).

27. Hackel, *Pearl of Great Price,* 136.

28. Ibid., 143.

29. Ibid., 29.

30. Ibid., 31.

REFLECTION AND DISCUSSION QUESTIONS

1. Julian the Apostate, a Roman emperor, "hated" Christianity because of certain heinous acts conducted by Christians during his life, not necessarily by the faith itself. What kind of things could be occurring today that would drive people of good will away from Christianity? How are we to respond?

2. The author offers an example of faithful persons telling an "out-and-out lie" in order "to bring about a greater good."
   a. Under what circumstances would "the ends justify the means" be acceptable to God?
   b. Under what circumstances would "the ends justify the means" be unacceptable to Him?

3. Discuss situations today in which we are challenged by Mother Maria's counsel: "Do not mistake the sin and horror of life for life itself."

4. Long before Mother Maria dedicated herself to a life in Christ, as a young woman she "found that talking and proposing ideas did not fill her deep desire to *do* something, to be active in service to other people." It is this love that led her back to the Lord and His Church.
   a. What do you suppose this "deep desire" actually could have been?
   b. Has anyone in your own life, including yourself, ever felt a similar kind of "deep desire"?

5. Mother Maria's story bears witness to important spiritual lessons. One of these lessons is how, even with many personal failures, it is possible for our lives to become something beautiful for God. Discuss the relationship between Mother Maria's failures as a parent and the hope that seemed to preside in her life, as well as in her children's, despite enormous difficulties. How did this happen?

6. Read once more the personal reflections shared by the author at the end of the chapter.
   a. Consider and discuss how people, including yourself, may experience the "push and pull" of reaching out to do a good deed, especially when it is inconvenient.

    b. Looking back, discuss situations which may have occurred when you experienced "second thoughts" about either having reached out or *not* having reached out to another.

7. Mother Maria led a colorful life.

    a. How do you imagine you would have responded to her in her pre-monastic life and later, in her monastic life?

    b. Does it surprise you that a person like this has been recognized as a saint? Discuss this.

8. The author identifies "the loss of personal relationships" as part of the "high price" Mother Maria paid for risks she took on behalf of the gospel. What do you imagine Mother Maria, or any of the other saints in this chapter, would say about "playing it safe"?

St. Barbara and the Martyrs
of the Armenian Genocide:
A Witness to Radical Forgiveness

Barbara K. Harris

*T*hroughout the ages there have been incredible acts of love and kindness demonstrated across religious groups, cultures, and ethnic populations. These actions reveal a selfless and sacrificial love for the other. Mother Maria Skobtsova, who is the focus of another chapter in this book, was one individual who demonstrated such love. As a Russian émigré in Paris during the German occupation, she tirelessly worked to provide baptismal certificates for Jews. This led to her arrest and deportation to the Ravensbrück concentration camp. While there, it is believed that she selflessly and sacrificially took the place of another who was in line for the gas chamber.

Tragically, despite such loving acts, individuals and communities have also shown an astonishing ability to inflict evil upon each other in all its various manifestations, including humiliation through murder, slander, slavery, torture, and discrimination, to name just a few. Virtually all ethnic, cultural, and religious groups have been at times both perpetrators and/or victims of such acts of degradation and inhumanity: African Americans, Native Americans, Tutsis, Hutus, Jews, Christians, Hindus, Shintos, Sunnis, Shi'as, Bahá'ís, black South Africans, and the list goes on. This article examines forgiveness as an expression of divine love and the Christian response to evil and intolerance as experienced

Barbara K. Harris is a graduate of Holy Cross Greek Orthodox School of Theology, with an MA in Church Service, and of Washington University in St. Louis, with an AM in Non-Profit Management. She resides in St. Louis, Missouri, where she is exploring the intersection of practical theology, leadership, and education. She also serves on the Board of St. Catherine's Vision.

by St. Barbara, an early Christian martyr, and by the 1.3 million Armenian martyrs of the early twentieth century. Their examples as intentional and unintentional martyrs have transformed me and my response when encountering abuse.

The witness of these martyrs vividly exemplifies the words of our Lord:

> You have heard that it was said, "You shall love your neighbor and hate your enemy." But I say to you, love your enemies, bless those who curse you, do good to those who hate you, and pray for those who spitefully use you and persecute you, that you may be sons of your Father in heaven . . . (Matt 5:43–45)

Yes, Christians must love and forgive even when faced with hatred from family members, close friends, and neighbors—those with whom there was thought to be a good relationship, one in which there was at least mutual acceptance, and at best total trust and surrender. Professor Kyriaki FitzGerald, Orthodox theologian and psychologist, eloquently speaks of the consequence of not responding with forgiveness and love, of turning away from God:

> When we fail to recognize our neighbor, not only do we increasingly become less than our "true self" but also we fail to follow the command of our Lord. In an insidious manner, we drift further and further away from and become ever more cold to the presence of the Kingdom. The Lord says to us: "You are the salt of the earth. But, if salt loses its taste, with what can it be seasoned? It is no longer good for anything but to be thrown out and trampled underfoot" (Mt. 5:13). These words are a powerful affirmation of our responsibility. They are also a warning![1]

ST. BARBARA THE GREAT MARTYR

Imagine living in a time and place in which a young woman is considered an extension of her family's *dignitas*.[2] In the fourth-century Roman Empire, power and social station were of utmost importance. *Dignitas* refers to one's perceived political and socio-economic status, an asset that demands attention and cultivation. The pursuit of *dignitas* requires that one dress, look, speak, and behave in a manner dictated by the prevailing social mores. In such circumstances, a woman is allowed very few choices. In fact, purity, beauty, family honor, and fortune—all vital dimensions of *dignitas*—are highly prized commodities in consideration of a marriage partner or, more accurately, a family alliance. Any deviation from this formula is severely punished. Respect for one's personhood is lost in this mix, and one becomes objectified by family and society.

St. Barbara the Great Martyr[3] was a young woman in such a society, defined by her father's name (Dioscoros), social standing (he was a man with high political ambitions), and pagan beliefs (in the Roman gods). She lived a privileged life as the only daughter of a wealthy and influential man and was raised in an influential Roman outpost. Dioscoros was an important political figure who had the responsibility to govern the district in which Barbara's family lived. This meant that they were expected to be models of Roman aristocratic life. They dressed, worshipped, entertained, and lived as full citizens, enjoying the benefits of an upper-class life. Roman citizenship afforded many rights, and Barbara's father's position afforded many privileges.

Anything she wanted was granted: delicious foods, elegant clothing, fine jewelry, excellent tutors, and luxurious furnishings. So cherished was Barbara by her father that he built a special tower to protect her from the many unwanted influences of that time. In his mind, her purpose in life was to increase the family's *dignitas* by marrying a person of equal or greater social rank and wealth. Dioscoros saw his household as an extension of his *dignitas*. Everyone in the household, including servants and family members, was expected to obey his desires and be attentive to him. This was quite natural, because everyone in the district was also expected to obey him.

The tower in which her father installed her did not prevent Barbara from having access to information, through the women who served her. She was barely eighteen when she learned through these relationships that "God so loved the world that He sent His only begotten Son, that whoever believes in Him should not perish, but have everlasting life" (John 3:16). How astonishing it must have been for her to discover that she was created in the image and likeness of God, and that this God became human so that she could become like God. With an open heart and mind, Barbara thirsted for truth, and in a short period of time, studied the veracity of these teachings.

Because she had no friends outside the home, her maids were her companions. Through them Barbara learned more of this new religion—one that was radically different from the idolatry of the Romans and their emperor worship. Barbara was informed about a belief in one God, in three persons. Her discussions with these friends turned into lessons, and these lessons continued over many days, until she made the decision to become a believer. The transformation was an interior one: her outward appearance remained the same, but her inward self was radically changed.

All this happened without her father's knowledge or approval. He was a traditional man, opposed to new religions because they were seen as a threat to the Roman Empire and the status quo. Anything contrary to the norm—anything that could potentially hinder his political ambitions—was unacceptable.

Barbara did not know how he would react. She was a beloved daughter who hoped for the best, separated as she was from the world. Yet the more she grew in this new faith, the more she desired to honor this Triune God. It is generally believed that Barbara did so in one small way. She asked the builders of her family's new bathhouse to have three windows installed, instead of the two that were planned. The legend states that she was so pleased with the result that she drew a cross on the wall with her finger.

When her father discovered this deviation from "the plan," she happily told him that: "These three windows prefigure clearly the Father, the Son, and the Holy Spirit, which be three persons and one very God, on whom we ought to believe and worship," and she proceeded to tell him about her new faith.[4] In an instant he became enraged and turned on her. She was no longer his cherished daughter whom he could manipulate to his best advantage; she immediately became a cancerous influence to be excised from the pristine Roman landscape. He beat his only daughter and locked her up as a prisoner in her own home.

Barbara had defied her father in order to respond to a calling from God. The consequences were real. She was dragged before the governor of the province, where she was encouraged to renounce Christ and to offer sacrifices at the local temple. She refused. For this she was tortured and sentenced to death. Simeon the Translator called her father "a child of the man-slaying devil"[5] because of his intense madness toward her as a person with abnormal religious beliefs. Such was his intolerance toward this Christian faith that Dioscoros carried out the death sentence himself by beheading his formerly beloved daughter. She is remembered in the following hymn of the Church:

> O honorable and triumphant Barbara,
> you believed in God the Holy Trinity
> and renounced the multiplicity of pagan deities.
> You fought for your faith with great courage
> and were not frightened by your persecutors' threats,
> but declared instead in a clear voice:
> "I adore one God in three divine Persons."[6]

Kyriaki FitzGerald would likely characterize the relationship between Barbara and God as *authentic*[7] and the one between father and daughter as *inauthentic*. It is conceivable that a man such as Dioscoros used "humiliation . . . as a weapon to control"[8] those around him. Dioscoros was playing the game of life by the "rules" he had been taught as a Roman citizen. Barbara learned a different set of "rules," and the cost of adhering to them was her life.

Orthodox Christians believe that all of humanity has been created in the image and likeness of God (Gen 1:26). Although people are free to choose whether or not to believe this, Orthodox Christians are expected to refrain from judging others for their choices in belief. Rather, it is their responsibility to respond to others by loving them as Christ would have (John 13:34). Archbishop Desmond Tutu confronts us with the reality that:

> The endless divisions that we create between [us] and that we live and die for—whether they are our religions, our ethnic groups, our nationalities—are so totally irrelevant to God. God just wants us to love each other.[9]

The Evangelist John reminded his flock that "he who says he loves God and hates his brother is a liar" (1 John 4:20). John of Damascus continues with this line of belief:

> God made him [humankind] by nature sinless, and endowed him with free will. By sinless, I do not mean that sin could find no place in him (for that is the case with Deity alone), but that *sin is the result of the free volition he enjoys rather than an integral part of his nature*; that is to say, he has the power to continue and go forward in the path

of goodness, by co-operating with the divine grace, and likewise to turn from good and take to wickedness, for God has conceded this by conferring freedom of will upon him. For there is no virtue in what is the result of mere force.[10]

The murder of Barbara by her father is reminiscent of the first murder recounted in Genesis 4, where Cain murders Abel out of envy for the gift offered to God. The exchange between Cain and God after the murder of Abel reminds us that God sees us as we are (not as we appear to be): "The Lord said to Cain, 'Where is your brother?' He said, 'I do not know; am I my brother's keeper?' And the Lord said, 'What have you done? The voice of your brother's blood is crying to me from the ground'" (vv. 9–10).

Both of these stories remind us of how final a choice murder is. Humanity has not yet learned the lesson of loving one's neighbor as one's self. Humankind has been (after the Fall) endowed with the knowledge of good and evil (Gen 3:22), in this way becoming more like God. Thus, there is no excuse for ignorance of the differentiation between good and evil. Although St. Barbara's father was vengeful because of her disobedience, and Cain was envious of Abel's gift to the Lord, their heinous actions are both based upon anger. In fact, St. John Cassian names this sin and the way out of it:

> Our forth struggle is against the demon of anger. We must, with God's help, eradicate his deadly poison from the depths of our souls. So long as he dwells in our hearts and blinds the eyes of the heart with his sombre disorders, we can neither discriminate what is for our good, nor achieve spiritual knowledge, nor fulfil our good intentions, nor participate in true life; and our intellect will remain impervious to the contemplation of the true, divine light . . . for it is written, "Man's anger does not bring about the righteousness of God." (Jas. 1:20)[11]

This message is further reinforced by Orthodox theologians Fr. Thomas and Kyriaki FitzGerald, who say:

> When we behave in an evil manner or speak in an evil way, we only contribute to the power of evil. It is as if we become an accomplice to the forces which struggle against God. When we respond to evil with good, on the other hand, we break the power of evil. We do not give it any further authority. And, we remain faithful to our vocation to live our life as the sons and daughters of God.[12]

It is important to establish a framework within which to live by look-ing to the endpoint of life as the starting point.[13] A choice to work toward eternal life with Christ begins here and now—today. This must by neces-sity be done in all aspects of life while at the same time forgiving, but not forgetting, the atrocities that have been committed against humanity by other human beings. This can be monumentally difficult for fallen hu-manity, yet with God all things are possible. On this point, St. Gregory of Narek, a late tenth- and early eleventh-century Armenian theologian and mystic, poetically reminds us that God can melt away our sins, debts, and despair in his *Prayer* 49:

> For wherever forgiveness reigns, sin is banished,
> and wherever your [God's] living word gives encouragement,
> there is no despair.
> And wherever your gifts abound, debts are dissolved.
> And the hand of God being close by, nothing is impossible.
> Rather, everything basks in the light, filled with strength and
> invincible potency.
> Yours is salvation, life, renewal, mercy, and at the same time,
> a sweet kingdom, incorruptible and glorified forever. Amen.[14]

St. John Chrysostom's commentary on "and lead us not into tempta-tion" from the Lord's Prayer elucidates the Christian response to the evil one as well as the consequences of this response:

> Here [Christ] teaches us plainly our own vileness, and quells our pride, instructing us to deprecate all conflicts, instead of rushing upon them. For so both our victory will be more glorious, and the devil's overthrow more to be derided. I mean, that as when we are dragged forth, we must stand nobly; so when we are not summoned, we should be quiet, and wait for the time of conflict; that we may show both freedom from vainglory and nobleness of spirit . . . For wickedness is not of those things that are from nature, but of them that are added by our own choice. And [the evil one] is so called pre-eminently, by reason of the excess of his wickedness, and because he, in no respect is injured by us, wages us implacable war. Wherefore, neither said [Christ], "deliver us from the wicked ones," but "from the wicked one;" instructing us in no case to entertain displeasure against our neighbors, for what wrongs soever we may suffer at their hands, but to transfer our enmity from these to [the evil one], as be-ing himself the cause of all our wrongs.[15]

MARTYRS OF THE ARMENIAN GENOCIDE

I am another Barbara whose own family has been the recipient of the same intolerance experienced by St. Barbara. Perhaps it was the same seed of envy and hatred identified above that came to full bloom in the hearts of those who perpetrated the Armenian genocide (1915–1923) in Turkey. My *yiayia's* (Greek grandmother's) last vision of her homeland—while she was running for her life toward the Mediterranean Sea—was of being chased by an armed and angry mob with an unquenchable thirst for the blood of non-Turks, because they believed that Turkey was for Turks only. She was in her late teens at that time, and she never returned to Palies Fokes, Turkey. She was fortunate. She escaped prior to 1915 with her life and with most of her family. Making her way to Morgantown, West Virginia, she lived a safer and perhaps less eventful life—although one might consider rearing four children in a new homeland just as eventful.

Many others were not so fortunate. Shamrig Marifian, the grandmother of an acquaintance, recounted the horrors of her family's forced march from Yerevan, her hometown, to Etchmiadzin. She talks about the separation from family members, starvation, forced marriages, and her eventual migration to orphanages in Istanbul and Athens; finally, she tells of her reunion with family in East St. Louis, Illinois. In the videotaped account of her life, the tension and sadness in her face, the shaking in her voice, and her hand-wringing brought to life the fear, pain, and utter helplessness she must have felt.[16] As I continued to watch Shamrig on the video, it was as if she had been transported back in time and place to relive those atrocities she experienced as a small child—thus retraumatizing her and continuing the abuse. Shamrig and one of her sisters were the only survivors of her immediate family.

Historical Framework and Tensions

The land that is present-day Turkey was predominantly Orthodox Christian in the years prior to 1453. In that year the Ottoman Muslims overthrew the Byzantine Christian empire in the East and proceeded to change the culture from Christian to Muslim through their laws and practices. The Ottomans were excellent military strategists who continued their conquest toward the West, venturing as far as Austria. It is important to note that in Turkey, tensions between Muslims and Christians as well as between other religious groups (Jews, Kurds, Assyrians, etc.) are deep seated and have evolved over the course of many centuries.

Discovering the reasons for escalation of Turkish intolerance toward non-Turks during the latter part of the nineteenth and early part of the twentieth centuries requires a bit of attention, because many complicated influences converged at this time. This chapter will not attempt an in-depth examination of all the factors contributing to the formation of modern Turkey or to the Armenian genocide.[17] Rather, the intent is to offer a brief examination of how these atrocities were perpetrated against an innocent people and to consider how Orthodox and other Christians, as inheritors of their martyric legacy, should respond.

The everyday reality in which Muslims and Christians lived under Ottoman rule was an imbalanced one. Muslims had conquered and were ruling, whereas Christians had lost, and were made to be subservient. So long as both parties accepted that premise, all was right with their world (at least from the Muslim perspective). However, the latter part of the nineteenth century saw the decline of the Ottoman Empire. In general, public law, particularly concerning finance and organization, was administered through edicts (*fermans*) from the Sultan. Civil law concerning personal issues (marriage and inheritance) was subject to the rulings of the Shari'a:[18]

> According to Islamic civil law, Muslims in an Islamic nation enjoy the full rights and duties of "citizenship," while the *dhimmî's* [conquered person's] rights are limited to protection from violence and depredation.[19] The *dhimmî* are to be endured. Their presence is not contested so long as they accept the authority and superiority of Muslims and the Islamic order . . . Under Ottoman rule the *dhimmî* were organized according to religion or sect, and these groups were known as *millets*. The autonomy of each *millet* was recognized through a sultanic letter of permission. Each *millet* administered the great majority of its own affairs, "not only the clerical, ritual, and charitable affairs of their flocks, but also education and the regulation of matters of personal status like marriage, divorce, guardianship, and inheritance."[20]
>
> Apart from such legal inequalities, the *dhimmî* were also subject to humiliating practices. They were forbidden to conduct their religious observance in a way that would disturb Muslims. The ringing of church bells and construction of churches or synagogues were forbidden. Permission from the state was required to repair existing churches. Additionally, *dhimmî* were prohibited from riding horses

and bearing arms and were obliged to step aside for approaching Muslims when traveling on foot. The color of the *dhimmī*'s clothing and shoes and the quality of fabrics had to be distinct from that of Muslims . . . Armenian shoes and headgear, for example, were to be red, while the Greeks wore black and Jews turquoise. Their homes too were painted different colors. They were forbidden to wear clogs and had to attach small bells to the coverings worn in the bathhouses.[21]

Due to various political and social influences, however, the landscape eventually began to change:

> From the late eighteenth century on, wars between the Ottomans and different European powers resulted in peace treaties that brought significant privileges to Ottoman Christian subjects which, in turn, paved the way for the eventual independence of these non-Muslim communities. The Christian minorities, infected with the spirit of progress and freedom blowing in from Europe, began to revolt against political and economic oppression and demand equality, followed by autonomy, and eventually territory. The Ottomans generally met these demands with violent suppression and terror, whereupon foreign powers would intervene, even to the point of war. After defeat, the Ottomans were then forced to accept the insurgents' demands and agree to reforms granting autonomy. But these were usually reforms only on paper, and new revolts would ensue, followed by new foreign interventions, beginning the cycle all over again. This process would continue until the rebellious community achieved independence.[22]

Non-Muslim communities wanted to be placed on an equal level with Muslims, and in fact some reforms were made in Turkey (for example, the Imperial Rescript of 1839, the Reform Edict of 1856, the 1876 Ottoman Constitution, to name a few). This was in part due to the influences of Protestant missionaries from the West functioning throughout the Turkish countryside.

> While the reforms were expected to bring about closer relations between Muslims and non-Muslims, in fact the very opposite occurred. The conceptual basis for such transformation simply didn't exist, either among the ruling elite or within the general society. According to leading Tanzimat reformer Mustafa Reşit Paşa, the full equality promised in the Imperial Rescript would erase the difference between the groups, and thereby end the 600-year dominance

of Ottoman Muslims. This was unacceptable to the general Muslim population. Mustafa Reşit Paşa maintained that without proper preparation, Muslims would resist the reforms, even possibly respond with violence. Just as he feared, Muslims created disturbances and these led to massacres.[23]

The Muslim-Christian balance had tipped toward a more equal position. The Muslims found it utterly intolerable to be equal to or subject to those they had formerly ruled (in Bulgaria, Greece, Serbia, etc.). Therefore, violent reactions on the part of the Muslims to Christians were seen by the Ottoman Turks to be entirely justified.

> The hatred that the Muslim population felt toward the Christians only increased with the Russian, English, French, and later German interference in Ottoman internal affairs. The loss of superior status had shaken the Muslims' confidence, which resulted in the loss of their tolerance. Massacres against Armenians, which by the late nineteenth century had become almost routine, can best be understood against this background.[24]

Sultan Abdul Hamid II was noted as saying:

> By taking away Greece and Rumania, Europe has cut off the feet of the Turkish state. The loss of Bulgaria, Serbia and Egypt has deprived us of our hands, and now by means of this Armenian agitation, they want to get our most vital places and tear out our very guts. This would be the beginning of totally annihilating us, and we must fight against it with all the strength we possess.[25]

In the early twentieth century, power was most assuredly in the hands of the Ottomans. Abdul Hamid II fully supported Muslim attacks against Christians and worked with Muslim clerics to encourage these sorts of actions as a fulfillment of their religious duty:[26]

> [The perpetrators of the 1894–96 massacres] are guided by the prescriptions of the Shari'a. The law prescribes that if the "rayah," or cattle, Christians try, through their recourse to foreign powers, to overstep the privileges allowed them by their Musselman [Muslim] masters and free themselves from their oppression, their lives and property are forfeited, and they are at the mercy of the Musselmans. To the Turkish mind, the Armenians tried to overstep those limits by appealing to the foreign powers, especially to England. They therefore consider it their religious duty and a righteous thing to destroy . . . the Armenians.[27]

As the Ottomans struggled through the fall of the sultanate and the rise of the Union and Progress movement to the rule of Young Turks, a "Turkish" identity was being formulated.

> For all their difference, these divergent currents—Ottomanism, Islamism, Turkism, and Westernism—shared one core premise: the nationalism of a dominant ethnic group, which was understood to mean the Turks.[28]

In fact, Namik Kemal, a leader of the Young Ottoman movement, reinforced this ideal when he said, "We can compromise with the Christians only when they accept our position of dominance."[29] He was openly racist, as was Ali Suavi, another member of the Young Ottoman movement, who believed "that the Turkish race [is] older and superior on account of its military, civilizing, and political roles."[30]

These and other Turkish nationalists worked against their recent history of defeats in Europe to regain their dominance, albeit of a smaller area, of their own remaining territories. They adopted openly racist policies to resubjugate Christian peoples within their borders and used violence to enforce these policies. Their stated concern was to develop a national Turkish identity—"Turkey is for Turks" (meaning Muslim Turks)—and to avoid partition by the Western Allies. The Ottomans returning half-starved and humiliated after defeats in the Balkans were intentionally settled into predominantly Armenian areas to help set the stage for future murders, tortures, kidnappings, and death marches. Imagine the depth and breadth of rage that may have been felt toward Christians "enjoying the privilege" of living in their homeland. They were defeated by Christians and then settled in predominantly Christian areas. The stage for the genocide was more clearly constructed,[31] and the atmosphere continued to worsen:

> After the Balkan Wars, the Armenians repeated their demands for reform. On 31 March 1913, the Armenian patriarch appealed to the grand vizier, delivering a letter stating that "the situation of the Armenians has deteriorated even further, to the point that we fear for their wholesale elimination." He announced that he was calling on the Ottoman state's sense of responsibility as a last resort. When the request went unanswered, the General Council of the Armenian Patriarch resigned on 4 May 1913, claiming that this was the only possible option, "because it had not, until now, seen a single result from initiatives and requests concerning the

situation in the provinces, which had been sent numerous times to the *Porte*."[32]

One of the key reasons why Ottoman Turks (and later the members of the CUP, or Committee of Union and Progress— the dominant party at the time) were so threatened by the Armenians was that if they suc-ceeded in partitioning to form their own country, modern-day Turkey would simply not exist.[33]

The Armenian Genocide

The pro-Turkish nationalists worked to obliterate the Armenian people through various atrocious acts (taking away their arms, restricting their movements, etc.).[34] It is noteworthy that although such acts were encour-aged by the nationalist Turks against Armenians, there were Turks who did offer assistance or relief to the Armenians. This is significant because these persons were under the constant threat of death for providing such aid. Taner Akçam, who is frequently cited in this paper, dedicated his book *A Shameful Act* to one such family. It is a sad commentary on those times and on present-day Turkey's lack of transparency that more ex-amples of such courage are not available to document here.

The abuse began slowly and slyly, then escalated to increasingly bla-tant acts of inhuman behavior, including raiding homes, confiscating knives, and hanging prominent citizens.[35, 36] Men were butchered, even dismembered.[37] Priests and others had horseshoes nailed to their feet.[38] Women and girls were raped.[39] Children were kidnapped from their fam-ilies to become servants in Muslim families. The vast majority of non-Muslims could not expect any help at all from Muslims because an edict was issued which said that "any Muslim who protected or hid an Arme-nian would be punished by hanging."[40] One of the most heart-rending and vivid examples of these heinous acts is described in an eyewitness account by a young girl, Dovey (Aghavni) Kassabian. It reveals the depths to which the Committee of Union and Progress Turks had descended in their choice to embrace the evil of genocide:

> The crowd lined the square, some people were sitting in chairs, some
> Arabs selling quinces, people burning incense, the Turkish women in
> burugs were sitting on hassocks eating simits. The sun was terribly
> hot, and on the black walls some cranes were perched. In the middle
> of the crowd there were fifteen or twenty Armenian women, some

a little older than me, some my mother's age. They were dressed in their daily clothes. Some in long fine dresses, others, who were peasants, in simple black. They were holding hands and walking in a circle slowly, tentatively, as if they were afraid to move. About six Turkish soldiers stood behind them. They had whips and each had a gun. They were shouting, "Dance. *Giaur.* Slut." The soldiers cracked the whips on the women's backs and faces, and across their breasts. "Dance. *Giaur.* Slut." Many of the women were praying while they moved in this slow circle. *Der Voghormya, Der Voghormya* (Lord have mercy), *Krisdos bada raqyal bashkhi i miji meroom* (Christ is sacrificed and shared amongst us[41]), and occasionally they would drop the hand next to them and quickly make the sign of the cross. Their hair had come undone and their faces were wrapped up in the blood-stuck tangles of hair, so they looked like corpses of Medusa. Their clothes were now turning red. Some of them were half naked, others tried to hold their clothes together. They began to fall down and when they did they were whipped until they stood and continued their dance. Each crack of the whip and more of their clothing came off.

Around them stood their children and some other Armenian children who had been rounded up from the nearby Armenian school. They were forced into a circle, and several Turkish soldiers stood behind them with whips and shouted, "Clap, clap!" And the children clapped. And when the soldiers said, "Clap, clap, clap," the children were supposed to clap faster, and if they didn't, the whip was used on them. Some of the children were two and three years old, barely able to stand up. They were all crying uncontrollably. Crying in a terrible, pitiful, hopeless way. I stood next to women in burugs and men in red fezzes and business suits, and they too were clapping like little cockroaches.

Then two soldiers pushed through the crowd swinging wooden buckets and began to douse the women with the fluid in the buckets, and, in a second, I could smell that it was kerosene. And the women screamed because the kerosene was burning their lacerations and cuts. Another soldier came forward with a torch and lit each woman by the hair. At first all I could see was smoke, and the smell grew sickening, and then I could see the fire growing off the women's bodies, and their screaming became unbearable. The children were being whipped now furiously, as if the sight of the burning mothers had excited the soldiers, and they admonished the children to clap "faster,

faster, faster," telling them that if they stopped they too would be lit on fire. As the women began to collapse in burning heaps, oozing and black, the smell of burnt flesh made me sick.[42]

Why did this happen? What had those young women done to be treated in such a horrific manner? The answer is: nothing! They were Armenian Christians, citizens the empire did not want. The CUP Turks were using them as instruments to teach the lesson "you are nothing, and we can abuse you as we wish," as well as to extract revenge for their losses and mistreatment in the Balkan wars. Those active and passive participants in such acts (soldiers and onlookers) did not realize that:

> The Son of Man will send out His angels, and they will gather out of His kingdom all things that offend and those who practice lawlessness. And will cast them into the furnace of fire. There will be wailing and gnashing of teeth. Then the righteous will shine forth as the sun in the kingdom of their Father. He who has ears to hear, let him hear. (Matt 13:41–43)

The guards and the lingering "passive," yet willing, observers all in their own way contributed to these atrocities. Their spiritual transformation, which occurred from the inside out, stands as a reminder of how any of us can, through our choices, either grow closer to or farther away from the God of love. In this context, one pauses to wonder what kind of reward the souls of the perpetrators,[43] submerged in hatred and intolerance as they were, will receive whenever their time comes to stand before His throne, trusting that judgment belongs to Christ. On the other hand, even though not asked to do so, the women and children had become martyrs. Through unspeakable humiliation, pain, and fire, they prayed as they offered their final witness, all the while facing unimaginable wickedness with a grace and dignity lost on their perpetrators.

Denial of the Armenian Genocide

To this very day, the Turkish government does not admit "the shameful act" (Kemal Atatürk's words) that it perpetrated on the Armenians. The current Turkish government only admits that a relatively "few" Armenians were killed as a response to the threat posed by them to incite a civil war. The facts bear witness to quite the opposite, as Armenians were responding in self-defense to the murders of their people, murders incurred through the assaults of the Ottoman, and later the CUP, Turks. It should also be noted that the Turkish government still ardently objects to the term "genocide" used in association with the "Armenian situation." The word "genocide" was coined by Rafael Lemkin to describe the atrocities perpetrated against the Armenians. The following statement from the Armenian National Institute's website on the genocide articulates the history of this word and its use:

> The United Nations Convention on the Prevention and Punishment of the Crime of Genocide describes genocide as "acts committed with intent to destroy, in whole or in part, a national ethnical, racial or religious group." Clearly this definition applies in the case of the atrocities committed against the Armenians. Because the U.N. Convention was adopted in 1948, thirty years after the Armenian Genocide, Armenians worldwide have sought from their respective governments formal acknowledgment of the crimes committed during W.W.I. Countries like France, Argentina, Greece, and Russia, where the survivors of the Armenian Genocide and their descendents live, have officially recognized the Armenian Genocide. However, as a matter of policy, the present-day Republic of Turkey adamantly denies that a genocide was committed against the Armenians during W.W.I. Moreover, Turkey dismisses the evidence about the atrocities as mere allegations and regularly obstructs efforts for acknowledgment. Affirming the truth about the Armenian Genocide, therefore, has become an issue of international significance. The recurrence of genocide in the twentieth century has made the reaffirmation of the historic acknowledgment of the criminal mistreatment of the Armenians by Turkey all the more a compelling obligation for the international community.[44]

Continuing Religious Intolerance

The intolerance of Turks towards non-Turks continues to this day; non-Turkish citizens of Turkey are suffering daily from the slow strangulation imposed on them by restrictive and discriminatory application of laws. This includes and is not limited to the Armenians, Assyrians, Greeks, Jews, and Kurds.[45] In a report on the elimination of religious intolerance in Turkey, the United Nations has described the situation in Turkey as one in which "the active policy of Turkization, as an expression of nationalism, has meant that the great majority of society has come to regard citizenship solely in terms of Turkish ethnicity and Muslim identity,"[46] to the exclusion of these non-Muslim elements. This report also states that "this particular form of nationalism pervades not only State institutions but society as a whole, and generally conveys a message that leaves no room for the Christian minorities. These policies have sparked the massive departure of members of these minorities from Turkey."[47] In sharp contrast to the situation in Turkey, Archbishop Tutu reminds us of our connectedness and our interdependence, citing blasphemy against God when we lose sight of this:

> Our humanity is caught up in that of all others. We are human be-
> cause we belong. We are made for community, for togetherness, for
> family, to exist in a delicate network of interdependence. Truly, "it is
> not good for man to be alone" [Gen 2:18], for no one can be human
> alone. We are sisters and brothers of one another whether we like
> it or not and each one of us is a precious individual. It does not de-
> pend on such things as ethnicity, gender, political, social, economic,
> or educational status—which are all extrinsic. Each person is not just
> to be respected but to be revered as one created in God's image. To
> treat one such as if they were less than this is not just evil, which it
> is, is not just painful, as it frequently tends to be for the one at the re-
> ceiving end of whatever discrimination or injustice is involved—no,
> it is veritably blasphemous, for it is to spit in the face of God. And in-
> evitably and inexorably, those who behave in this way cannot escape
> the consequences of their contravention of the laws of the universe.[48]

It is most ironic that today Turkey officially claims to be a secular state even though the Muslim faith is the only fully accepted religion. This is due to the repeatedly stated fear that desecularizing the country "will pave the way for Muslim extremists" to further dominate the politi-cal landscape in Turkey.

What are the effects on Turkey of perpetuating lies, and discrim-inatory policies and practices for so long a time? The vast majority of Turkey's own citizens today may unknowingly be colluding with "ethnic cleansing" in their own country. Perhaps all too many Turkish citizens allow themselves to remain naïve yet complicit partners in ef-fectively eliminating all but one voice, one religion. Imagine, instead, a culturally diverse Turkey—one in which Armenians, Assyrians, Greeks, Jews, atheists, agnostics, and others are all allowed the same rights in practice, not just in theory. This appreciation for cultural and religious diversity could translate into a previously unknown national strength. In turn, this strength, based in mutual respect, could lessen the chances of the nation falling prey to radical or fundamentalist entities intent on imposing a culture of domination, intimidation, and violence. Such a fresh and creative venture would have the potential to eliminate a large obstacle blocking Turkey's application to the European Union.

Perhaps there are ways in which United States foreign policy has been complicit in perpetuating present-day Turkey's denial of its past. The United States-Turkish relationship is complex and multilayered. On a political level, Turkey allows the United States to operate strategic airbases along its eastern border. But the Turkish government is quite aggressive in threatening to prohibit the use of its land if the United States officially recognizes acts against the Armenians as genocide, or tries to force Turkey to admit that what was done to the Armenians was in fact genocide. By allowing Turkey to dictate these terms, the United States falls short of its own moral standard on this issue.

In this difficult situation there are no clear-cut or easy solutions. To accomplish a resolution would require interested stakeholders (including Turkish officials, Armenian Church officials, etc.) to sit down and work out a mutually respectful understanding of the situation. At present, it seems that the stakeholders are not interested. Even today, Turkey supports activities and individuals in the US who deny the Armenian genocide.[49] This is as absurd as attempting to hide an elephant in a broom closet. Sadly, Turkey is not alone in denials of genocide. Other countries and ethnic groups have experienced and/or perpetrated genocide: Rwanda, South Africa, Sudan, Nazi Germany, Cambodia, China . . . and this list is by no means complete. What has humanity learned through the centuries about how to respond (individually and corporately) to such situations? How have we allowed ourselves to be changed by these events?

FORGIVENESS AND LOVE IN ACTION

In such circumstances, it is extraordinarily difficult to separate the sin from the sinner. The sinner always has the possibility to change, to choose to depart from evil and walk toward the good. Such *metanoia*[50] requires courage and strength. Christians today are challenged not only to forgive, but also to love. In the end, perpetrator and victim alike stand in judgment before God, where they will account for their actions. There are no excuses.

There are, however, recent examples of such courage and strength found in the efforts of the South African Truth and Reconciliation Commission.[51] Archbishop Tutu described this commission as

> quite appalled at the depth of depravity to which human beings could sink and we would, most of us, say that those who committed such dastardly deeds were monsters because the deeds were monstrous. But theology prevents us from doing this. Theology reminded me that, however diabolical the act, it did not turn the perpetrator into a demon. We had to distinguish between the deed and the perpetrator, between the sinner and the sin, to hate and condemn the sin while being filled with compassion for the sinner. The point is that, if perpetrators were to be despaired of as monsters and demons, then we were thereby letting accountability go out the window because we were then declaring that they were not moral agents to be held responsible for the deeds they had committed. Much more importantly, it meant that we abandoned all hope of their being able to change for the better. Theology said they still, despite the awfulness of their deeds, remained children of God with the capacity to repent, to be able to change.[52]

In South Africa, the Truth and Reconciliation Commission granted amnesty to the guilty when they confessed. This was difficult not only for the guilty and the victims, but for the families of both. As awful as it was to read the ugly truths spoken by perpetrators and victims, it seemed that truth-telling released poison festering in the souls of both. True healing occurred because the wound was lanced by telling the truth, and the poison was drained. In many instances, victim and perpetrator did not allow their sins to continue to corrode their souls—they reversed the effects of sin. The power the sin held over them all was dissipated simply by their stating the truth before God, before one another, and even before the entire world.

Survivors of Abuse: Forgiveness and Love

For survivors of atrocities to expect an admission of guilt as a prerequisite to forgiveness becomes in itself a stumbling block to salvation. Desiring and working toward an authentic relationship with Christ require a measure of defiance of societal expectations and a surrender to the example of Christ, the suffering servant and Savior of all. Jesus "made Himself of no reputation, taking the form of a bondservant, and coming in the likeness of men. And being found in appearance as a man, He humbled Himself and became obedient to the point of death, even the death of the cross" (Phil 2:7–8). We are also called to become like Christ by emptying ourselves of our self-centeredness, instead inclining ourselves to do His will so that we may "shine as lights in the world" (Phil 2:15). We are reminded by St. Paul that "the message of the cross is foolishness to those who are perishing, but to us who are being saved it is the power of God" (1 Cor 1:18). Paul continues, "We preach Christ crucified: a stumbling block to Jews and foolishness to Gentiles, but to those whom God has called, both Jews and Greeks, Christ the power of God and the wisdom of God. For the foolishness of God is wiser than man's wisdom, and the weakness of God is stronger than man's strength" (1 Cor 1:23–25).

So what appears to be a "weak" position in worldly terms in actuality requires a great deal of strength. Civil engineers acknowledge that the strength of a building lies in its ability to be flexible through the use of concrete reinforced with steel rods. Under stressful environmental conditions such as high winds or earthquakes, the building may vibrate and sway, but will not crumble. A building without the flexibility of steel rods is more likely to become unstable, crack, and be destroyed. In like manner, a Christian without forgiveness is not flexible enough to withstand all the challenges in this life.

Those who perpetrate evils on innocent victims (and even on not-so-innocent victims) unwittingly drink condemnation unto themselves. Such perpetrators need prayers all the more. This seems paradoxical. Christians maintain that Christ came "for the life of the world—that is, for the life of the *whole* world. How, then, can one not be compelled to pray for those who blame the victims? As noted earlier, the Turkish government continues to deny the outright torture, murder, and intentional extermination of 1.3 million Armenians. History books have been rewritten. The current generation of Turkish citizens generally believes that only a few Armenian insurgents were justifiably killed.[53] They have been blinded by a fabricated, counterfeit history projected onto them, and collectively lack the moral resolve, inquisitiveness, and courage to uncover the truth. In a recent incident, a small number of respected Turkish scholars courageously sought to discover the whole truth and write about it. As a consequence of their actions, they were either imprisoned or banished from their homeland.

As impossible a change as such a fresh initiative may seem to be for some, Archbishop Tutu remarked that people emerged transformed by the Truth and Reconciliation experience:

> But there is another side, a more noble and inspiring one. We have been deeply touched and moved by the resilience of the human spirit. People who by rights should have had the stuffing knocked out of them, refusing to buckle under intense suffering and brutality and intimidation; people refusing to give up on the hope of freedom, knowing they were made for something better than the dehumanizing awfulness of injustice and oppression; refusing to be intimidated to lower their sights. It is quite incredible the capacity people have shown to be magnanimous—refusing to be consumed by the bitterness and hatred, willing to meet with those who have violated their persons and their rights, willing to meet in a spirit of forgiveness and reconciliation, eager only to know the truth, to know the perpetrator so they could forgive them.
>
> We have been moved to tears. We have laughed. We have been silent and we have stared the beast of our dark past in the eye. We have survived the ordeal, and we are realizing that we can indeed transcend the conflicts of the past, we can hold hands as we realize our common humanity . . . The generosity of spirit will be full to overflowing when it meets a like generosity. Forgiveness will follow confession and healing will happen, and so contribute to national unity and reconciliation.[54]

Let us examine and learn from the courageous example of those in South Africa struggling against their past atrocities. They faced their "demons" head on and offered no amnesty without an admission of guilt. Archbishop Tutu outlined their approach:

> In the South African case there was to be no general amnesty. This amnesty was not automatic and the applicant had to make an individual application, then appear before an independent panel which decided whether the applicant satisfied the stringent conditions for granting amnesty. So the other extreme, of blanket amnesty, was also rejected. Apart from the reasons mentioned above, it was felt very strongly that general amnesty was really amnesia. It was pointed out that we none of us possess a kind of fiat by which we

can say, "Let bygones be bygones" and, hey presto, they then become bygones. Our common experience in fact is the opposite—
that the past, far from disappearing or lying down and being quiet,
has an embarrassing and persistent way of returning and haunting
us unless it has in fact been dealt with adequately. Unless we look
the beast in the eye, we find it has an uncanny habit of returning to
hold us hostage.[55]

Archbishop Tutu has also said that there can be "no future without
forgiveness." Indeed,

> our nation sought to rehabilitate and affirm the dignity and person-
> hood of those who for so long had been silenced, had been turned
> into anonymous, marginalized ones. Now they would be able to tell
> their stories, they would remember, and in remembering would be
> acknowledged to be persons with an inalienable personhood.[56]

There can be no spiritual growth without forgiveness, because when
I dehumanize you, I dehumanize myself. When Cain murdered his
brother, Abel, something died in Cain, too. When we think we know better than God, we act as did Lucifer, whose pride led to his expulsion from
the ranks of angels. We are told, "Do not fear those who kill the body but
cannot kill the soul. But rather fear Him who is able to destroy both soul
and body in hell" (Matt 10:28).

The Orthodox nun, theologian, and philosopher Mother Maria of
Normanby has said, "To suffer injustice can, at the utmost, destroy the
body, but to do injustice would of necessity harm the soul and in the
end destroy."[57] Again, Archbishop Tutu speaks from his experience while
instructing us:

> True reconciliation is based on forgiveness, and forgiveness is based
> on true confession, and confession is based on penitence, on contri-
> tion, on sorrow for what you have done . . . How can you forgive if you
> do not know what or whom to forgive? When you do know what or
> whom to forgive, the process of requesting and receiving forgiveness
> is healing and transformative for all involved.[58]

Christians must take the high moral road and do the work that leads
to salvation. I myself must continually, at a deep level and in a dispassionate manner, examine my motives and opportunities. The New Testament
is replete with examples of Christ teaching which actions are and are
not acceptable to God. These acceptable actions prepare us and open us

up to receive His merciful love. The following stories provide only a few examples: the Parable of the Publican and the Pharisee illustrates the contrast between self-emptying (the publican) and self-righteousness (the Pharisee);[59] Christ's admonishment of Peter to forgive his brother who sins against him;[60] and again, in the Parable of the Unmerciful Servant, Christ exhorts us to forgive and show mercy.[61]

We can only follow this course when we are authentically acting with humility by doing the right thing, like the publican, as opposed to acting self-righteously, like the Pharisee. This is a difficult but necessary condition to receive the transformational love of God. Think of Peter's question: "How many times must I forgive?"

We can learn from the response of Marietta Jaeger to the events that occurred on a camping vacation in Montana. She and her husband's youngest daughter, seven-year-old Susie, went missing on the last night of the trip. Susie was killed. Marietta describes her eventual response to the murder:

> I had finally come to believe that real justice is not punishment but restoration, not necessarily to how things used to be, but to how they really should be. In both the Hebrew and Christian scripture whence my beliefs and values come, the God who seeks not to punish, destroy or put us to death, but a God who works unceasingly to help and heal us, rehabilitate and reconcile us, restore us to the richness and fullness of life for which we have been created. This, now, was the justice I wanted for this man who had taken my little girl.
>
> Though I readily admit that initially I wanted to kill this man with my bare hands, by the time of the resolution of his crimes, I was convinced that my best and healthiest option was to forgive. In the 20 years since losing my daughter, I have been working with victims and their families and my experience has been consistently confirmed. Victim families have every right initially to the normal, valid, human response of rage, but those persons who retain a vindictive mind-set ultimately give the offender another victim. Embittered, tormented, enslaved by the past, their quality of life is diminished. However justified, our unforgiveness undoes us. Anger, hatred, resentment, bitterness, revenge—they are death-dealing spirits and they will "take our lives" on some level as surely as Susie's life was taken. I believe that the only way we can be whole, healthy, happy persons is to learn to forgive. That is the inexorable lesson and experience of the gospel of Marietta. Though I would never

have chosen it so, the first person to receive a gift of life from the death of my daughter . . . was me.[62]

PERSONAL REFLECTION AND CHALLENGES

I am outraged by the events that have occurred and profoundly saddened by the loss of family members resulting from the coerced "Turkification" of Turkey. I am forced to face my own prejudices without feeding them. I remember that these catastrophic events began as a seed in a heart and mind that had turned away from God. How often during the day do I turn from God? Can I stand in truth before God and confess innocence? Absolutely not! I am a sinner. I struggle with forgiving others who have harmed and betrayed me, albeit in a far less extreme manner than the examples of St. Barbara and the Armenian people. I struggle with praying for those who hate me. I struggle when praying for the situation in present-day Turkey. I struggle to separate Turkish policies from Turkish citizens when I remember that all are created in the image and after the likeness of God. I struggle when people who think they know me make inferences about my life that are not based in truth. I struggle with being around such people.

I groaned in Istanbul when the state-licensed tour guide in Hagia Sophia[63] told all in my group what a great monument the edifice was to the Christian and Muslim faiths. A part of me wanted to take over the tour group narrative to reveal the lies the guide was extolling as fact.[64] My "good sense" prevailed only when I thought that type of response might put me in prison, and I was not prepared for that. I was on vacation, after all! So I console myself with the knowledge that "there is nothing covered that will not be revealed, and hidden that will not be known" (Matt 10:26). Truth-telling is important and should not be motivated by self-righteousness, because self-righteousness eats away the purity of the truth-telling.

And yet, for my own good, I must forgive all. Christ presses this point after instructing his disciples how to pray (the Lord's Prayer): "For if you forgive men their trespasses, your heavenly Father will also forgive you. But if you do not forgive men their trespasses, neither will your Father forgive your trespasses" (Matt 6:14–15). If I do not forgive and love my enemy, I condemn myself. But if I do surrender, I open myself to God's grace, mercy, and love. What a choice! I can be like St.

Barbara: confess Christ, forgive all, and surrender myself to the consequences. I could even be like the women who chanted the communion
hymn while enduring their excruciatingly humiliating and painful
death—always looking to the endpoint as my starting point. Recalling
the gentle yet firm words of St. Gregory of Narek's *Prayer* 49 helps me
to choose Christ:

And now remembering the image of your royal kingdom above,

> God of light for all,
> do not let iniquity rule me.
> Do not let the haughty rebel steal the grace
> of your breath from this creature you made.
> Do not let sin trap and rule my mortal body, enslaving me.[65]

John of Damascus reminds us to continually incline ourselves toward
our Creator:

> Here, that is, in the present life, his [humankind's] life is ordered as
> an animal's, but elsewhere, that is, in the age to come, he is changed
> and—to complete the mystery—becomes deified by merely inclin-
> ing himself towards God; becoming deified in the way of partici-
> pating in the divine glory and not in that of a change into the divine
> being.[66]

I don't know why the genocide happened. Maybe God allowed it not
because of the horrors the martyrs endure, but because of the "after"—
what we have done with this experience. Have future genocides been
avoided? Has awareness of the Armenian faith grown? Have displaced
Armenians taken advantage of opportunities for growth, development,
and witness in their new homelands? Have we in the West been exposed
to a faith, culture, and experience we would not otherwise have known?
Is there an independent Armenian homeland? Yes, much has been lost:
women, children, men, churches, art, literature, homes, businesses, and
much, much more. Yet, had this horrible event not happened, a little boy
might never have come to America and married the mother of a cherished friend. She might not even have ever existed, and yet she does. Had
my grandparents not left Smyrna, I might not exist. And I do value all
that I am and am becoming. No matter what plan we think we have for
our lives, if we are attentive we will find that we are like fallen leaves—
picked up by the wind and carried away, resting when the wind rests,
carried away again when the wind picks up. The Lord sends us all over.

Not to trivialize the situation, it is as if the Armenians in Turkey were "ploughed under," only to come up as beautiful flowers, fragrant flowers not just in heaven, but on earth—in the faces of the people we meet and come to know. We are all connected through these rich relationships, horizontally to those on the earth and vertically to those who have ascended before us:

> Whether we recognize it or not, the Triune God has "knit us together" in His love (Eph. 4:16). Each of us shares the same Heavenly Father. And, this Father offers His love to each of us.[67]

Every day we should remember the endpoint as our starting point, while rejoicing in the Resurrection by chanting the final ode of the Paschal canon:

> It is the day of Resurrection!
> Let us shine forth in splendor for the Festival,
> and embrace one another.
> Let us say, "O brethren," even to those who do not love us;
> let us forgive all things in the Resurrection,
> and thus, let us exclaim:
> "Christ has risen from the dead, trampling death by death,
> and bestowing life to those in the tombs."[68]

NOTES

1. Kyriaki Karidoyanes FitzGerald, *Persons in Communion: A Theology of Authentic Relationships* (Berkeley, CA: InterOrthodox Press, 2006), 55–56.

2. "*Dignitas*" is defined as the quality of being worthy, honored, or esteemed. In Roman times a person's *dignitas* also included family name (lineage), patronage, and fortune.

3. Some scholars claim that the life of St. Barbara is fictitious: "There is considerable doubt of the existence of a virgin martyr called Barbara and it is quite certain that her legend is spurious. There is no mention of her in the earlier martyrologies; her legend is not older than the seventh century, and her *cultus* did not spread till the ninth" (*One Hundred Saints: Their Lives and Likenesses Drawn from Butler's* Lives of the Saints *and Great Works of Western Art* [New York: Bulfinch Press, 2007], 86). If Barbara did in fact exist, there is disagreement about the actual location of her home (some possibilities: Heliopolos, Egypt; Heliopolos, Lebanon; Tuscany; Rome; Antioch; or possibly Nicomedia). If Barbara lived in Lebanon during the second century, then she would have lived near three great temples: the Temple of Jupiter (depicted on

the coinage of the time), the Temple of the Sun, and the Circular Acropolis. There is also disagreement about her date of birth and repose. Some date her repose to the early to mid-200s, whereas others place her nearly one hundred years later (ca. 310). In either case, the late second and early third centuries were times of turmoil throughout the Roman Empire, and consequently, Christians were in constant danger.

A traditional account of St. Barbara's life can be found in *The Lives of the Holy Women Martyrs*, translated and compiled from the Greek of *The Great Synaxaristes of the Orthodox Church* (Buena Vista, CO: Holy Apostles Convent, 1991), 528.

4. *One Hundred Saints*, 85.

5. *Lives of the Holy Women Martyrs*, 534.

6. Joseph Raya and José De Vinck, *Byzantine Daily Worship* (Allendale, NJ: Alleluia Press, 1969), 532.

7. Dr. FitzGerald describes an authentic life in Christ as one "marked by coherence between our deepest identity as a child of God and the manner in which we live our life. Such a life is marked by continuity between our beliefs and our actions, between our words and our deeds. Such a life is marked by continuous honesty with our own self before God and others. Such a life is marked by integrity before God and others" (*Persons in Communion*, 38). She continues by identifying humility as "arguably the most powerful virtue in assisting us to become our true selves in the presence of God. Genuine humility requires courage, and in many ways wielding it is counter-intuitive for most of us" (ibid.). St. Barbara's actions were consistent with her beliefs, and thus they were authentic.

8. FitzGerald, *Persons in Communion*, 39. Dr. FitzGerald differentiates humility and humiliation by describing humiliation as "a dangerous and poisonous mechanism used by one human being seeking to diminish and distort the value of other persons . . . it is toxic and life-effacing. Humiliation does not enhance the life of another person. The objective of humiliation as a weapon is very precise. The action of humiliation seeks to control and ultimately annihilate the other experientially 'from the inside out'" (ibid.).

9. Archbishop Desmond Tutu, *God Has a Dream: A Vision of Hope for Our Time* (New York: Image Books, 2004), 47.

10. John of Damascus, *An Exact Exposition of the Orthodox Faith*, bk. 2, chap. 12, in vol. 9 of Nicene and Post-Nicene Fathers, Second Series, trans. E. W. Watson, L. Pullan, et al., ed. Philip Schaff and Henry Wace (reprint, Grand Rapids, MI: Eerdmans, 1979), 31; italics added.

11. *The Philokalia: The Complete Text*, vol. 1, compiled by St. Nikodimos of the Holy Mountain and St. Makarios of Corinth, trans. and eds. G. E. H. Palmer, Philip Sherrard, and Kallistos Ware (London: Faber and Faber, 1983), 82.

12. Kyriaki FitzGerald and Thomas FitzGerald, *Happy in the Lord: The Beatitudes for Everyday* (Brookline, MA: Holy Cross Orthodox Press, 2000), 170.

13. Mother Maria of Normanby, *The Fool and Other Writings*, ed. Sister Thekla (Normanby, UK: Greek Orthodox Monastery of the Assumption, 1980), 98.

14. St. Grigor Narekatsi, *Speaking with God from the Depths of the Heart: The Armenian Prayer Book of St. Gregory of Narek*, trans. Thomas J. Samuelian, poetic ed. Diana Der Hovanessian (Yerevan, Armenia: Vem Press, 2002), 219.

15. St. Chrysostom, *Homily* 19.10, in vol. 10 of Nicene and Post Nicene Fathers, First Series, trans. George Prevost, eds. Philip Schaff and Henry Wace, online at Christian Classics Ethereal Library, accessed May 3, 2007, http://www.ccel.org/ccel/schaff/npnf110.iii.XIX.html.

16. Shamrig Marifian, 1910–2005, in a videotaped account recorded by her loving family, speaks of her explusion from Turkey and arrival in America. I was provided with a copy of this videotape by Shamrig's granddaughter, Jane Matoesian.

17. "The definition in the United Nations' Convention on the Prevention and Punishment of the Crime of Genocide, which the United States finally ratified in 1988, offers a useful standard for judgment. Article II of the convention states: In the present Convention, genocide means any of the following acts committed with intent to destroy, in whole or in part, a nation, ethnical, racial or religious group, as such: (a) killing members of the group; (b) causing serious bodily or mental harm to members of the group; (c) deliberately inflicting on the group conditions of life calculated to bring about its physical destruction in whole or in part; (d) imposing measures intended to prevent births within the group; (e) forcibly transferring children of the group to another group" (Donald E. Miller and Lorna Touryan Miller, *Survivors: An Oral History of the Armenian Genocide* [Berkeley: University of California Press, 1999], 45).

"Armenians take considerable pride in having been the first nation to accept Christianity. The Apostles Thaddeus and Bartholomew brought the Christian gospel to the Armenians as early as A.D. 43, and this event is commemorated in the name of the mother church, the Armenian Apostolic Church. The Armenian Church is sometimes also called the Gregorian Church, in honor of Saint Gregory the Illuminator, who converted the Armenian sovereign Trdat III to Christianity in about A.D. 301. In A.D. 506 the Armenian Church reaffirmed its independence from both Constantinople and Rome and has remained separate to the present. Currently, there are two rival branches of the Armenian Church: the Mother See is Etchmiadzin, Armenia, and the Cilician (Sis) See in Antelias, Lebanon, each of which appeals to Armenians of somewhat different political inclinations" (ibid., 33).

18. Taner Akçam, *A Shameful Act: The Armenian Genocide and the Question of Turkish Responsibility*, trans. Paul Bessemer (New York: Metropolitan Books, 2006), 21.

19. "The meaning of '*dhimma*,' a notion in Islamic jurisprudence, reflects the Islamic obligation to protect the *dhimmî* [conquered people]; the word also connotes 'right,' 'agreement,' or 'mercy.' According to the understanding reached by the *dhimmî* and the Islamic state, their lives and property are inviolate, and their freedom of religion and worship are guaranteed. In exchange, the *dhimmî* are obliged to display subservience and loyalty to the Muslim order and to pay a tax known as the *jizya*'. The relationship is not one of equals, but one of tolerance and forbearance" (ibid., 22–23).

20. Ibid., 22–23.

21. Ibid., 24.

22. Ibid., 27.

23. Ibid., 31–32.

24. Ibid., 35.

25. Ibid., 27.

26. Ibid., 45.

27. Ibid.

28. Ibid., 49.

29. Ibid.

30. Ibid.

31. "This last point is crucial for the subsequent Armenian genocide, because it was precisely those people who, having only recently been saved from massacre themselves, would now take a central and direct role in cleansing Anatolia of 'non-Turkish' elements. The dimension of this migration and its results become easier to understand when we recall that between 1878–1904 some 850,000 refugees were settled in predominantly Armenian areas alone" (ibid., 87).

32. Ibid., 98. *"Porte"* means "gate"; the term referred to the court in the Ottoman Empire where government policies were established.

33. Ibid., 101.

34. Peter Balakian, *The Burning Tigris: The Armenian Genocide and America's Response* (New York: HarperCollins, 2003), 189–90. Balakian continues: "One remarkable document was discovered and translated in early 1919 by British officials in Turkey, who labeled it 'The Ten Commandments.' It is a blueprint of the Armenian extermination operation and appears to have been the centerpiece of a secret party meeting, which took place sometime in late December 1914 or in January 1915. The document was obtained by Comm. C.H. Heathcote Smith, the right-hand man of Adm. Somerset Calthorpe, the British-high commissioner in Constantinople. Fluent in Turkish, Smith had served as British consul in Smyrna before the war, and he first learned of the 'The Ten Commandments' from the former Brit-

ish intelligence agent Percival Hadkinson, in Smyrna" (ibid.). The text of the document is as follows (ibid.):

(1) Profiting by the Arts: 3 and 4 of Comite Union and Progres, close all Armenian Societies, and arrest all who worked against Government at any time among them and send them into the provinces such as Bagdad or Mosul, and wipe them out either on the road or there.

(2) Collect arms.

(3) Excite Moslem opinion by suitable and special means, in places as Van, Erzeroum, Adana, where as a point of fact the Armenians have already won the hatred of the Moslems, provoke organised massacres as the Russians did at Baku.

(4) Leave all executive to the people in provinces such as Erzeroum, Van, Mamuret ul Aziz, and Bitlis and use Military disciplinary forces (i.e., Gendarmerie) ostensibly to stop massacres while on the contrary in places as Adana, Sivas, Broussa, Ismidt and Smyrna actively help the Moslems with military force.

(5) Apply measures to exterminate all males under 50, priests and teachers, leave girls and children to be Islamized.

(6) Carry away the families of all who succeed in escaping and apply measures to cut them off from all connection with their native place.

(7) On the ground that Armenian officials may be spies, expel and drive them out absolutely from every Government department or post.

(8) Kill off in an appropriate manner all Armenians in the Army— this to be left to the military to do.

(9) All action to begin everywhere simultaneously, and thus leave no time for preparation of defensive measures.

(10) Pay attention to the strictly confidential nature of these instructions, which may not go beyond two or three persons.

35. "Virginia Meghrouni wrote that 'continually, day and night, officers searched for weapons in Armenian homes . . . even small kitchen knives were confiscated; so were historical materials and books listing names of Armenian leaders.' She described the shock that went through the community when deportation notices were posted in Kayseri on June 15. All over the city Armenian shops and businesses were ordered closed immediately, and Armenians were informed that they must be prepared for a deportation; in doing so they were instructed to leave their goods and belongings behind and their money in the bank, and that all would be safeguarded. Shortly thereafter, twenty prominent Armenian men were hanged in the town square" (ibid., 228).

36. Ibid., 270: "Farther west in the great port city of Smyrna, the American consul, George Horton, documented a similar Turkification frenzy in a report to Secretary of State William Jennings Bryan in February 1915 . . . [Horton said,] 'lawless Turkish bands are appearing in increasing numbers in this dis-

trict and are spreading a reign of terror among the Christians of all races.' Horton closes his letter to Bryan with the refrain of a song Turkish students in Smyrna were singing:

Revenge! Revenge! Revenge!
Let us kill, let us cut to pieces,
Let us swim in blood up to our knees,
Revenge! Revenge! Revenge!
Let us wipe the stain from our clothes.

37. Ibid., 230–31, 244–45, 247.

38. Peter Balakian, *Black Dog of Fate: A Memoir* (New York: Broadway Books, 1998), 214.

39. Balakian, *Burning Tigris*, 255.

40. Ibid., 266.

41. This is the hymn sung during the offering of Holy Communion in the Divine Liturgy. The words remember Christ's sacrifice unto death. The women sang this in anticipation of their own sacrifice unto death.

42. Balakian, *Black Dog of Fate*, 216–17.

43. It may seem that I have made the assertion that perpetrators remain in a stagnant state of hatred. Because no data is available about the present state of the perpetrators of this recorded incident, one cannot know. I remain steadfast in the knowledge that with God all things are possible, that forgiveness is given and received even at the eleventh hour.

44. "Frequently Asked Questions about the Armenian Genocide," Armenian National Institute, accessed May 22, 2006, www.armenian-genocide. org/genocidefaq.html.

45. United Nations General Assembly, *Elimination of all forms of religious intolerance: Interim report of the Special Rapporteur of the Commission on Human Rights on the elimination of all forms of intolerance and of discrimination based on religion or belief, Addendum 1: Situation in Turkey*, A/55/280/ Add.1 (August 11, 2000), 15–23.

46. Ibid., 26.

47. Ibid.

48. Desmond Mpilo Tutu, *No Future without Forgiveness* (New York: Image, 1999), 196–97.

49. William H. Honan, "Princeton Is Accused of Fronting for the "Turkish Government," *New York Times*, May 22, 1996.

50. "*Metanoia*" is the customary Greek word for repentance. Genuine repentance is closely associated with confession. It literally means a radical turning away from something; this also involves a reciprocal turning toward something else.

51. The Truth and Reconciliation Commission in South Africa was a government agency established after the fall of apartheid in 1990.

52. *No Future without Forgiveness*, 83.

53. *The Armenian Genocide*, directed by Andrew Goldberg, aired on Public Broadcasting Service April 2006 (New York: Two Cats Productions), DVD.

54. Tutu, *No Future without Forgiveness*, 120.

55. Ibid., 28.

56. Ibid., 30.

57. *The Fool and Other Writings*, 98.

58. *God Has a Dream*, 53.

59. "Also [Jesus] spoke this parable to some who trusted in themselves that they were righteous, and despised others: Two men went up to the temple to pray, one a Pharisee and the other a tax collector [or publican]. The Pharisee stood and prayed thus with himself, 'God, I thank You that I am not like other men—extortioners, unjust, adulterers, or even as this tax collector. I fast twice a week; I give tithes of all that I possess.' And the tax collector, standing afar off, would not so much as raise his eyes to heaven, but beat his breast, saying, 'God, be merciful to me a sinner!' I tell you, this man went down to his house justified rather than the other; for everyone who exalts himself will be humbled, and he who humbles himself will be exalted" (Luke 18:9-14).

60. "Then Peter came to Jesus and asked, 'Lord, how many times shall I forgive my brother when he sins against me? Up to seven times?' Jesus answered, 'I tell you, not seven times, but seventy-seven times'" (Matt 18:21-22).

61. "Therefore, the kingdom of heaven is like a king who wanted to settle accounts with his servants. As he began the settlement, a man who owed him ten thousand talents was brought to him. Since he was not able to pay, the master ordered that he and his wife and his children and all that he had be sold to repay the debt. The servant fell on his knees before him. 'Be patient with me,' he begged, 'and I will pay back everything.' The servant's master took pity on him, canceled the debt and let him go. But when that servant went out, he found one of his fellow servants who owed him a hundred denarii. He grabbed him and began to choke him. 'Pay back what you owe me!' he demanded. His fellow servant fell to his knees and begged him, 'Be patient with me, and I will pay you back.' But he refused. Instead, he went off and had the man thrown into prison until he could pay the debt. When the other servants saw what had happened, they were greatly distressed and went and told their master everything that had happened. Then the master called the servant in. 'You wicked servant,' he said, 'I canceled all that debt of yours because you begged me to. Shouldn't you have had mercy on your fellow servant just as I had on you?' In anger his master turned him over to the jailers to be tortured, until he should pay back all he owed. This is how my heavenly Father will treat each of you unless you forgive your brother from your heart" (Matt 18:23-35).

62. Marietta Jaeger, "The Power and Reality of Forgiveness: Forgiving the Murderer of One's Child," in *Exploring Forgiveness*, ed. Robert D. Enright and Joanna North, foreword by Desmond Tutu (Madison: University of Wisconsin Press, 1998), 13-14.

63. Hagia Sophia is the Church of Holy Wisdom in Istanbul (formerly Constantinople), Turkey. It was once the main church for the Eastern Christian faith and home of the ecumenical patriarch. After the Ottoman Turks conquered Constantinople in 1453, the church was turned into a mosque. In more recent years Hagia Sophia has become a museum, and is touted as a great example of the best of both the Muslim and Christian faiths.

64. Construction of this church began under Emperor Justinian I in 532 and was completed some five years later. Ancient visitors were impressed by the structure both inside and out. Some seven hundred years later, when Hagia Sophia was converted into a mosque, the mosaic icons were whitewashed and all Christian symbols were removed. Muslim additions included a mihrab (niche in the wall indicating the direction to Mecca) in the apse where the altar used to stand, a sultan's gallery, a dais for sermons, and a loggia for muezzin, as well as the construction of external minarets. In 1935 Hagia Sophia was converted into a museum by Kemal Atatürk. Sources used in this paper indicate that relations between many Muslims and Christians have been less than hospitable over the course of the centuries. For the tour guide to indicate otherwise seemed a misrepresentation of reality.

65. St. Grigor Narekatsi, *Speaking with God*, 215.

66. John of Damascus, *An Exact Exposition of the Orthodox Faith*, bk. 2, chap. 12, 31.

67. FitzGerald, *Persons in Communion*, 57.

68. George L. Papadeas, *Greek Orthodox Holy Week and Easter Services: A New English Translation* (South Daytona, FL: Patmos Press, 1963), 460, adapted.

REFLECTION AND DISCUSSION QUESTIONS

1. Discuss the range of feelings you experienced while reading this chapter.

2. St. Barbara was defined by her father's position in Roman society. Essentially, her main purpose in society was predetermined for her: she was to help promote her father's social and economic stature. Are there situations today in which people are used to promote the social and/or economic stature of others? Please discuss this.

3. St. Barbara's father held a very powerful and prominent position in society. He is described as someone suffering from excessive self-importance due to the sin of self-love (or self-absorption) and entitlement. Discuss some of the ways people today may fall into this kind of trap.

4. *Due to the sensitive nature of the questions in this section, feel free to discuss or skip this particular section:*
   Marietta Jaeger talks about becoming a second victim of the murderer. This experience is called "secondary trauma" in certain circles.
   a. Have you ever experienced being a victim of secondary (or other) trauma, even if the trauma was not so extreme?
   b. Have you ever survived an overwhelmingly difficult time or traumatic experience after which you were able to see some personal growth or other redeeming factors come out of it?
   c. In what ways have you seen in hindsight that God was with you during a very challenging time?
   d. Have you ever felt abandoned or "forsaken," even by God (cf. Mark 15:34)? Consider and discuss this as much as you are able.

5. This chapter may be seen as a bridge between the two "sides" of the Orthodox family: the Eastern Orthodox and the Oriental Orthodox.
   a. Consider and discuss your experience with Orthodox from other jurisdictions or from outside your faith community.
   b. What do you find similar, and what do you find different?
   c. How have Orthodox Christians from other jurisdictions touched your life and faith?

6. How does it make you feel knowing there are people who deny occurrences of genocide? How should Christians respond to this misinformation?

7. The author tells us about a law prohibiting, under pain of death, the Muslim Turks from assisting the Christian Armenians. Can you reflect on a time when you too felt prohibited from assisting another person because, for whatever reason (a law or rule, peer pressure, some social more), it was not "safe" to do so?

8. Discuss the following statement made by the author: "A Christian without forgiveness is not flexible enough to withstand all the challenges in this life."

St. Mary of Egypt:
A Provocateur of Parrhesia
Iulia Corduneanu Curtright

INTRODUCTION: ON SILENCE AND LISTENING

I remember being startled by the straightforward yet provocative response I received to a question I posed during a visit to an Orthodox monastery many years ago. I asked the gerontissa,[1] "Why are people coming to the monastery?" She answered, "Because here, they find the silence to listen to God."

This reply set in motion a host of thoughts and questions upon which I have been reflecting for a very long time. In prayer, as well as in everyday discourse, I wonder: whenever communication occurs, do we always have to be speaking? What would be the opposite of talking—is it silence? And if it is, is there something special about this silence for which we should be listening?

Nowadays, unfortunately, it seems as if we are always talking more than listening. Surely, whenever we pray, the one to whom we should listen is not primarily ourselves or even our fellow human beings, but God. We deprive ourselves of the possibility for living encounter whenever we drown ourselves in empty chatter, all the while calling it prayer! What could happen if we stopped the chattering of our thoughts and instead listened to what God might be telling us?

Iulia Corduneanu Curtright is a graduate of the School of Theology of the University of Iasi, Romania, and of Holy Cross Greek Orthodox School of Theology, where she earned a master of theology (ThM) degree. She is presently working on her dissertation for her PhD degree in Systematic Theology at Marquette University, Milwaukee, Wisconsin. Deeply fond of teaching theology, she has led retreats and Bible study classes at Annunciation Greek Orthodox Church, Kansas City, Missouri. She also serves on the Board of St. Catherine's Vision.

LEX ORANDI EST LEX CREDENDI

In my chapter in the first volume of *Encountering Women of Faith,* I indulged my fascination with the Church's use of the word "boasting." I presented a study of the original Greek term *kavhomene,* and showed that this is a rather unusual word to use in service of the gospel message. It is found in the resurrectional troparion in the fourth tone.[2]

While examining the original meaning of the word, I was caught off guard by the powerful and provocative implications that were conveyed through the troparion (a type of hymn), especially noting how the word was deliberately used. This hymn is challenging me even now to take more risks with you, the reader, in the service of Christ. As we proceed, it is important to stress that words we read, pray with, and chant in scriptural and liturgical hymns are not merely artistically articulated sounds, linguistically ornate songs, or religious poetry. Rather, based on the ancient theological principle of *lex orandi est lex credendi,*[3] these words become tools, vehicles, or channels, if you like, that are meant to reveal and transport us into the Presence[4] of God. It is through our being open to the inherent Truth[5] conveyed through these words that our frail human attention is restrained from its wandering and brought back to worship God.

This pattern, a pattern that encourages us to "corral" our wandering thoughts and bring them back toward God, is also stressed in the Psalms. The psalmist directs us to put God's words in our hearts: "I have laid up Your word in my heart, that I might not sin against You" (Ps 119:11). Our intentional remembrance of specific memorized verses from Psalms may prove to be a helpful spiritual exercise, especially when we are too tired to reflect on how we have conducted ourselves over the course of the day. Even when we are on—or perhaps in need of—a vacation, this kind of prayerful meditation may help our body, mind, and soul experience relief from the fatigue of the daily grind, mysteriously finding *rest* in God's mighty arms.

And when, indeed, this allowing the Word of God to rest in our hearts happens, who would care about any other convoluted philosophical or linguistic concept? Isn't our society torturing us with its futile modern hermeneutics and vain maneuvers of construction and deconstruction? Nevertheless, a certain living exchange is taking place through and in the language of worship. Not only the language used in worship, but the whole Liturgy is so incarnate, so real, that we are called to experience and receive it fully.

SILENCE AND DOXOLOGY[6]

The Greek word for Liturgy, "*leitourgia*," signifies the work of all the people, of the "people of God" (*o laos tou theou*). Being part of the liturgical assembly requires our intentionally putting forth the effort to act "liturgically," thus offering "ourselves and one another" completely to Christ our God. By so doing, we make ourselves ever more open to experiencing the Presence of God through the Holy Spirit.

From this perspective, we are not merely spectators of a mystical show performed on the Holy Table. Rather, we offer ourselves and one another as living tabernacles. As much as we are able, we offer ourselves and one another body and soul, becoming temples ready to receive Christ in our hearts and minds through and in the Holy Eucharist. This is the mystical experience of the Church that the saints are inviting us to be part of now, today. There is no time or age limit; there are no barriers to be crossed. All that is needed is our willingness to be part of this liturgical ascension on the mountain[7] and to abandon ourselves to the most real, and yet mystical, reality that God gives us in this world: seeing and partaking of His incarnate Glory.[8]

THE SILENCE OF GOD AND THE BOLDNESS OF THE SAINTS

The response of the gerontissa many years ago returns to my mind here. Her words bear witness that people seeking spiritual nourishment come to the monastery in order to "find the silence to listen to God." Not our talking, but silence, absolute silence, was her point.

The life of the Church conveys this silence to the cosmos. This silence is the *something* or *somebody* by which God is surrounded. Even the psalmist tells us that God[9] speaks out of His silence in a luminous way, a way that is unique to God. In fact, the biblical language is quite explicit in describing God's radiant epiphany; Psalm 93, for example, uses a Greek word, *parrhesia*, which in Hebrew means "to shine forth," "to appear in brightness."[10] This luminosity, or inaccessible light, as it was experienced by the apostles on Mount Tabor before Christ's Crucifixion, does not belong to this world, that is, to the creation. It is divine, and thus uncreated. In genuine prayer, could we in some way be listening for the Light?[11]

By the ineffable mercy of the loving God, we are called to become bearers of this same Light, the "Gladsome Light," as the Orthodox hymn of Vespers identifies it. This is no less than our bearing the Light of the living God Himself. The Church affirms this teaching through many hymns. These declare how the saints become "pure and spotless as the angels"—just as is depicted in the next chapter of this book, which also concerns St. Mary of Egypt. And due to this gift of purification, the light of God's glory rested upon them. Thus, they have "become a hallowed dwelling-place of the Spirit."[12] As bearers of the Holy Spirit, the saints freely and boldly stand before the throne of God. They are confident and exult, with no fear. Their praise is full of joy: "And the righteous and the elect will have lifted up themselves from the earth and will cease to look down to the earth and will be invested with the robe of glory . . . and your [the saints'] glory will not perish before the Lord of spirits."[13]

A CASE IN POINT: THE BOLDNESS OF ST. MARY OF EGYPT

We find in the story of St. Mary of Egypt the image of a hardened prostitute who, to her surprise, is confronted by love and who by God's grace becomes the "greatness of the ascetics and glory of all saints."[14] The story of her life, as it has been conveyed to us long ago by Sophrony, Patriarch of Jerusalem, describes Mary as a woman who committed adultery not so much for money as for the irresistible pleasure of the sexual act, which dominated her. At a certain moment she decided to leave Egypt for Jerusalem, a trip which was to change her life. Her conversion from a life of sin to a life in the Spirit, as the liturgical hymns describe it, is so spectacular and out of the ordinary that the Church places it during Great Lent for our special consideration.

Egypt, the homeland of St. Mary, is also a land where part of the history of our salvation has been written. In Hebrew, Egypt means "a matrix of water," a narrow place that encapsulates life, like a womb keeping tight the fetus inside. Forced to stay there in captivity, Israel will come out of Egypt only by God's will and providence. In a metaphor based in Biblical language, one could say that Egypt symbolizes the Fall, while Israel is the Fulfillment.

This biblical imagery also may apply to us human beings. Each of us experiences an interior "Egyptian,"[15] or the more unconscious part of our being, and an interior "Israel," or the more conscious part, which is able to hear and recognize the divine name. Knowing, and hence recognizing, God's name is very important for old Israel. God's name—YHWH,[16] or "I Am Who I Am"—was revealed to Moses in the burning bush and has been kept reverently in the inside pocket of the tunic of Israel. Israel, or our soul, is leaving the land of sinful passions, Egypt, where Israel could not know YHWH. Israel receives the grace of baptism by crossing the Red Sea and is made radiant through the *askesis*[17] of the wilderness, so that one day Israel will be able to reach the Promised Land and Jerusalem, the place where the divine name dwells. The same path was followed by Mary, an Egyptian woman living in darkness, who was led by Christ, as once was Israel, toward the Light. Thus, she abandons the interior Egypt to become part of the New Israel (the Christians) and to enter the heavenly Jerusalem. The Jordan River serves not only as a natural border, but also a spiritual one. It is a demarcation between the land of slavery and sin, and the land of repentance, of tears, and, paradoxically, of freedom.

One might wonder: What is so spectacular about the wilderness that so many saints go there for the rest of their lives? As we can see from the stories of St. Mary of Egypt and numerous other desert ascetics, it was their desire to be closer to God and to give Him glory day and night that led them to the desert. In those times urban areas were not as crowded as they are today. In all probability, they could have lived somewhere in the outskirts of cities and still have been with God, and yet they chose the wilderness. There is nothing harder than living in the wilderness, where there is nobody to say the most casual "hello" to, and where the assaults from evil spirits do not cease.

Mother Gavrilia, a spiritual mother for our times, said about this life of asceticism in the wilderness: "One can think of nothing but the Glory of God. From one morning to the next . . . Day and night . . . With the sun, with the stars, with the birds, with everything . . . Nothing else . . . Whom else can you think of?"[18] More than anything else, someone does not retreat from this world to find God, but to find himself or herself as he or she truly is in front of God.[19]

The hymnography of the Church proclaims about St. Mary of Egypt:

> Having gone to dwell in the wilderness, thou hast blotted out
> from thy soul the images of thy sensual passions, and hast
> marked upon it the God-given imprint of holiness.
> Thou hast attained such glory, blessed Mother, as to walk upon
> the surface of the waters, and in thy prayers to God thou wast
> raised up from the earth.
> And now, all-glorious Mary, standing before Christ with bold-
> ness, entreat Him for our souls.[20]

Another hymn describes her life in the wilderness with the following
words: "In the silence of the wilderness, the octaves of her cry touched
the Logos,"[21] and her tears, like the baptismal waters, were washing away
the "leprosy of her sins."[22] Into her heart, the upper room where the mystical encounter with the Bridegroom was going to take place, she brought
herself "as a sweet spiritual offering to Christ."[23]

Taking a closer look at these hymns, it is surprising to discover an
interesting combination of themes which are so descriptive of the life
in the wilderness: "The armies of the angels rejoice, O holy Mary, seeing
in thee a life equal to their own," and then, "The hosts of dark demons
tremble at the strength of thine endurance: how thou, a woman, solitary
and naked, hast in a marvelous manner put them to shame," and, not to
be forgotten, the last one: "thou hast shone like the sun and illumined
all the desert with thy brightness: do thou make me also glorious with
thy light."[24]

Another beautiful hymn reconnects us with the understanding of
how the saint, through God's loving mercy, cleansed her body from passions, transforming it into a tabernacle of God's Light: "Longing, like the
Psalmist, to behold the majesty of Thy temple and the spiritual tabernacle of Thy glory, she who had profaned Thy temple cried: 'O Christ,
through the spiritual prayers of the Virgin that became Thy temple,
make me a temple of the all-creating Spirit.'"[25]

Being indwelt by the divine Light, the bodies of the saints received
the *boldness of immortality*. Even after physical death, in many cases
their bodies did not decompose; rather, they became sources of healing
and miracles. As faithful pilgrims, we seek to venerate and touch the
bodies of these holy persons, who have been touched and purified by
the flames of the Holy Spirit and have become illumined like pillars of
fire[26] in the desert of this world. Some of them lost their garments in the

austerity of their desolate habitat and had to live for many years almost naked[27] until they received a visitor, and hence new clothes.[28]

Enlarged Hearts and the Holy Ones of God

Why emulate the angels? Or perhaps it is better to ask why the life of the saints is compared to the life of the angels within the spiritual Tradition of the Church. The angels do not possess a material body, and their ministry is to give glory to God unceasingly. In the same way, the saints, through their dispassionate life,[29] empty themselves of their fallen human (or selfish) ego and, paradoxically, through humility enlarge their beings—especially their hearts—for bearing "the fullness of love for Christ."[30] Such an enlarged heart does not have the smallest room for self because it embraces the whole creation in prayer: "I pray Thee, O merciful Lord, for all the peoples of the earth, that they may come to know Thee by the Holy Spirit."[31]

While focusing on the saints, one does not want to overlook the unique experience of Mary, the Theotokos,[32] whose entire body was "enlarged more than the heavens" because she received the Son of God into her womb. In Orthodox churches, there almost always appears above the altar an icon of the Theotokos with her hands wide open and with the Child Jesus in the center of her being.[33]

There is more to say about why and how the saints emulate the angels. The transformation of their entire being, described as an enlargement, is caused by the fact that their whole self, not just the physical body, but also the soul, is being transformed by the *indwelling* of the Word of God. At the same time, their physical bodies lose any heaviness[34] and are eager to follow the soul in its ascension toward fuller communion with God. This indwelling bestows on the soul a blessed silence, because in this silence one receives an authentic, ineffable experiential knowledge of God. Also, when this blessed silence takes over, any distracting memories from the past, attachments to the present, or worries about the earthly future have no echoes in one's mind and soul.[35]

"Let us who mystically represent the cherubim, and who sing the thrice-holy hymn to the life-giving Trinity, now lay aside all the cares of this life, so that we may receive the King of all, who comes invisibly escorted by the angelic hosts." This is the hymn of the Great Entrance intoned at every Divine Liturgy. And this is also the only time, liturgically speaking, when we are called to represent the angels (cherubim) here on earth. In this image (we are the image, or icon, of the bodiless powers) is established "the deepest relationship"[36] between us human beings here on earth and the angelic powers in heaven. There is no way except iconically[37] that we can be present in the church at that time when the "King of all" (Jesus Christ) comes in our midst. It is imperative to stress that this is not magic, but the very reality of the encounter between us and the divine. Do we, truly, need to see the angels escorting the King? Or do we really need to hear their unheard-and-yet-not-silent, thrice-holy hymn while they are rippling the air with their golden wings? As the hymn declares, this can happen only if and when we drive out all mundane cares and abandon them—and ourselves—to God. When left to our own fallen self-centeredness, these cares block our senses and blind our entire being from seeing God in His amazing glory.[38] We truly need to be wrapped in liturgical time and space in order to acquire new senses. And with our senses thus purified, we will be able to contemplate the stillness and the silence of the age to come.

We have arrived at a place in our discussion at which we can stop and ponder deeply the following question: can silence be doxological, and if so, how? Or perhaps our doxology must be silent, so we can hear the angels praising God.

OUR BOLDNESS, IN THE MAKING—A PERSONAL REFLECTION

"And give us *boldness* without condemnation to call you Father and to say . . ." This is an invitation we receive from the servants of the altar—that is, the priests—at every Divine Liturgy. A different liturgical version of the same call says, "Make us worthy, O our Lord and God, that we may stand before You without blemish, with a pure heart and 'with uncovered face' [cf. 2 Cor 3:15–18] and with *boldness* (*parrhesia*), which You in Your mercy have given to us." It is obvious that this *boldness*, or *parrhesia*, is a gift from God; it does not belong to, nor come to, us in an obvious way. What comes to us "naturally"[39] to us is covering our heads or faces out of shame or out of reverence for God. The Bible gives us the examples of Moses, Elijah, and the seraphim,[40] who all covered their faces in front of God because they acknowledged the awesomeness of God's Presence. At the same time, *uncovering* does not necessarily mean a lack of shame or humility, but is a sign of an authentic communion with God.[41]

Now, I ponder and ask myself, am I brave enough to *uncover* my head or face in front of God, especially when I am calling Him Father? When thinking about doing so, I either have in mind several meanings—"open-hearted," "without fear," "openly"—or not. Am I ready for the secrets of my being to be revealed to the entire world or to God, today? Or am I deceiving myself, thinking that only at the Last Judgment will all things be revealed about my life, so that I still have some time left to *cover*, or to veil, what I do not want anybody, including God, to know?

Now I see how the "nakedness" of the saints serves a spiritual purpose for all of us. Their bodies became icons of the Truth, and the truth (a glimpse into the revealed Truth of Christ). On the one hand, in their sainthood, they mysteriously mirror Christ, who is the Truth; and on the other hand, they have nothing to hide about themselves. A relevant example here again is this wonderful saint, Mary of Egypt, who was not ashamed to tell Father Zossima about her past; nevertheless, she did not she reveal to him all the charisma God gave her through her *askesis*.

There are moments when I find my *boldness*, and I can touch and feel it. It is somewhere hidden in my heart, and when I am confident that I have found it, I lose it again. Where does it go? Or who takes it away from me? The human mind is always asking questions and trying to find answers. And yet the answer is right there waiting at the door of my heart. It comes in only if and when I leave my fallen ego aside and humble myself, so that the emptiness of my heart vacuums *boldness* in. Yes, indeed, being humble is the opposite of being proud, but I cannot take humility like a vitamin or a prescribed medicine from the wisdom of the Fathers of the Church, and wake up one day perfectly cured. There is no such spiritual panacea.

What God does give us is a lifelong endurance, an acceptance of who we are that lasts a lifetime. He is also the only One able to heal us, with and in His silence. And this healing silence is found, my friend, in the silence of the Cross. There, on the Cross, the Son of God, like a silent lamb, did not protest, did not argue, did not complain. Rather, He offered His healing love to the entire world. He was wounded, but soon after His Resurrection even the marks from the nails of the Crucifixion became a source of healing for the broken, doubting heart of the Apostle Thomas.

Christ's *healing silence* is offered to all of us from the Holy Table at every Divine Liturgy when "with fear of God, with faith and love" we draw near to receive Him, the Fire, and we hear the priest whispering in a soft voice, "this Holy Communion is granted to the servant of God *N.* for the forgiveness of sins and for eternal life."[42] It is in and through this precious moment that the divine *Pearl*,[43] Jesus Christ Himself, comes to dwell in and adorn our hearts with the healing silence of eternity.

May He who is always glorified among His saints come and dwell in our hearts forever. Amen!

NOTES

1. "Gerontissa" is the Greek, and often general Orthodox, equivalent for the English "abbess," designating the superior of an Orthodox monastery.

2. This hymn declares the following: "When the women disciples of the Lord learned from the angel the joyous message of Your Resurrection, they cast away the ancestral curse, and boasted to the apostles: 'Death is overthrown! Christ our God is risen, granting the world great mercy!'"

3. *Lex orandi est lex credendi* means that what we believe is reflected in the way we worship.

4. I am again capitalizing this word with the intention of focusing our attention on God as the "Presence" par excellence. This Presence was experienced by Israel when God's glory was *dwelling* among them in the wilderness. "Dwelling" is the word that describes the divine action in the biblical narrative of Exodus, and I have italicized it in several places for emphasis.

5. "Truth" capitalized refers to Christ, while "truth," lowercase, is a glimpse into the revealed Truth of Christ.

6. The word "doxology" does not refer solely to the preliturgical hymn, but to the general attitude of prayer the angels and the saints have before God—an attitude that we are called to emulate.

7. The mountain I have in mind here is Mount Tabor and the experience of God's glory that the apostles witnessed during the Transfiguration of Jesus Christ on that mount. Coming to church and preparing through the whole preceding week to be part of this unique event—the Divine Liturgy—is similar to preparing for mountain climbing.

8. The Holy Eucharist is the sacrament par excellence, in which the bread and the wine are transformed through the Presence of the Holy Spirit into the very Body and Blood of Jesus Christ. This real encounter with Jesus Christ that takes place within the Eucharist is for the "benefit of our souls and body, for the remission of sins, and for life everlasting," as the liturgical prayer before receiving the Holy Gifts affirms. The expres-

sion "incarnate Glory" stands for Christ, and can be encountered in many liturgical hymns because it reminds us that the Son of God has been the One present at all times, during both the Old and the New Covenants, in the history of salvation.

9. It is quite significant the way God reveals His holy name to Israel: "He Who Is," or "I Am Who I Am" (Exod 3:13–14). Such a revelation is not addressed in the Bible only to the *former* Israel (of that time), but to the *now* or *new* Israel, which is the Church.

10. Psalm 93:1, "The Lord is the God of vengeance; the God of vengeance declares Himself *boldly.*" Translation from *The Orthodox Study Bible* (Nashville, TN: Thomas Nelson, 2008), 744, emphasis mine.

11. The word "Light" requires capitalization because it stands for Christ, who is the Light of this world.

12. From the Matins of the fifth Sunday of Lent, in *The Lenten Triodion*, trans. Mother Mary and Kallistos Ware (South Canaan, PA: St. Tikhon's Seminary Press, 2002), 460.

13. Ethiopian Enoch 63:1ff.

14. *Lenten Triodion*, 460.

15. Annick de Souzenelle, *L'Égypte intérieure ou les dix plaies de l'âme* (Paris: Albin Michel, 1997).

16. YHWH is also known as the "tetragrammaton," and I prefer it to the word "God," which has been so abused in our language.

17. "*Askesis*" refers to the Christian practice through which one has the willingness to purify one's being from destructive passions (a passion is a repeated and uncured sin). The practice involves sustained, if not continuous, prayer and fasting. It is not relegated to only cave or desert dwellers; it is also for the modern person living a life "in the world." More than a practice, it is a determination to respond to God's love through a personal effort to conquer one's ego.

18. Mother Gavrilia, *The Ascetic of Love*, trans. Helen Anthony, 2nd ed. (Athens: Eptalofos, 1999), 222.

19. Ibid., 276.

20. *Lenten Triodion*, 447–48.

21. The "Logos," or "Word of God," is another biblical name for Christ, the Son of God.

22. *Lenten Triodion*, 452.

23. Ibid., 455.

24. Ibid., 456.

25. Ibid., 455.

26. Saints are often described in the hymns as pillars of fire. This is not just a metaphor, but an accurate description of their spiritual transformation through their struggle to emulate Christ, who was prefigured by the pillar of fire guiding Israel in the desert.

27. This becomes obvious through iconography in which the ascetics have covered their bodies with a minimum of clothes. Here I have in mind St. John the Baptist and St. Mary of Egypt, to name only two.

28. I would say that this is not an insignificant detail from the lives of the saints. The loss of the material garment is in anticipation of the forthcoming robes of glory. "As many as have been baptized into Christ have put on Christ, Alleluia!" (cf. Gal 3:27) is a hymn sung at baptisms in the Orthodox Church. Also, we need to have in mind the Syriac tradition according to which, at His baptism in the Jordan, Christ deposited robes of glory (the robes Adam and Eve possessed before their Fall) into the baptismal waters so that those who will receive His baptism will put on these robes of glory.

29. A dispassionate life is the life lived by those who put God first, especially when it comes to exercising their own wills.

30. Archimandrite Zacharias, *The Enlargement of the Heart: "Be ye also enlarged" (2 Corinthians 6:13) in the Theology of Saint Silouan the Athonite and Elder Sophrony of Essex*, ed. Christopher Veniamin (South Canaan, PA: Mount Thabor Publishing, 2006), 37.

31. Archimandrite Sophrony (Sakharov), *Saint Silouan the Athonite*, trans. Rosemary Edmonds, 274, in *Archimandrite Zacharias, Enlargement of the Heart*, 37.

32. "Theotokos" was the name given to Mary at the Fourth Ecumenical Council, in Ephesus, and it indicates that Jesus Christ, the Child born of her, is both God and man. In other words, the title "Mother of God" specifically does not exclude Jesus' human nature.

33. This icon is called *"Platitera ton ouranon,"* or "more spacious than the heavens."

34. One might recall here the first encounter between St. Mary of Egypt and Abba Zossimas in the *Life* of St. Mary of Egypt, when, due to the lightness of her body, she was not touching the earth.

35. See Archimandrite Zacharias, *Enlargement of the Heart*, 41.

36. Archimandrite Vasileios, *Hymn of Entry: Liturgy and Life in the Orthodox Church* (Crestwood, NY: St. Vladimir's Seminary Press, 1984), 72.

37. "Iconically" refers to the mode of representing a (divine) reality when we do not have direct access to it through our senses.

38. Christ was always wearing His luminous garments, but the only time that the apostles could see them was on Mount Tabor, during His Transfiguration.

39. "Natural" here does not refer to what God has given to humanity through creation, but to the shame that humanity inherited after the sin of Adam and Eve.

40. Exod 3:6; 1 Kings 19:13; Isa 6:2.

41. In the Jewish Bible, covering of the face or of the head means mourning (2 Sam 15:30) or shame (Jer 14:3–4). By contrast, uncovering of the face or

head means the absence of shame or the end of mourning, but also more than that. As we read in the Prophet Isaiah, 25:7–8, and in St. Paul's letter to the community in Corinth (1 Cor 15:55; cf. Rev 7:17; 21:4), God will remove the veil at the end of the time. See W. C. van Unnik, "The Semitic Background of Parrhesia in the New Testament," in *Sparsa Collecta: The Collected Essays of W. C. van Unnik*, pt. 2 (Leiden, Netherlands: Brill, 1980), 290–306.

42. *The Divine Liturgy of Our Father among the Saints John Chrysostom* (Oxford: Oxford University Press, 1995), 55.

43. The word "Pearl" is commonly used among the early monks of Syria, Mesopotamia, and Persia when referring to Christ. For example, Isaac of Nineveh, a seventh-century monk, compared the wise monk, who "will go naked through the desert places to find the Pearl, Jesus Christ himself," with a diver who "plunges naked into the sea to find a pearl" (quoted in *The Wisdom of the Pearlers: An Anthology of Syriac Christian Mysticism*, trans. Brian E. Colless [Kalamazoo, MI: Cistercian Publications, 2008], 1).

REFLECTION AND DISCUSSION QUESTIONS

1. Describe what came to mind for you in the introduction about "silence and listening."

2. Inspired by the words of the gerontissa, the author states: "We deprive ourselves of the possibility for living encounter whenever we drown ourselves in empty chatter, all the while calling it prayer!" Consider and discuss what this may mean for us in our context today.

3. We are informed about the ancient theological principle of *lex orandi est lex credendi*, which tells us that the words of the liturgical services "become tools, vehicles, or channels . . . that are meant to reveal . . . the Presence of God."
    a. Reflect and discuss how the "typical" Christian of today may be approaching the words of the liturgical service.
    b. Reflect and discuss how this teaching affirms or challenges your present practice.

4. The author takes issue with those who approach the Word of God in an imbalanced manner through "convoluted philosophical or linguistic concepts" and "futile modern hermeneutics and vain maneuvers of construction and deconstruction" as opposed to a "living exchange" between us (as members of the Church) and the living God. Have you ever noticed something like this? What does this mean for you? Discuss this.

5. "Silence is the *something* or *somebody* by which God is surrounded." The author goes on to state that "biblical language is quite explicit in describing God's radiant epiphany; Psalm 93, for example, uses a Greek word, *parrhesia*, which in Hebrew means 'to shine forth,' 'to appear in brightness.' This luminosity, or inaccessible light . . . does not belong to this world, that is, to the creation. It is divine, and thus uncreated." The author later states, "We are called to become bearers of this same Light." This ancient Christian perspective may sound new or foreign to a number of readers. How does this teaching invite, challenge, or encourage your prayer and relationship with God? Discuss this.

6. St. Mary of Egypt is used as an example of an ascetic who, while living in darkness, was led to the Light of Christ through "the silence of the wilderness."
   a. Discuss what this may mean.
   b. How does this impact you?
   c. Are there contexts today in which "the silence of the wilderness" could be emerging in new ways?

7. Most people today may think of acquiring an "enlarged heart" as a problematic medical condition. In this chapter, however, the author bears witness to the spiritual heart of the person growing in the holiness of God. The purpose of this very different kind of "enlarged heart" is "for bearing 'the fullness of love for Christ.' Such an enlarged heart does not have the smallest room for self because it embraces the whole creation in prayer."
   a. Are there any people you may know personally or have heard about that personify this kind of change in some manner? Discuss this.
   b. What may be some of the blockages or challenges our hearts may be bearing that impede this type of growth? Consider and discuss this as you are able.

8. Rather than entreating God out of shame, the author states that we are called to "'stand before You [that is, God] without blemish, with a pure heart and "with uncovered face" [cf. 2 Cor 3:15–18].'"
   a. Review this section and discuss this.
   b. Have you noticed practices today that may not coincide so well with this teaching?
   c. How does this relate with the "boldness" and "nakedness" of the saints to which we are all called, as discussed in this section?

Healing the Unspeakable: The Life of St. Mary of Egypt

Kyriaki Karidoyanes FitzGerald

*T*he power of Your Cross, O Christ, has worked wonders,
for even the woman who was once a harlot
chose to follow the ascetic way.
Casting aside her weakness, bravely she opposed the devil;
and having gained the prize of victory,
she now intercedes for our souls.[1]

INTRODUCTION

St. Mary of Egypt is remembered annually by Eastern Orthodox Christians on the fifth Sunday of Great Lent. It is no coincidence that the Orthodox liturgical calendar brings her life into particular focus during this special season. As we prepare for celebrating the Lord's Resurrection at Pascha (Easter), we are encouraged to reflect more deeply upon our relationship with God, neighbor, our own selves, and creation in order to bring our lives more in line with the gospel and the will of God for us.

Her life story, in particular, is an invitation for repentance and healing because she survived a profoundly difficult life. Many practicing Christians would be scandalized to know that this St. Mary led a life of

Kyriaki Karidoyanes FitzGerald, MDiv, PhD, serves as Adjunct Professor of Theology at Holy Cross Greek Orthodox School of Theology. She represents the Ecumenical Patriarchate at theological meetings, and she founded (along with Clara Nickolson, of blessed memory) St. Catherine's Vision. Dr. FitzGerald is also a licensed psychologist, pastoral counselor, author, and lecturer. She maintains a private practice in Sandwich, Massachusetts, and serves on the Board of St. Catherine's Vision.

extreme debauchery, aggressively selling her services as a prostitute for many years. Some would even use the old movie designation of "X-rated" to describe her and her exploits. She was X-rated due to her sexual practices. She was X-rated due to her willful, callous connection with others. And she was X-rated due to the way others in return had dehumanized her in their minds and hearts.

Because of these extreme and perilous dimensions of her life, more than one sermon about her over the years has left me feeling uneasy, even cold, because of the perspective of the speaker. All too often, there seemed to be more of a titillating focus on Mary's early life than appreciation for the arduous journey of a human person starting from virtually unspeakable circumstances. There seemed to be little recognition that as a result of experiencing profound forgiveness, healing, and transformation, St. Mary of Egypt became an emissary of God, serving as a provocative witness to His endless mercy, love, and joy for others.

The Tradition of the Church records her life in a disturbing and graphic manner. My portrayal in this chapter is perhaps less graphic than what has been written in some liturgical and historical texts.[2] St. Mary of Egypt was restored to health from a chaotic and loveless existence that could be called a living death; furthermore, she was changed in ways that many of us today would never even imagine.

Over the course of many years, the study of the life of St. Mary of Egypt was one to which I would return. With each attempt to engage her life, I found that cumulative experience from the private, vocational, and professional dimensions of my life all contributed to obtaining a richer appreciation, as well as sparking new questions. Partly because of things that affected my life, her story became more compelling every time I would "visit" with her in the presence of God during the past twenty years.

In the last few decades, more than any other time in living memory, science has begun to scrutinize the ways that people are impacted by rejection, abuse, and trauma, in the family and elsewhere. I have had the privilege to study and receive clinical training regarding these issues. I have also enjoyed the honor of working closely with a number of great and inspiring people who have survived various types of abandonment, maltreatment, and trauma. The images of abuse survival in my depiction of St. Mary's early life are expressed truthfully, yet conservatively. In other words, whatever really happened to her that led her to a life of such gross abasement of self and others was probably worse than the circumstances described in this chapter.

The account I am about to share is written as if Mary entered my office, sat down before me, and began to speak. I find myself seeking the mercy and help of the Lord, as well as asking for the saint's direction and entreating you, the reader, for your patience and forgiveness as I dare to share her story with you in the first person.

✛ PART ONE ✛

My name is Mary. I lived during the fifth century and was born not too far from the illustrious city of Alexandria in Egypt. My early life is not much to write about. In fact, there is not much about my childhood in surviving historical documents. But what I can tell you is that my family life was far from happy. When I grew up I ran away from home and headed straight for the great city, so that I could begin building a better life for myself. I was twelve years old.

You may wonder, "What would cause a twelve-year-old child of that era to run away from home?" By looking into the next phase of my life, you may obtain some insight into this. You will notice that at twelve, I ran toward a life of squalor, depravity, and gross sexual misconduct. For the next seventeen years, I was a prostitute. I sold my body indiscriminately and as often as I could, to anyone who interested me. I was particularly famous for my sarcastic wit and aggressive exploits in tracking down my patrons. I mocked them mercilessly, and I sometimes even stalked them down, not unlike wild game. I remember, especially, the sour disgust and contempt I felt toward them, even as I desperately chased after their caresses. These extremes did not faze me. Deep within me I felt nothing. I felt dead.

For the sake of decorum, I will not divulge too many details about how abysmal my life became. Bear in mind, however, that some Church historians have been honest enough to record that I would have performed my sexual favors "on the house," so to speak—gratis, nada, free of charge! There were times when I performed these acts simply for the thrill. Yes, these Church historians were correct in their portrayal.

Please consider how this could be so, as my biographers in centuries past did not. My behavior is not unusual for children who grow up in an atmosphere of overwhelming, ongoing unreliability. From my earliest days, there was a dearth of authentic human connection and safety to direct my path. I lived in an environment where inconsistencies and abuse abounded, including sexual abuse. Rather than being tenderly guided and cherished by emotionally healthy parents, I was progressively neglected and devalued. Rather than being seen as a beloved daughter of God, I became invisible. I was treated like an object, a worthless commodity. I was used to satisfy my pitiful father's whims and business dealings.

Many survivors of abuse, including sexual abuse, do not grow up to become abusers of others, as I did. In fact, many persons experience healing and transcend very difficult childhood histories, leading to wonderful and fruitful lives, praise God! Nevertheless, we must bear in mind that when certain powerful, life-effacing circumstances are right, it is not uncommon for people to lash out in the only way they know how: targeting themselves and others. This is partially because most of the abuse they survive occurs in secret. Acts of neglect and abandonment, lack of concern for safety, weak interpersonal connections demonstrating a failure of trustworthy, mutual love, even psychological intimidation and oppression, happen unseen. The casual observer is usually oblivious to this powerful "anti-gospel" (or *kakovagelion*, in Greek) reigning within the life of the family. Perpetrators, knowingly or not, are conveying stunning contempt for the mystery of the human person, created in the "image and likeness of God."

When the needed healing does not occur, children may seek restitution for their indescribable loss by acting out the abuse anew in their adult lives. This may be their only way to experience some form of connection, even if "connecting" means passing on to others what was done to them in the past. Acting out in this manner was the only way I felt *alive* . . . and home is where it all started.

After I left home, I had no family, no friends, and no hope. It did not even dawn on me that I needed to save for the future, let alone invest my money in order to prepare for it. I just barely subsisted by using my street smarts and whatever my body could get for me. In a deep sense I was continuing the same pattern of abuse perpetrated against me. I was only fooling myself in thinking that at least I was free finally, living on "*my* terms."

This extreme manner of trying to feel alive served me poorly and was only a temporary means of relief. Like one who misuses a medication or alcohol to numb pain, I would soon enough wake up and return to my senses, finding myself back in the same cold, empty and flat existence called "my life." Yes, mine is an extreme yet genuine example of someone running away from home in search of the "geographical cure." I was too fragile and afraid to ask the difficult, brutally honest questions, the questions inviting me to examine what really went wrong in my life. For many of these later years, I may have helped contribute to my own problems. This is because wherever I went, I still had to face myself.

After about seventeen years of living this way, my routine had begun to feel *very* old. Like an alcoholic or a drug or sex addict who knows he or she can no longer continue in the same way, I was desperate for a change, only there was none in sight. I did not even have the language or the thought forms in my mind to conceptualize the possibility that things could be different. All I knew was that I was growing increasingly uncomfortable living in my own skin and I could no longer bear it. But there was no way I could admit this to myself. So, I continued in my familiar, miserable way of living.

During this time, I caught myself paying attention to a growing group of people in the illustrious city of Alexandria. They seemed to treat each other and their neighbors differently from the way others did. They were called "Christians." Even while on the job, I managed to study them from afar for some time. They behaved with unusual humility and kindness, addressing each other often as "brother" or "sister," "mother" or "father," when they were not even related! I found this very odd, because the few blood relatives I knew never treated anyone with such attention and gentleness.

These Christians were consistent, too! They did not employ the "double-speak" so easily mouthed by the movers and shakers of my society. Their "yes" was "yes" and their "no" truly was "no." They were even merciful to strangers. Although I had trapped numerous weaker members of their fellowship in my bed, there were still many among them I could not ensnare, and I never could quite figure out why. Some of these people, even knowing who I was, treated me kindly. This really confused me.

Yes, by now I was "damaged goods" in the extreme. Even in today's better circumstances, persons like me often do not live to a very old age. Beginning in childhood, the inner ravages of mistreatment and neglect perpetrated on the soul and body may extract their toll in numerous ways. These extreme and painful circumstances of childhood are often at the root of serious physical illnesses, which may develop later on in adult life. This sad fact, especially in recent years, has been repeatedly documented through the explosion of clinical research examining the effects of trauma, abandonment, and abuse.

My life was certainly a living death. I could not grow as a person because I was never engaged consistently with love by another human being. I could not grow in the "image and likeness of God" in which I was created because no one was there to convey the love of the living God to me. Even now, to say this to you causes me to twinge in pain. God abhors the abuse of all His children!

Our loving God profoundly understands that many of these, His beautiful creations from desperate backgrounds, could not come to know Him during their earthly lives. My story is all the more incredible, for I certainly "beat the odds" for children who find themselves in my kind of situation. But there was much suffering before the story reached its conclusion. The unbearably heavy boredom of my bleak and meaningless life led me to follow, even stalk, Christians more closely . . . and, oh my, I am now embarrassed to say, I really did begin to annoy them.

One day, as I was amusing myself by watching from afar the movements of a group of Christian men from Egypt and Libya, I realized they were preparing to board a ship heading for Jerusalem to celebrate the solemn feast day of the Exaltation of the Holy Cross. Brazen as I was, I wanted to go as well, thinking that any change would be an entertaining distraction. Surely, there would be plenty of customers on board and in the city of Jerusalem, once the ship arrived there.

Sarcastic and persistent, I harassed the poor fellows so much that they finally snuck me on board. On the ship I continued my old practices. In fact, I was virtually insatiable. I enticed, seduced, even coerced the unwilling . . . as many as I could, to lie with me. A desperate gnawing, a hunger that some would even call insane, exploded deep within me. I would do anything not to face it.

More than ever before, I gave my body away. But the more I tried to give myself away through each sexual exploit, the emptier and more dead I felt afterward. No matter how much I tried to distract myself from the blight of my existence, it seemed to return to me with compounded interest. And so I kept performing the only "work" I ever knew at this literally unstoppable pace.

I can only attribute the fact that God did not deal with me then to His ineffable mercy and loving-kindness. He knew everything I was feeling and thinking. He knew, especially, how utterly void and dead I felt inside. I learned only later that sometimes, before a person "bottoms out" preceding a crisis that leads to healing from a life of sin, addiction, and/or compulsive behaviors, that person's behavior may change for the worse—sometimes, much worse[3]—before it becomes better. This was true, at least, for me. That God was able to love me even during this, the lowest point in my life, still overwhelms me and brings me to tears. I was hardened, dead, and extremely cynical. At age twenty-nine, I was old and at the very end of my game.

Finally we reached Jerusalem. I was able to follow the crowds as they prepared for the liturgical celebration. Even then, I was actively engaged in the only profession I ever knew, watching from a distance as the ecclesial events progressed, while seeking the amorous affections and downfall of my next client.

I share these details with you not so much to shock you, but to show you how any person, no matter how internally lifeless he or she may be, as I was, can be brought to an encounter with the loving God Himself. Please bear this in mind.

The Lord Jesus came to the world proclaiming that the love of God is already with us, as He inaugurated the Kingdom through His Person. All God asks of us is to repent. Repentance, as I am sure you already know, refers to the Greek word *metanoia*. This word means a radical change of mind and heart; it is a transformation of the human person's *nous*. And although *nous* is usually translated from biblical Greek as "mind" or "intelligence," its fullest meaning points to its Semitic roots. These roots refer to the depth of our souls, the place of "the mind in the heart," which lies at the foundation of our being. It is in this place that what we value most deeply and who we are come together, for "where your treasure is, there your heart lies also" (Matt 6:21). A number of holy lovers of God (that is, saints) have even sometimes identified the *nous* with the "heart" or "core" of a person.[4]

From the secret recesses of our depths, God calls us to turn to Him, as He is our Source and the Author of life. The more we turn away from the Truth, from the loving God, the more we throw ourselves into our own self-absorbed darkness. And without this true Light, left to our own devices, we so easily mistake our darkness for light (cf. Matt 6:23). This is precisely what happened to me. The "light" and "life" I was chasing through all of my existence was actually my own finite, ego-based, self-absorbed, inner darkness. It was a living death, and I didn't even know it.

Even at this point in my story, I was brazenly managing my craft, but somehow I still kept following the pilgrims to the courtyard of the cathedral, and from there I watched. At daybreak I saw throngs of pilgrims entering the cathedral to venerate a portion of our Lord's Holy Cross that had been brought out for that special day. Intrigued, I blended into the middle of the crowd so that I could enter and see what was taking place. But as I reached the threshold of the entryway, I was thrown back. Not even thinking twice about it, I tried a second time . . . a third time . . . even a fourth time. Each time I struggled to sneak into the church, it felt as if powerful sentries would block my way. The force was so strong that I felt bruised and beaten up. For quite some time I was utterly broken and transfixed.

Suddenly, in a moment of clarity, I realized that in no way was I pure enough to enter this gateway. Yes, by purity I do mean my sinfulness, my profoundly hardened, cynical existence, and the way I treated my life and my body, as well as the lives and bodies of many others: like garbage. But I mean far more here.

I am pointing to the Greek word "*parthenia*," which is often translated into English as "virginity." "*Parthenia*" and "virginity" do indicate an unconditional physical abstinence from sexual relations. But "*parthenia*" refers first of all to our *purity of heart in the presence of God*. This is a foundation of radical integrity, and it is unconditional; it takes hold from the inside out. This integrity refers to our personal unconditional surrender, from the very depths of our being, to the life and love of the living God. Being "pure" in this way grounds us in Reality, which is our abiding in the presence of the living God of absolute love. This is truly how Christians traditionally experience and approach reality.[5]

And my life was *so far* from this! I realized all of this as I was standing there, transfixed at the threshold of the church. I had hit bottom. I recognized the fact that I was an utter counterfeit in the way I lived my life. It was not based in Reality. I had become so accustomed to turning my face away from Truth that I needed help from beyond me just to become honest with myself. I needed help from beyond my experience of the world in order to face the depths of despair in which I had been living all these years. And help did finally come.

There, in that instant, I noticed the beautiful icon of our Lady, Mary, the Mother of our Lord and God. From the bits and pieces of stories I had managed to glean during the previous months, I knew who she was. She was so beautiful! As I gazed upon her, it seemed that I felt for the very first time in my life the indescribable, sweet purity of a Mother's love.

She seemed to hold me there—yes, even cradle me—in the depths of her loving gaze. I felt as if she could see right through me. The entire area between us was flooded with Light beyond description. The crowds of pilgrims seemed to fall far away into the background. It was as if only she and I were there together. This Light penetrated my own being and somehow, with an ability that did not originate from me, I drank this in. I was not unlike a famished baby nursing, gratefully, with adult tears in her eyes, at her Mother's breast. Please believe me, my brothers and sisters, that I had never, ever experienced a Mother's unconditional love until then.

I do not know how much time passed. No words were exchanged. Only ineffable relief and love were communicated. Finally, when it seemed that I had fed enough on this inexpressible, life-giving sweetness, I began to come to my senses for the very first time.

At that point, I cried out to her, "Help me, beloved Mother. I am unworthy of entering this sacred place. Only now do I realize why I have not been able to enter. Uphold me, embrace me and help me! Help me to enter, and I will do whatever you instruct me to do. I desire True Life. I will listen and obey you, O Beautiful Mother of our God, with a grateful and happy heart even as the very least of your children."

A weight of unspeakable proportions had been lifted from me. The dark and ominous cloud of doom evaporated in that very moment. Because of this Mother's love, I was no longer alone, trapped, or, rather, frozen in the chaotic darkness of my own finitude, cut off from true connection with others, as well as from the loving, thrice-holy God Himself.

This cleansing and healing offered me relief and joy. And this joy spawned a new, deep inner urgency to proceed more deeply into the church so that I, too, might venerate our Lord's Precious and Holy Cross. This newborn connection with our Beautiful Mother made my initial baby steps toward Christ seem effortless. Even though the edifice was noisy and crowded, I walked peacefully. In a way that cannot be described, it felt as if I was being physically drawn in by Love, and that I was finally home. Do not underestimate what the power and love of God can do for the healing and transformation of human souls!

At this point, not unlike the many throngs of pious pilgrims, I, too, was permitted the gift of falling down in utter thanksgiving and joy, to pray before the Cross of her Son and our Lord. And when I did, in that one instant, I was ambushed—again—by the indefinable divine sweetness! Dazed and overwhelmed, this time I was caught up in the sublime mystery of Life and Love eternal, bestowed upon all of fallen creation through this piece of Wood. Heaven and earth would never be the same, and neither would I.

I worshipped our loving Lord at the foot of His Precious Cross for the first time that day. With all of my heart, I did not want this to end. Turning to her, I opened my heart to my and our loving Mother and Intercessor. In that moment, I heard with my spirit and ears: "If you cross over the Jordan, you will find rest."

Immediately, I perceived what this meant. I left the church then, at about 9:00 a.m. Out of the blue, in the courtyard a kind stranger appeared and out of pity gave me three small coins, with which I bought three loaves of bread. This was a surprise blessing from God for my journey! With these three loaves under my arm, I set off on my way, and by sunset I had arrived at the Church of St. John the Baptist by the Jordan River. It was there that I was baptized and received the sacrament of Holy Communion for the first time. In retrospect, I recognize that at this moment, the first half of my life's journey had been fulfilled.

On the next day, I passed to the other side of the Jordan, and there I prayed again to our Beautiful Mother and Intercessor. I asked, I implored her to direct me to go wherever it pleased her Son, and our life-giving God, to send me. And indeed, I was led on a very long journey through the desert, where eventually I came to a small cave that would be my cell for the next forty-seven years.

The Truth urges me on to tell you two more things about my life. First of all, this next very long period of my life became my honeymoon, so to speak, with Christ. I came to know Him and depend upon Him in the daily spiritual and physical struggles of the desert. By getting to know Him, I also came to become more fully the person God had intended me to be.

But just as in any marital honeymoon, difficulties arose. These difficulties were not the fault of my Beloved and Divine Bridegroom, but of fallen, earthbound, and unworthy me. The battle of getting to know myself, growing in the manner God intended, was coming.

Yes, the floodgates of love and paradise had been opened to me. Nevertheless, my accepting and trusting the ever-present Light, Love, and Person of our Lord in the unknown depths and secret recesses of my soul was still a work in progress. Gently, ever so gently, through the extremes of Jordanian sun and cold, He healed the damage caused by a lifetime of sin, despair, and abuse. Of course, this took much time and effort on my part. Since the Church's foundation many have received this divine gift of quiet struggle and ongoing healing. It is a gift based on the fact that *God loves us first.* He is always the one who reaches out to us, even if it seems to us on our finite human level that we are the ones initiating the contact.

Once we experience the gift of this loving connection, we also receive a second gift of sorts. After we taste the refreshment of our Lord's sweetness, we begin to obtain a greater sense of how altogether unprepared we are for the visitation of the all-loving God. We notice more and more our own inner cobwebs, which were invisible to us before because of the lack of Light. And so in the following years, over and over again, I had the privilege of facing all of the demons that diverted and prevented my heart, soul, and mind from experiencing the love of the living God—in other words, from experiencing Reality. This inner hardness had also kept me from discovering my true identity as a unique and cherished child of God.

The Church, guided by the Holy Spirit, graciously has refrained from recording what these specific personal demons, difficulties, and challenges were, as a way to protect my privacy. But the general categories have been recorded, and even these indicate that they were "legion." Some of them spewed loathsome, self-condemning, and life-effacing messages toward me, toward others, and sometimes toward both. These demons very successfully distracted me from seeking the "one thing necessary" (Luke 10:42) and helped deaden me in many ways. During those early days of my lackluster life, I had tried to feel alive and sometimes even thought I was alive, but I truly did not know what life was, until Life tackled me.

Cradled in the arms of the living God of love, a new journey began both in my heart and in the safe confines of the Jordanian desert. What a surprise! Slowly, ever so slowly, I was changing as a result of His tender loving-kindness. This was almost as marvelous a discovery as the initial encounter with God Himself—namely, to realize with every fiber of my being that I, too, unworthy as I was, had been created for the love of the living God, by this same loving God whose love saturates and contains all of creation.

✚ PART TWO ✚

At this point, brothers and sisters, I am compelled to go on with my story. I will now go out on a limb with you and reveal something that it was not my original intention to share. Circumstances beyond my control have obliged me to reveal this part of the story. Some may say that I have saved the best, or most amazing witness, for last.

I lived a solitary life of prayer in the desert all of those forty-seven years. Some who have met me before you have wondered and asked how the Church ever came to know about my life. This is a good question. Surely, my life would never have become known if it was not God's pleasure to reveal it to you. But this next part of the story teaches us much about faith, courage, and integrity, though not my own.

Forty-six years into my honeymoon with Christ, I was "found," or "discovered," so to speak, by the holy presbyter-monk Zossimas. He also became my friend, pastor, and confessor. It is he who heard me confess my life story, recorded it, and eventually shared it with the world, reflecting God's pleasure. I would like to tell you more about him now, and will try to do so as if I were a third person, an observer.

Before he met me, Fr. Zossimas had been serving as the abbot and spiritual father of a large monastic community for men in Palestine. At the opposite end of life experience when compared to mine, he grew up in safety and in the bosom of the Church. From the time he was a toddler, he was raised in the same Christian monastery. This reflects an ancient Christian custom, dating back to the early Church, of dedicating at least one child in a Christian family to monastic and/or ordained service in the Church. This custom is still practiced in parts of the ancient Orthodox Christian world even now, particularly in the Middle East, Africa, and many parts of Greece.

From the very beginning of his life in the monastery, Zossimas demonstrated great love for monastic life and excelled quickly in every known ascetic discipline. As he grew into adulthood, through no effort of self-promotion, he earned a reputation as the "perfect" monk. He had become so well respected for his rigorous discipline and ability to offend no one that monks from his own community, as well as others living at a distance, sought his spiritual direction.

At the heart of his discipline was his fervent desire to achieve "purity of heart." This is a response to the Lord's teaching found in the Beatitudes: "Blessed are the pure in heart, for they shall see God" (Matt 5:8). As I mentioned earlier, "purity of heart" refers to a kind of unconditional integrity in our relationship with God. It is the foundation of holiness. Through "purity of heart" our self-centeredness and sins no longer cloud our vision, allowing us to perceive and respond in truth to God. This seems, and indeed is, impossible for human beings to achieve, but as Christians we believe that "all things are possible with God" (Matt 19:26; Mark 10:27).

Throughout the Christianized Roman Empire (also known as the Byzantine Empire), numerous monasteries had been established in the larger cities. As early as the fifth century, being abbot of a large monastic community was a highly respected ecclesial vocation. By the time Zossimas was in his mid-fifties, he had already been serving within his monastery as abbot and spiritual father for many years. He was "at the top of his game." He accepted his responsibilities without complaint, aware and appreciative of the many gifts God had given him, and respected the confidences of his fellow monks. But he was also aware that, according to everything he knew, he had achieved all there was to achieve in the monastic life.

As this awareness grew, he started to feel a kind of spiritual uneasiness, even psychological anxiety. As much as he profoundly loved his spiritual sons and brothers in the monastery, he began to be assailed by disturbing thoughts and feelings, wondering, in effect, "Is this all that faithful discipline brings?" or "Is this everything?"

In time he came to appreciate that these were important questions; the disturbing concerns were the product of a growing relationship with God. As he considered them, he realized that even though he was a spiritual father, he, too, needed spiritual direction. He, too, needed the guidance of someone more spiritually mature.

He began to ask more probing and courageous self-searching questions: "Is there anyone out there who can help me?" "Is there anyone who could serve as my spiritual guide and teacher, and as intercessor to God on my behalf?" "How do I go about searching for this person?" He began to feel some hope when the thought occurred to him that the loving God was near and always ready to help. So he began more earnestly to pray and fast about this, asking God to help him discern what to do next.

During prayer, as he was yet again deeply considering what to do next, he saw a man standing before him who told him, "Indeed, Zossimas, you have gone far in your monastic effort, but your life here has taken you as far as it can. If you truly desire to know more, to know God Himself, you must learn from the example set by Abraham. Leave the comfort and familiarity of your father's house and seek God in foreign terrain. Go to the monastery that is located near the Jordan River."[6]

This was a difficult directive for Zossimas to hear, as he had never left his monastery before. Nevertheless, he left immediately for the River Jordan and eventually found the monastery, even though it was in such an obscure location that most monks in the region did not know about it. Truly, his being able to find this community reflects the desire of God for his growth and salvation.

Zossimas was a bit of an enigma to the abbot and the brothers there. They realized that he was no foreigner to the spiritual life, yet he refused to identify himself to them fully. To the abbot he said, "I have heard about your monastery, that your community's life helps one grow in an intimate relationship with Christ our God. I wish to seek our Lord here if you will give your blessing, Father." The wise abbot reminded Zossimas that it is God who heals and restores our relationship with Him, and welcomed him into the brotherhood, though he still had not fully disclosed who he was.

Zossimas soon came to admire the level of spiritual experience and discipline of his new brothers. Above all things they sought to know and grow in Christ. For the first time in what seemed a very long time, Zossimas was happy. Released from the constrictions of his previous responsibilities, he found it an honor and joy to be in the company of such spiritually mature persons, all seeking together the "one thing necessary." He certainly had nothing new to teach them. He was edified by their example and inspired to strive all the more earnestly to know God.

There was one aspect of the monastery's discipline with which Zossimas was unfamiliar. This was their most important spiritual rule. On the Sunday that initiates Great Lent, all of the brothers would gather together after the celebration of the Liturgy. They ate one last simple meal, privately collected whatever provisions they each deemed necessary, and gave each other a farewell embrace. Then, each of them crossed the Jordan River, heading for the desert, in order to begin his personal Lenten vigil. At the heart of this rule was a rigorous silence. They separated from one another during this time as a way to safeguard the privacy of every brother's prayer and fasting discipline. They did not want to be a source of comparison, scandal, or temptation to each other.

Except for one or two priest-monks who stayed behind to conduct services, the monks remained in the desert, fasting and praying, and returned six weeks later to celebrate together the feast of Palm Sunday. Zossimas enthusiastically looked forward to following this discipline. And as he set out on this arduous desert journey, he noticed that the desire to receive a blessing from a holy person of God returned to him, stronger than ever before. A deep longing originating from the depths of his soul urged him to travel further and further, deeper and deeper, into the desert.

"Perhaps now," he thought, "God will bless me with meeting the spiritual father from whom I have so long desired to receive a blessing." He felt an almost palpable expectation that this beloved person was close at hand, somehow.

For twenty days he prayed and walked. During his journey he saw no one, not an animal or a bird or even the shadow of one. This absence of encounters fed his strange sense of joyful, palpable expectation, a feeling that never left him. Then at about noon on the twentieth day, facing east and nearing the end of his noonday prayers, he thought he saw with his peripheral vision the outline or shadow of a human being darting about among the large boulders. Fearing that this could be some kind of malevolent spirit, he made the sign of the cross and finished his prayers.

His prayers completed, he looked back and realized that he did see something, or, rather, someone. It was an old woman, with skin scorched black by the sun, and short, wooly white hair. She was completely and utterly naked. Zossimas leaped for joy at the sight of her! Yes, I am referring to myself here. It is awkward speaking to you about myself in the third person. But, who else but the loving God could direct a person to the very relationship he or she needed in the middle of nowhere? Forgetting his age and exhaustion, Zossimas began to chase me. "Please, stop, let me meet you!" he shouted. "Grant me, an old man, a prayer and a blessing for the sake of God, who despises no one!" he cried.[7] But despite his tears and imploring, I kept eluding him. At this point in our stories, both figuratively and literally, I was vulnerable and exposed in new ways!

After what turned out to be a long chase in the midday desert sun, Zossimas could go no further. He was unable to run any more, and stopped in what seemed to be the middle of a dry riverbed. I raced up an embankment and hid behind a large rock. Zossimas burst into tears, grieving over this lost opportunity. The sounds of his weeping broke my heart.

As he wept, I could not bear watching him in pain, so I called out to him, "Father Zossimas, please forgive me, as I am a sinful woman, naked and unable to face you for reasons of decency. Grant, I beg you, the prayer of this sinful woman and toss me your outer cloak, so that I may cover my weakness and turn to you and receive your blessing."[8]

Zossimas seemed to tremble as he heard my voice. God granted him the ability to sense that I knew who he was. Through the eyes of our tender-hearted God, I saw *him*. He realized that this could only have been revealed through the Holy Spirit. He finally found the humble servant of God for whom he had been waiting all this time.

Taking off his faded, tattered cloak, he tossed it over to me and turned his back. A minute later I approached him and asked, "Why is it that you have come all this way, Father? Why do you wish to see such a sinful woman as me? You have gone through so much trouble; what could I possibly have to offer you?"

For some reason, my addressing him in this manner frightened Fr. Zossimas, and he knelt down in the sand, bowed low, and asked me for a blessing, saying the customary, "*Eulogeite!*" ("Bless!"). He did not dare to look up at this point. This scene overwhelmed me, and I, too, knelt down in the sand, bowed low to him, and asked him for his blessing, also saying the customary, "*Eulogeite.*" And so there we were, two aged adults, prostrating before each other in the hot desert sand.

"Eulogeite!" "Eulogeite!" "Eulogeite!" "Eulogeite!" We remained on the ground asking one another for a blessing, several times. This scene must have seemed funny to everyone in heaven, but I feel sure God warmly received our actions, pleased by the sweetness of the tender love and humility expressed by each toward the other.

After what must have been a very long time, I insisted that Zossimas offer his blessing to me, reminding him that "it is only proper for you to give your blessing to me, as you serve our gracious God through the dignity of the priestly office. For many years you have served Him faithfully at His holy table and offered the sacrifice of Christ."[9]

For some reason, this seemed to cause Zossimas to panic. His heart raced, and he began to perspire. With great difficulty he was able to say, "O mother in the Spirit, it is plain from this insight that all of your life you have dwelt with God and have nearly died to the world. It is plain above all that grace is given you, because you called me by my name and recognized me as a priest, although you have never seen me before. But because grace is recognized not by office, but by gifts of the Spirit, bless me, for God's sake, and pray for me out of the kindness of your heart." Overwhelmed by his love, I gave in to the plea of this deeply cherished man of God and said, "Blessed is God, who cares for the salvation of souls," and he responded with, "Amen."[10] We then helped one another up, sore knees and all, and found a more shady and suitable location to talk. Together we prayed and shared our stories.

This story recorded by Fr. Zossimas is about how repentance affected the two of us. There is more to the story, but suffice it to say that he offered me the precious Body and Blood of our Lord, and later, with the help of God, he also buried my body after I had departed this world. The Lord blessed him with a very long and happy life as a monk at the monastery by the River Jordan. He died peacefully at one hundred years of age.

I share this part of the story as an act of respect to those who asked in the past, "How did the Church ever come to know you?" Surely, as many in the world have now become acquainted with both our stories, it is of the will of God.

✠ ✠ ✠

Allow me to end this visit by sharing three important lessons that I learned during my forty-seven-year honeymoon with Christ. Perhaps you will consider packing these along with you, like the surprise gift of three loaves I received as I set out for the Jordan, as you proceed with your own spiritual journey.

First of all, know that the loving God has never ceased loving you. Do not be fooled by other voices that may, with boisterous and convincing authority, say otherwise. Every day, even every minute of the day, marks a new opportunity to begin afresh our side of our relationship with the loving God. Despite profoundly difficult circumstances, every moment of life can invite us to turn our gaze back to Christ. If this is the only thing you do, dare to trust and turn the eyes of your deepest heart toward Him—and hold on fast.

With God's help, all are called to life-giving encounter with Him. Bear in mind that both the preparation and the encounter itself take place solely as a result of His love for each one of us. Although these occur solely by the will of God, our most honest effort is needed. This requires courage, humility, and trust to seek "the one thing necessary." As a result of this ongoing discipline and dialogue of love, we become more spiritually "supple," surrendering the immature, yet hardened, self-defeating "chips on our shoulders" that make us sure we know how life "should" treat us. The more supple, humble, and open our hearts are, the more receptive they are to His fashioning them into thrones of rest for His pleasure.

With this in mind, it is high time to put away childish things! Pursuing the love of God and neighbor, in other words, the "Other," may have more in store for each of us than we could ever have imagined. It is vital to remain open to the possibility that our entire universe could change at a moment's notice as a result of the love of God.

Second, look to my example and to the example of all of the saints. Learn from us! Turn to us! Even from these reflections offered to you concerning the lives of Fr. Zossimas and me, bear witness that we are only two from among a whole "cloud of witnesses" (Heb 12:1). Our examples are as varied and plentiful as the stars in the heavens. Despite countless personal differences, we testify in unison that *no* obstacle can keep us from the love of the living God. Although most people today may not be called to ascetic solitude, everyone is called to the life-giving journey.

Third, ask for help. Reach out in prayer to God, and do not fear asking for what He takes great pleasure in giving. Do not be shy in reaching out to good and trustworthy persons around you whom God Himself places in your path. Also, as strange as this may sound to many modern ears, do not fear reaching out to your friends who have departed from this life yet are nevertheless very much alive in Christ and abide among His saints. Do not neglect this. Through His merciful love the saints, your friends, are all gathered about you. Your path in this life indeed may not be easy, but you will never be alone. The loving, Triune God is always there.

I must take my leave of you now. I beseech that the love of our living God, thrice-holy, will protect, sustain, and guide you on your journey toward Him. As I leave you, please allow me to offer the gift of these words from another friend of God, who beautifully describes this journey. He bears witness to the following:

> Christ gives to human persons life and growth, nourishment and light and breath.
> He opens their eyes and gives them light and the power to see.
> He gives to human persons the bread of life, and this bread is nothing else than Himself.
> He is life for those who are living and a sweet scent for those who breathe.
> He clothes those who desire to be clothed.
> He strengthens the traveler, and He is the way.
> He is at once both the inn along the road and the destination of the journey . . .
> When we struggle, He struggles at our side.
> When we argue, He is the reconciler.
> And when we win the victory, He is the Prize.
> (St. Nicholas Cabasilas, 14th c.)[11]

NOTES

1. Adapted slightly from the "Canon of St. Mary of Egypt," in *The Lenten Triodion*, trans. Mother Mary and Kallistos Ware (London: Faber and Faber, 1978), 448.

2. For a brief, yet excellent, study on this saint, see Benedicta Ward, *Harlots of the Desert: A Study in Repentance in Early Monastic Sources* (Kalamazoo, MI: Cistercian Publications, 1987), 26–56. See also the related chapter in this volume, "St. Mary of Egypt: A Provocateur of *Parrhesia*," by Iulia Corduneanu Curtright.

3. Often placing others and ourselves in the way of far more danger, as well! Tragically, countless souls have never succeeded in passing through this stage of acting out. These lives now rest in the loving hands of the living God.

4. See Kyriaki FitzGerald and Thomas FitzGerald, *Living the Beatitudes: Perspectives from Orthodox Spirituality* (Brookline, MA: Holy Cross Orthodox Press, 2006), 219–58.

5. For more on this issue, see my *Persons in Communion: A Theology of Authentic Relationships* (Berkeley, CA: InterOrthodox Press, 2006).

6. *Harlots of the Desert* offers a more detailed, beautiful rendition of this encounter, directly translating patristic texts; see 37–38.

7. Cf. Ward, *Harlots of the Desert*, 40–44.

8. Ibid.

9. Ibid.

10. Ibid.

11. *The Life in Christ* 1.4, adapted.

REFLECTION AND DISCUSSION QUESTIONS

1. Reflect on the graphic nature of St. Mary of Egypt's story during the years before she was healed by God. Discuss how this version of her life affected you.

2. a. What was it like reading how St. Mary became a follower of Christ?

   b. Were there places in her story that surprised you?

3. With the above question in mind, could some persons be surprised that she began to notice Christians, even becoming attracted to them, yet at the same time she became much worse in her sin?

   a. How does this part of her life strike you?

   b. What could this say about people in our own society?

   c. What could this say about our own close family members and loved ones?

4. Consider the section of the story in which St. Mary could not enter the church and found herself being "ambushed" by Love.

   a. Describe how this part of her spiritual journey touched you.

   b. Are there places in our lives where we may need to be "ambushed" by Love today? Discuss this as you are able.

5. What can we learn from the saint's example of living for so many years in the desert, fighting her inner demons while on her "honeymoon with Christ"?

6. The story later discusses the life of St. Zossimas, a respected spiritual father and abbot, who left the life that he knew so well in search of a spiritual companion to help him with his journey in Christ. What may this have to say to us, adult Christians, today?

7. The meeting of the two ascetics in the desert is deeply touching and even a little humorous. In his humility, and through the wisdom granted to him by God, St. Zossimas seeks out and finally receives St. Mary's blessing.

   a. How does this part of the story touch you and your experience within the life of the Church?

   b. St. Mary's love, humility, and spiritual authority is sought after and recognized by St. Zossimas. Could there be other women saints in our midst, or at least potential saints in the making, who may prove to be resources of love, humility, and spiritual

       benefit for others? If so, where are they? How may we as mem-
       bers of the Church be accountable to them?

    c. What would the Lord have us do?

8. a. Discuss how your understanding of the saints may have changed
       as a result of reading this (and other) chapters.

   b. If we were to turn to the saints as our friends who are alive in
       Christ right now, surrounding us (cf. Heb 12:1) on a daily basis,
       how could this impact our lives? Discuss this.

EPILOGUE

Discerning and Building
New Relationships

We thank you for reading our book! *Encountering Women of Faith*, volume 2, was produced by St. Catherine's Vision, Inc. (SCV), an organization endorsed by the Assembly of Canonical Orthodox Bishops of North and Central America. Most of our Board is comprised of women graduates of Holy Cross Greek Orthodox School of Theology and St. Vladimir's Orthodox Theological Seminary. Other trusted partners in our initiative include faithful men and women committed to advancing the mission of the Church.

Through this series, subsequent books we hope to write, and other initiatives, we desire to bear witness to and facilitate new opportunities and venues for the "abundant life" in Christ (John 10:10) to be shared with others. The calling to this life is as true for us today as it was for the first disciples and friends of the Lord many centuries ago. We desire to contribute toward "the building up of the body of Christ" (Eph 4:12). We strive to carry out this discipline through prayer, humble listening and discussion, investigation and study, as well as active support of the many ways God may be calling women and men to serve within the life of the Church, today. In other words, this work is founded in a discipline of love, seeking the discernment of the Holy Spirit. As a result of this ongoing effort, we have discerned three vital concerns to which we commit ourselves with every endeavor. These are:

Orthodox unity
Spiritual renewal
Education

If reading these chapters has inspired you to do something more, please consider the following:

1. Pray for the work of St. Catherine's Vision and for those whom this work may touch.

2. Suggest this book to your parish clergy, religious and community educators, students of the Bible and Christian history, religious organizations, women's group, students, friends, family, or others. If you are able, purchase additional copies and share them with your friends!

3. Suggest that your parish bookstore, local bookstore, and local community and/or college library carry this volume.

4. At church, home, and/or work, start a reading and discussion group, contemplating one chapter at a time.

5. Write a review of this book at www.amazon.com and elsewhere.

6. Invite one or two of the authors to speak at your local parish.

7. Visit the St. Catherine's Vision website for more updates about our work (www.orthodoxwomen.org).

8. Volunteer to assist with the work of St. Catherine's Vision.

9. Send us an e-mail with your suggestions for future endeavors, topics, and/or saints to study. Our e-mail address is: orthodoxwomen@gmail.com.

10. Consider helping this unique ministry grow through your financial support. *SCV receives most of its revenues through private donations.* We anticipate that much work may be waiting for us (cf. John 4:35). Your support will be deeply appreciated.

11. Be patient and continue to pray for us, *please.* SCV is a very young initiative!

ST. CATHERINE'S VISION CONTACT INFORMATION

Website: www.orthodoxwomen.org
E-mail: orthodoxwomen@gmail.com
Office address: Sextant Hill, 90 Route 6A, Suite 4C
              Attention: Dr. Kyriaki FitzGerald
              Sandwich, MA 02563

www.ingramcontent.com/pod-product-compliance
Lightning Source LLC
Chambersburg PA
CBHW021359090426
42742CB00009B/920